Navigating by the Stars presents the (written for the layperson as well as the p sun-sign astrology, beyond (though inc~~l~~~~uding, ----- ------~~~~p~~ -- -- encompass the full range of astrological techniques. In the process, it provides astrologers with information found in no other one source.

You may not want to become a professional astrologer or even a student of astrology, but in these pages you will learn how you can receive the greatest advantage from an astrological reading, and how other well-known people have been affected by the astrological parameters of their lives, whether or not they actually sought advice from an astrologer.

This book presents concise definitions of some of astrology's major tools, its philosophical underpinning, and specific examples of how events and outcomes in people's lives reflect the reality of astrology. The author draws from 45 personal stories, 33 of them told in greater detail. These include well-known figures from history, politics, show business, and the annals of crime. There is also a focus on corporate and political decision-making.

You do not have to know anything about astrology to start reading this book. But when you are done, you will have a better understanding of all that astrology can do. Not that it is the only guideline to action and insight, but it is a resource of astounding richness and potential.

"Accessible to the beginner and informative to the seasoned professional as well, Navigating by the Stars *is a Geminian feast for the mind. It explores Astro·Carto·Graphy and several other new astrological techniques with intelligence and understanding. For those who have never attended one of my seminars, this book may be the next best thing; for those who have, Edith Hathaway has added depth and insight to standard A·C·G interpretation techniques, plus suggesting a few new ones! And she does all this by using the nativities of modern culture heroes, so fashioning a book both fun to read and eminently worthwhile."* **—Jim Lewis**
Co-author of *The Astro*Carto*Graphy Book of Maps*

"This book is very interesting and very ambitious. Edith Hathaway covers the A to Z of astrology, and she does it with a different approach. Though written to inform the general public of the intricacies of the subject, she manages to have enough new material to keep even the pros absorbed."
—Marion D. March
Co-author of *The Only Way to ... Learn Astrology* Series

About the Author

Edith Hathaway is a consulting and counseling astrologer based in Santa Fe, New Mexico. She has lectured at international astrological conferences, and is a member of the National Council for Geocosmic Research, from which she holds a Professional Certificate as Consulting Astrologer. Ms. Hathaway is also a certified Astro•Carto•Graphy interpreter.

Her clients span a wide range of ages and occupations, from international businessmen, physicists, and artists to young students and housewives.

Ms. Hathaway received a B.A. in English literature from Wheaton College in Massachusetts. She began her astrological studies in New York City in 1976. Before becoming a professional astrologer in 1980, she was active in the performing arts as a dancer, actress, and composer/musician, performing her own works for solo piano and chamber ensemble.

To Write to the Author

We cannot guarantee that every letter written to the author can be answered, but all will be forwarded. Both the author and the publisher appreciate hearing from readers, learning of your response to this book. Llewellyn also publishes a bi-monthly news magazine with news and reviews of practical esoteric studies and articles helpful to the student, and some readers' questions and comments to the author may be answered through this magazine's columns if permission to do so is included in the original letter. The author sometimes participates in seminars and workshops, and dates and places are announced in *The Llewellyn New Times*. To contact the author, write to:

Edith Hathaway
c/o THE LLEWELLYN NEW TIMES
P.O. Box 64383-366, St. Paul, MN 55164-0383, U.S.A.

Please enclose a self-addressed, stamped envelope for reply,
or $1.00 to cover costs.

The Llewellyn Modern Astrology Library

Navigating by the Stars

Astrology and the Art of Decision-Making

Edith Hathaway

1991
Llewellyn Publications
St. Paul, Minnesota 55164-0383, U.S.A.

FIRST EDITION

Cover painting by June Zenner

Library of Congress Cataloging-in-Publication Data

Hathaway, Edith
  Navigating by the stars : astrology and the art of decision-making / Edith
     Hathaway. — 1st ed.
       p. cm. — (The Llewellyn modern astrology library)
  Includes bibliographical references and index.
  ISBN 0-87542-366-3 : $14.95
     1. Uranian astrology. 2. Horoscopes. 3. Astrology—Maps. 4. Celebrities—
Miscellanea. I. Title II. Series.
  BF1708.1.H365 1991
  133.5—dc20 91-620

                                                                    CIP

Llewellyn Publications
A Division of Llewellyn Worldwide, Ltd.
P.O. Box 64383, St. Paul, MN 55164-0383

About the Llewellyn Modern Astrology Library

Books for the *Leading Edge* of practical and applied astrology as we move toward the culmination of the 20th century.

This is not speculative astrology, nor astrology so esoteric as to have little practical application in meeting the needs of people in these critical times. Yet, these books go far beyond the meaning of "practicality" as seen prior to the 1990's. Our needs are spiritual as well as mundane, planetary as well as particular, evolutionary as well as progressive. Astrology grows with the times, and our times make heavy demands upon Intelligence and Wisdom.

The authors are all professional astrologers drawing from their own practice and knowledge of historical persons and events, demonstrating proof of their conclusions with the horoscopes of real people in real situations.

Modern Astrology relates the individual person to the Universe in which he/she lives, not as a passive victim of alien forces but as an active participant in an environment expanded to the breadth, *and depth,* of the Cosmos. We are not alone, and our responsibilities are infinite.

The horoscope is both a measure, and a guide, to personal movement—seeing every act undertaken, every decision made, every event as *time dynamic:* with effects that move through the many dimensions of space and levels of consciousness in fulfillment of Will and Purpose. Every act becomes an act of Will, for we extend our awareness to consequences reaching to the ends of time and space.

This is astrology supremely important to this unique period in human history, when Pluto transits through Scorpio and Neptune through Capricorn, and the books in this series are intended to provide insight into the critical needs and the critical decisions that must be made.

These books, too, are "active agents," bringing to the reader knowledge which will liberate the higher forces inside each person to the end that we may fulfill that for which we were intended.

—Carl Llewellyn Weschcke

Acknowledgements

In writing this book I am indebted to my clients and students for teaching me about their lives, and to the many astrological teachers and writers whose work has contributed to a higher level of understanding, expertise and practice in this field. Among those I would especially like to acknowledge are the following:

Robert Hand, for his elegant and profound style of teaching and writing about astrology. He has been a consistent standard-bearer of excellence for astrologers everywhere, never fearing to tread into new territory, while keeping a wisely balanced and open frame of mind.

The late **Neil Michelsen,** for his prolific output of astrological reference materials of the highest quality of accuracy and attention to detail.

Gary Christen, a teacher of Uranian astrology who has the gift to ignite that ineffable spark in his students. His wit and inspiration galvanized my entire approach to astrology.

Jim Lewis, who continues to break new ground in our conception of the geographical components of astrology. His work in exploring how Astro•Carto•Graphy operates, especially with political figures and events, has been invaluable.

Lois Rodden, whose prolific chart collections exemplify her tenacious insistence on the most accurate birth data. She has raised the standards for all astrologers in the area of research. I appreciate her checking all the birth data used in this book.

In the preparation of this manuscript for publication I would like to thank the following:

Tom Bridges, who championed this book in the early stages of its pre-publication life, and **Kathy Halgren,** who assisted in that process.

David Godwin, my editor, for his patience and understanding in the final stages of production.

And finally, I would like to thank my husband, **Richard Stevens,** for his love and support—and his extraordinary generosity of spirit.

Contents

*The birth data given in this book is based on the best information currently available. However, like any data, it can be superseded by new information which may come to light in the future.

List of Illustrations

I
Introduction to the Nature of Astrology, How it Works, Its Place in Science and History

It is only when a traveler has reached his goal that he is justified in discarding his maps.[1] During the journey, he takes advantage of any convenient shortcut.... There are certain mechanical features in the law of karma that can be skillfully adjusted by the fingers of wisdom.
—Paramahansa Yogananda,
Autobiography of a Yogi, ©1946,
11th ed., 1987, p. 189.

With the crescendo of so-called "New Age" ideas in the 1970s and '80s have come many voices telling us how we can get where we want to go and be who we want to be—as soon as possible, or as soon as we can clearly visualize our goals. To a certain extent these voices are right, especially under two known conditions: 1) if you are a highly enlightened being capable of manifesting on the physical plane, such as some of the great spiritual Masters, or 2) if the time and circumstances are right for you to have what you want and/or be what you want to be.

In the meantime, there are many clues along the way which enable us to determine what is desired. Because, as strange as it may sound, it is not always that clear to us, very personally, what we want or who we want to be. Astrology is one such big clue or road

---

1. The maps referred to here are astrological maps or charts (also called horoscopes) derived from the moment that a human being takes his or her first breath. (In the case of the birth of a nation, corporation, or a marriage, the map is determined from a pivotal ceremonial moment from which there is no turning back.) Such maps are not the sun-sign blurbs called "Daily Horoscopes," commonly found in newspapers, which may apply to you in a very marginal or remote way only if you have a number of planets or chart factors in that zodiacal sign.

1

map, if deciphered properly and used as the truly sacred art and science that it is.

Astrology in History: Its Reemergence

So, you might ask, if astrology is such a fine tool and source of clues, why has it remained so much in the background and so little in the public arena for the last several centuries, at least in the Western Hemisphere?[2] One of the major reasons astrology, or the serious use of astrology, disappeared from sight in the West (and from its role as an acceptable and valid subject for study in the universities)[3] after around 1700 was that it did not coincide with the prevalent viewpoint of the scientific establishment which ushered in the Age of Reason. According to that viewpoint, any important and valid position scientifically, whatever the subject or theory, must be rational, objective, mechanistic, and totally provable by the Law of Causality, i.e. cause and effect. (A mechanistic view of the universe, which arose largely out of Newtonian physics, proposed that reality consists of solid objects and empty space, that within this context time and space are separate and independent factors, and that an observer's perceptions of reality do not in any way affect that reality.) Vis-à-vis astrology, this was also a convenient position for much of organized religion in the West, because the Church had wavered for centuries as to whether people had a right to examine their own destinies without a church-appointed official, such as a priest or minister, guiding the way according to accepted theological principles.[4] Even so, civilization has managed to achieve a great deal in nearly 300 years by focusing most of its attention on the rational mind, or the left brain. Unfortunately, a great deal has also been lost in the process of largely ignoring one whole side of the brain: the right side, which governs our emotional, intuitive sources

---

2. The beginnings of astrology and astronomy date back ca. 5000 years ago.

3. Through this same time period, astrologers in India have continued up to the present to obtain university degrees in Jyotish, a complex study of the precise mathematical and astronomical principles of the planets. This can take up to eight years and is followed by many years of apprenticeship to learn to apply both the spiritual principles and the mathematical techniques of Hindu astrology to daily practice.

4. "Thus a rift arose between man's traditional Christianity and his rational or intellectual mind. Since that time éi.e., the late Renaissanceù these two sides of modern man have never been brought together. In the course of the centuries, with man's growing insight into nature and its laws, this division has gradually grown wider; and it still splits the psyche of the Western Christian in the 20th century." Carl Jung, *Man and His Symbols,* ©1964, Laurel Edition (Dell), 1979, p. 275.

of wisdom.

Astrology and Science

In recent decades, modern scientists, especially physicists, have begun to make discoveries about how life operates on a subatomic (or microscopic) level that defy what was previously thought to be "unreasonable" and "irrational." They have found that certain events take place on a subatomic scale which cannot be explained through laws of cause and effect, and which even defy the law that underlies all of classical modern physics, which says that the fastest known speed is the speed of light (186,000 miles per second). This conflict within the scientific world started to develop with Einstein's discovery that light was not only a wave but also a particle phenomenon, and thus energy and matter simultaneously. No longer could reality be correctly perceived as solid objects and empty space. In his Theory of Relativity, first proposed in 1905, Einstein also said that concepts of space and time are inseparable and interdependent. That is, the movement of an object in space is never absolute but dependent upon the vantage point of the observer. In 1927 Werner Heisenberg took this a step further with his Uncertainty Principle and said that the observer actually alters the observed by the mere act of observing. This means that we not only influence our reality, but to some extent we create it. All of this brings the Newtonian physicist's concept of objectivity into question, since it is now proved that what is out there is very dependent upon what is inside the observer—i.e. his or her opinion, physical vantage point, or point of view.

Quantum mechanics also blew the lid off the classical idea, based in Newtonian physics, that there are separate objects in the universe which are categorizable and understandable in and of themselves, without reference to outside objects and/or events. Quantum mechanics, especially Bell's theorem (first proposed in 1964 and confirmed by experiments in 1972 and later) shows definitively in the behavior of subatomic wave/particles that separate parts of the universe are interconnected in ways that are both intimate and immediate, and move faster than the speed of light, or at superluminal speeds. The laws governing these subatomic events are beyond a totally rational understanding. While Newtonian physics predicts events, quantum mechanics predicts the probability of events. The laws of quantum mechanics would seem to explain, among other things, telepathy, which most physicists do not acknowledge as existing; concepts of synchronicity, of which psychiatrist Carl Jung spoke a great deal; and, of course, astrology, which assumes an intimate connection and interrelatedness between all of the planets and important connecting points in our solar system, and most often uses the earth as the central vantage point from which to measure planetary configurations.

There are several important issues here. One is that we reevaluate what a "science" is about. Another is that we make the connection between discoveries in science and how they relate to the rest of our lives.

Clearly, *science*, or a scientific establishment is not, nor should it ever be, an impenetrable academic stronghold through which the force of worthwhile new ideas and concepts never enters. The word "science" comes from the Latin "to know" and is described in the dictionary as a "systematized body of knowledge derived from observation, study, and experimentation carried on in order to determine the nature or principles of what is being studied."[5] With an insistent and increasingly rigid objectivity, rationalism, and causality propelling modern science, there is nowhere for that to go but inwards on itself. The idea that science holds *pure and absolute truths* is crumbling, because new information constantly contradicts and supercedes the old and because all experiments are affected by the perception of the observer. In addition, there is nothing *pure and absolute* which fails to take into consideration concepts of the whole, which metaphysicians refer to when they speak of "holograms" or being "holistic." Some quantum physicists are, in fact, beginning to sound like mystics or metaphysicians in their use of language, implying the use of both right and left brain functions, a constant throughout the history of Eastern thought. You cannot examine the part without examining the wholeness and the unity of all the parts. By itself, the left brain functions in a completely rational and compartmentalized way. Unfortunately this is the way much of modern science has been functioning for the past 300 years. The astonishing discoveries in the realm of subatomic physics have been made public since the 1920s and '30s, and especially with Bell's

---

5. *Webster's New World Dictionary*, 2nd college edition, 1984.

Theorem in 1964. However, only a small minority of the public and an even smaller minority of physicists are aware of the profound implications which life on a subatomic level has for life on a macroscopic level.[6]

In ancient Greece, as well as in many other periods throughout history, religion, philosophy, and science were accepted and acknowledged as closely interrelated. Discoveries or ideas in one of these areas were seen to have an immediate effect on the development of the other two. Unfortunately the Age of Reason put an almost 300-year halt to that process, and its effects can be seen in many arenas. With the Age of Reason came the separation of philosophy and mathematics, intuition and reasoning. So currently we often have scientists and engineers with a great deal of mathematical knowledge and very little of the emotional, intuitive wisdom which could alter and enhance the level of ethics and integrity pervading the scientific and industrial establishment.

Astrology demands that we function with both sides of the brain, though it is possible to get involved in its technicalities and overlook the emotional, intuitive information and vice versa. If you took a survey of all current practicing astrologers, you would run into these polarities. That happens in astrology and other disciplines because people feel the pressure not only to be respectable professionally, but also to appear to be in sync with modern technology, which, though it's changing, is still very left-brain oriented and wedded to the concept of causality and rationalism.

The Law of Correspondences

Up to the late 1600s astrology and astronomy were one. (Johann Kepler and Galileo Galilei were among the last of the great astronomer-astrologers living in the 17th century.) The stars and the planets were studied not only for the precision of calculating their mathematical positions and interrelationships, but also for the correlation of these planetary positions and interrelationships to human affairs, collectively and individually. This correlation is called the Law of Correspondences. Central to Hermetic theory,

---

6. Some highly readable books for the layperson on this subject are: 1) Fritjof Capra, *The Tao of Physics*, 1975; 2) Michael Talbot, *Mysticism and the New Physics*, 1980; 3) Gary Zukav, *The Dancing Wu Li Masters: An Overview of the New Physics*, 1979.

which had its origins in the early Christian era, is the idea that everything in nature has its parallel in the human being and in human affairs. In other words, in the macrocosm may be found the microcosm and vice versa.

Hippocrates, who lived ca. 4th century B.C. and is still called "the father of medicine," insisted that his medical students study astrology and the Law of Correspondences within astrology, especially those relating the planetary positions to the various parts of the physical body. The highly innovative Swiss astrologer and physician Paracelsus (1493-1541) was also adamant that doctors consult astrology before making their final diagnoses or writing prescriptions. He developed a theory he called *magnale magnum,* and a system in which all contemporary medicine, astrology, and alchemy (including chemistry and metallurgy) were in harmonious mutual accord. In his system the seven major organs of the body corresponded to the seven planets (out to Saturn), and he cataloged each bodily part with its astrological correspondence—for which a further catalog of vegetable remedies, minerals, precious stones, colors, fabrics, herbs, and animal substances were in turn directly applicable through their astrological rulerships. In such a way subtle imbalances or disharmonies could be caught early, before they manifested into full-fledged disease. For several centuries (from ca. 1491), the general populace, especially the rural populace, was kept aware of this medicine-astrology tradition through the almanacs, particularly with regard to the use of medicinal plants and their association with certain planets. This knowledge was conveyed to doctors in Nicholas Culpeper's *The English Physician Enlarged* (1653).

Again, a reminder that we are moving *beyond* causality, the principle that cause must precede and account for effect. Here we are dealing with a simultaneous reflecting and reverberating action. What is happening in the heavens mirrors what is happening on the Earth. Paracelsus thought of it as a kind of cosmic magnetism. There are similar implications in biologist Rupert Sheldrake's books, *A New Science of Life: The Hypothesis of Formative Causation* (1981) and *The Presence of the Past: Morphic Resonance and the Habits of Nature* (1988), in which he talks about morphogenetic fields that persist in time and that have a resonance, implying that everything around us affects us, and sometimes from great distances in time and space.

In a true interweaving of right and left brain, we can see that for astrologers, complex mathematical calculations demand the attention of our left brain, and the correlations to human affairs demand the attention of our right brain to make the intuitive leaps to those symbolic connections. With the information that the left brain provides, the right brain can then apply the planetary configurations to human events. The planetary symbols and the vast and ancient body of astrological and astronomical knowledge underlying them must of course first be an everyday working language for the astrologer. But once we have this successful interweaving of planetary knowledge, we have at our disposal an incredible road map which, as Yogananda reminds us in the opening quote, we only need for as long as we are on life's journey.

A Divine Plan, Karma, Fate, Destiny

That the planetary patterns for any given moment in time and space can describe the character and thus the probable destiny of any person, group, nation, or event born at that moment is indeed an awesome realization. That our Creator would have given us such a gift, and that we would have chosen the planetary imprints and thus our lives is a profound idea. Some would argue that these lives were assigned to us, and that we had no choice in the matter. But after examining a large number of astrological charts and watching the people living out these charts, my feeling is that the gift of life is so intensely connected with our desire to partake of it that they cannot be separated. In the East, they call it the Law of Karma. In the West, we are not as comfortable with concepts of fate and inevitability. We call it "destiny," which implies a greater choice in the outcome. The irony is that, like many things we have been rediscovering about the East vs. the West, both are right. The astrological chart shows us something we have apparently mapped out for ourselves in order to complete something we need to do, and within that context we have the opportunity to make good or bad choices, all of this with or without an awareness of what some would call a Divine Plan, a Divine Presence, or simply a Higher Consciousness. It is more and more impossible to consider the usefulness of an astrological chart without also considering a basic framework which has some spiritual purpose as a driving force. That is, if we consider that each of our lives on Earth has a very specific and meaningful reason for being, then it is urgent that we try to discover what we are doing here and how we can best go about it.

A Philosophy of Decision-Making

This book is about astrology and the art of decision-making. The word "decision" comes from the Latin *decisio*, meaning a cutting short, also the act of deciding or making up one's mind. Presumably what is being cut short is the process of weighing all the alternatives, all the possibilities in terms of one's choice of direction. To come to a decision implies a finality of choice, although interestingly enough, those not happy with the first decision may wish to review the alternatives and keep cancelling out and replacing the first decision —which will reverberate in time and space nonetheless. Sometimes this is appropriate. Other times we call it a Life of Indecision. And still other times there is no possibility of changing the decision, because a myriad of complex events have catapulted into being that cannot be reversed.

When we read the stories of the lives of certain Masters, we have the sense that they made all the right decisions. Implicit, somehow, is the idea that they knew how to move always along the path of least resistance in achieving what was desired. For example, Jesus knew that his capture and crucifixion would lead to a greater lesson for humanity than if he had lived out a normal life. Thus arise several key questions: What is the path of least resistance? What is the desired end result? And are they not both closely connected to the concept from the Latin "decision," cutting short? Perhaps a great decision is in some way a "shortcut" to growth.

Astrology as a Teller of Time and Character

When we become acquainted with our natal horoscopes,[7] we become more deeply acquainted with who we are. The astrological chart stands alone in its ability to give us not only complex and precise details about our characters but in its ability to act as a clock or timing mechanism in which various cycles spiral into each other and tell us, literally, what time it is for us. It is important to realize

---

7. The natal horoscope is the planetary map that becomes an imprint at the moment in time and space when a person is born. The word "horoscope" comes from the Greek *horoskopus,* observer of the hour.

also that what time it is for me may not seem so connected to what time it is for you, but in fact they are very interconnected. This is especially true if we belong to the same generation, in which case in certain ways we will be reacting collectively to events that are happening now and throughout our lives.

Being Attuned to Time and Space

In a world that once existed, human beings had sharp intuitive senses about what was happening and almost a smell for what was due next. There was no need for manmade watches to tell people what time it was or what they ought to be doing next. (Perhaps this is still true in some rare primitive cultures.) In such a world tools imparting astrological law would be unnecessary, since the souls of these human beings would be naturally and correctly attuned to the movements of the planets and the laws of nature governing their destiny and its timing.

In fact, it becomes almost redundant to speak of the timing of one's destiny in astrological matters, because *who you are is also where you are going in time.* Where you are going in time is very much determined by the human attributes and character that you have started out with and which are described in the birth map. Similarly, with a road map, when considering how best to get from point A to point B, one has to consider where point A is. All that seems linear enough, but in fact when we also see that where we are on the road reflects where we have been on the road, then an element of elasticity enters in.[8] For convenience and communal reference we use linear concepts of time, but what really happens to us is very unlinear. It is as if space and time are not only folding in on each other but spiraling around each other in ways that make present, past, and future simultaneous. The older generations in their 70s, 80s and 90s speak about this repeatedly, and are often called

---

8. "... Physics does not in fact forbid the transmission of information from the future to the present. It happens all the time. If you run an electric current through a system for a while and then suddenly cut it, several things happen, and the actual blackout is the last of these to occur. Two precursor waves go out ahead of the cutoff event. One of these travels ... at the speed of light. The other is almost as fast, but is slowed down a little by the properties of the medium through which it passes. And then finally, at a very much slower speed, the event itself arrives. Signals about what is to happen thus actually go out ahead of the happening ... The future can be predicted without being predetermined. The biggest problem we have with precognition is a personal one. We are so used to causality, cause preceding effect that we accept it as a fact of life and have trouble believing that it is not a law of the universe."—Lyall Watson, *Gifts of Unknown Things,* ©1976, Bantam, 1978, pp. 56-57.

disoriented because they do. But what is really happening is that the longer we live, the more the time and space spirals are forming and the more we are forced to deal with them—even if our habitual mental attitude might tend to be logical, rational, and linear.

Time Present-Past-Future (Time Spirals Within Spirals)

This natural sense of living life in a simultaneously present-past-future time framework is also innate to a child, especially from birth to the age of seven. In that period of life the naturally creative flow and intuitive connectedness and centeredness is strongly related to that spiralling sensation of time and space. The consciousness is attuned to it without much outside interference, and the child experiences life as having many possibilities as well as many probable realities. Civilization is often eager to label such behavior as the eccentricity and fantasy of the very young. As soon as possible after the child enters first grade (age six), our educational system attempts to set all this straight.

But astrology presents us with a great gift: 1) The birth chart or any astrological chart assumes that matters of time and space are inseparable. In fact, you can't erect a horoscope without having the month, day, year, hour, minute, *and* longitude and latitude representing the geographic location. In other words, the planetary patterns of that moment in time and space give us a picture of your character and probable patterns for your destiny. 2) Furthermore, the birth chart assumes that a person, an organization, or an event is affected at all times by cycles, measured in planetary positions and movements, which are spiraling backwards and forwards in time.[9] For example, one timing technique that most modern Western astrologers use is called "secondary progressions." In this system, the formula is more or less a day for a year, which means that whatever is happening to the planetary movements and interactions 20 years after you were born is equivalent to what is happening 20 days after you were born, and so on.[10] Some

---

9. "[The physicist Richard] Feynman ... suggests that the space-time path interpretation of the quantum principle shows that an electron can be scattered *backwards* in time by an electromagnetic vacuum fluctuation...[See diagram on next page.] An electron moving backwards in time would be detected as a positron of opposite charge, but having the same mass moving forward in time." Michael Talbot, *Mysticism and the New Physics*, ©1980, 1981, p. 95.

10. The computed positions of all the planets are listed in a publication called an "ephemeris." The data for the *American Ephemeris* comes from the U.S. Naval Observatory.

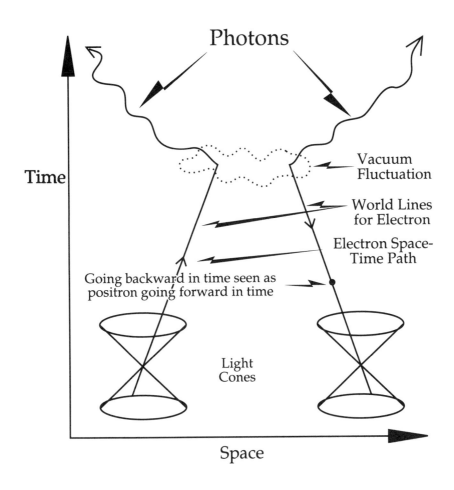

An electron being scattered backwards in time
(Disgram by Michael Talbot illustrating a principle in quantum physics, as interpreted by physicist
Richard Feynman. Reproduced with permission.)

astrologers even use converse secondary progressions, which
consist of the same principles, only going back in days prior to birth
rather than after birth.

Other prominent timing systems include the transits, which are
the daily movements of planets and are especially important when
slower-moving outer planets hover over certain natal positions,

such as the Personal Points (described on pages 29-37). Also, there are solar arc directions, in which the measurement of the movement of the Sun (in Earth-centered, or geocentric, astrology) is used to calculate relationships between all of the planets and various other points in space (described in Chapter 2).[11] Those other planets are said to be "directed" by solar arc, and sometimes (especially with the Uranian system of astrology) by half of that solar arc measurement, and also double that solar arc, giving different timing nuances.

All of this may begin to sound quite elaborate, and indeed astrology becomes complex in its mathematical technicalities, but the principles throughout are consistent with this sense of the fluidity and spiraling nature of time and space. And what we find, as in life, is that certain time cycles clock in with what is happening to everyone at certain ages (such as the Saturn returns at ages 29 and 58), and other time cycles, much more mysterious and frustrating when they don't occur according to society's dictates, represent our own truly personal timetables.

Astrology and Psychology

As we look at the recent history of astrology and the issues it raises, one obvious question arises. How do astrology and psychology fit together? Do they overlap? Do they complement each other? As I have said, astrology is over 5000 years old in its development and evolution, whereas psychology as a discipline is somewhere around 100 years old. Arriving as it did during the Age of Reason, its tenets are predicated upon cause and effect. Sigmund

---

11. Some astrologers use both the heliocentric (Sun-centered) and geocentric (Earth-centered) astrology. But more often astrologers look at the planets from the point of view of the Earth (or geocentrically), because that metaphor is truer to what it is like being a human being on planet Earth. We would use the same astrological principle living on any other planet (Mars-centered on Mars, for example), not to depart from what we know to be the actual fact astronomically (i.e. that all the planets in our solar system orbit around the Sun), but in order to be true to a profoundly meaningful metaphor.

When the 16th century astronomer Copernicus "discovered" the heliocentric theory, some thought it would create the permanent downfall of astrology—since presumably astrologers should have known better all along. Ironically, there were no inherent contradictions within the principles of astrology even with this discovery. What is less well remembered in modern times is that the Christian Church reacted violently against the heliocentric theory. They couldn't accept it because it conflicted with the Christian theology of the time and its view of the Holy Scriptures. Later on, in the early 17th century, when the astronomer-astrologer Galileo tried to support Copernicus' position and reconcile the heliocentric view with Christian theology, he was taken before the Inquisition and forced to recant. So again and again, we observe how concepts of correctness, logic, or rationality are guided by the prevalent and often temporary views of Church, State, and/or Science.

Freud (1856-1939) put psychotherapy on the scientific map when he proposed reasons and theories for why people behave as they do, focusing especially on infantile sexuality and the Oedipus complex. In America today, there are myriad approaches to psychology and over 450 types of psychotherapy. The major ones are no longer Freudian and can be classified as either behaviorism or cognitive psychology.[12]

B. F. Skinner was the chief modern proponent of behaviorism, though its origins began in the early 1900s with the conditioned-reflex experiments of Pavlov. It focuses on explaining behavior in terms of patterns of responses to external stimuli, mainly rewards and punishment. It rejects that which cannot be understood as observable responses to environmental stimuli. Cognitive psychology, on the other hand, is a broad discipline which has a fundamental interest in mental processes and products, its object being to reach for an increased understanding of the human mind.[13] Its research is done by studying the actual human brain and its workings or by using artificial models via computers.

As a student and colleague of Freud (between 1907 and 1912), Carl Jung (1875-1961) has an important place in the history of psychology and psychoanalysis. However, his break in 1912 from Freud and Freud's largely sexual orientation freed him to set off in a direction that allowed more room for a spiritual orientation in psychology.[14] Although in certain parts of the world, especially in California, Europe, and South America, Jung's ideas and theories are still used and studied, neither his position nor Freud's is

12. Whereas psychologists obtain either a Master's degree or a Ph.D. in psychology, psychiatrists go through medical school training, and diagnose and treat primarily mental disorders. The two main approaches of psychiatry are 1) biological, treating the problem with drugs, and 2) therapeutic, treating the problem through analysis. Though their analytic methods sprang from Freud and his ideas, he is rarely given credit in recent years, due to what is considered his overly sexual orientation. Carl Jung, the Swiss psychiatrist and founder of analytic psychology, is even less mentioned or acknowledged in medical schools. His works and his methods are examined very little to not at all in modern psychiatry, and he is generally considered too mystical to be included in most medical school psychiatry programs. (Jung's entire life's work focused on the human consciousness, the uniting of all its various layers and its spiritual nature.)

13. A relatively recent phenomenon, cognitive psychology started to be officially recognized within the profession with the publication of a book on the subject in 1967 by Ulrich Neisser.

14. Not present in psychology for most of its 100 year history, with the exception of Jung as a major force, a spiritual or religious emphasis in psychology was soundly repudiated by Freud, and has not reappeared until very recently with Roberto Assagioli's "psychosynthesis," also in the mid-1960s.

currently central to the orientation of the American Psychological Association (the largest psychological organization in the United States). No doubt Freud's overemphasis on sexuality explains his decline, but it's even more predictable to see why Jung's position has declined somewhat, at least temporarily, given the cause and effect orientation of psychology and psychiatry and of all of modern science for some 300 years.

Carl Jung's thinking was clearly not bound by causality. His voluminous work with dreams as a mirror of the unconscious mind is very much linked to the Law of Correspondences. Jung made extensive use of horoscope charts in diagnosing his patients and in studying the relationships between marriage partners. The latter is described in *Synchronicity: An Acausal Connecting Principle* (1955). Jung's daughter, Gret Baumann-Jung, went on to integrate astrology completely into her work as a psychologist, a pattern which is becoming more common around the world today. In doing so, she and others are adding a dimension to psychology otherwise absent. Without the use of astrology, psychology has no precision tools for measuring time and space influences on its patients and clients. Precise cyclical information becomes guesswork without it.

Astrology has its therapeutic dimension, although currently most astrologers do not establish regular weekly meetings with a given client. Commonly, an astrologer may see or talk by phone with a particular client several times a year at most, although there are always exceptions. This situation may change, but perhaps not, because astrology does not focus, like psychology and psychotherapy, on the dysfunctions and imbalances of human behavior. Herein lies one of the big differences between the two professions. Psychology, psychotherapy, and the wide range of therapies considered under the umbrella of mental health treatments began as concepts to treat dysfunctional personalities and pathologies. And although spokesmen for current mental health treatments talk of the vast array of therapies, especially those outside psychiatry per se, as dealing with problems of contemporary living and not pathologies, the orientation still seems to be towards diagnosing and treating a wide range of neuroses and dysfunctional behaviors.[15] Astrologers, on the other hand, often

15. Only recently has someone in the field such as Abraham Maslow started focusing on what makes a winner, what are the components of a peak performance, and so on.

deal with people and organizations and corporations who want to maximize their potentials, with greater use of timing and character information, and sometimes geographic information.

The need for an extensive interview with the client or hours of testing is not necessary in astrology. That information is in the chart, a comprehensive picture of the client's concept of himself or herself, and though it does not contain explicit details of past events, nevertheless it gives the essence of where the person has been and where he or she is going. Even so, the number of precise details is awesome. Except for those astrologers deeply involved in a psychotherapeutic profession or medical astrology, astrology is generally not oriented towards disease and dysfunctional behavior. Astrology is an incredible tool for self-knowledge of the individual as a *whole being*, and typically attracts clients for the first time at a major turning point or crisis in life when the individual is deeply questioning his or her level of self-knowledge. Because of the way astrology was created and constructed, it is impossible to separate concerns of mind, body and spirit. You cannot separate concerns of time and space, or of energy and matter. Carl Jung was vitally aware of this when he said, "Everything born or done at this moment of time has the qualities of this moment of time." If you become truly acquainted with your birth map, and the specific Law of Correspondences therein, you develop a deeper sense of who you are, who you can be, and of your time framework, especially the likely peak and low periods and their probable manifestations. You have an incredible built-in avenue to inner and outer serenity.

The best professionals do their jobs to the point where their presence is no longer needed. Speeded up, frazzled, and disoriented lives and relationships, common to the 20th century, seem to engender the need for psychotherapy, especially when there is no one close, trustworthy, and/or objective to talk to about your troubles except your therapist. For this purpose, a greater exchange between astrology and psychology would be beneficial, especially in time saved for the psychologist in diagnosing the character and personality of the patient/client, and in informing him or her under what timing cycles they are currently operating. What may be the most valuable tool from psychology for astrologers is learning some of their methods of counseling, especially in crisis situations. It is not about borrowing their language, because astrology already has its own rich language.[16] But if we had perfect self-knowledge and were perfectly attuned to the movements of time and space, astrology itself would not be necessary.

There is much to be gained in collaboration between astrologers and psychologists, although that fact is more obvious right now to astrologers than to psychologists, who are more likely to be burdened by the prejudices of our times, participating as they do in a mainstream social science. The general public should take a look at its almost total acceptance of some 450 or more forms of psychotherapy, alongside its almost total ignorance of astrology. Astrology describes the psyche rather precisely, as well as the whole human being; his or her relationships; physical, emotional, and mental well-being; social and economic tendencies—in fact the historical trends on all levels at the time of birth. Though specific hereditary and genetic traits and environmental influences can somewhat affect the interpretation of the initial planetary blueprint, it is still a large and detailed picture of a person and a time.

Where Prejudice Arises, or Intellectual Sloth

A Zen story tells of Nan-in, a Japanese master during the Meiji era who received a university professor. The professor came to inquire about Zen. Nan-in served tea. He poured his visitor's cup full, and then kept on pouring. The professor watched the overflow until he no longer could restrain himself. "It is overfull. No more will go in!" "Like this cup," Nan-in said, "you are full of your own opinions and speculations. How can I show you Zen unless you first empty your cup?"

—Gary Zukav, *The Dancing Wu Li Masters: An Overview of the New Physics*, ©1979, Bantam, 1986, p. 118.

Many of our leading scientists have a solemn sense of mission in their disdain for astrology, in which there is much vehemence, little or no serious investigation, and much intellectual sloth. In Zen terms, they come at it with a full cup.

In 1975, for example, 186 scientists, some of them Nobel Prize

---

16. It could be said that any profession has its language, but in astrology the real transition from student to professional status comes not simply in technical proficiency but in *translating* the language of the planets to the mind and heart of the client and of the general public.

winners, signed a statement in the Sept.-Oct. 1975 issue of the *Humanist* magazine denouncing astrology as a "pseudoscience" and condemning it as "a cult of unreason and irrationalism being foisted on an unsuspecting public." The cumulative effect of this anti-astrology manifesto suggests hysteria against a science and art which does not adhere strictly to principles of causality and rationalism, as neither does quantum physics or quantum mechanics.

These 186 scientists never studied or investigated astrology, and their premises and facts were therefore invalid, as was pointed out to them by knowledgeable and practicing astrologers. They were forced to recant their proclamation—however, they did so in the back pages of a later issue of the magazine, and the fact was kept quiet by the scientific community.

Even so, such an intellectually authoritarian group influences public opinion. In the spring of 1988, journalists in print and television bashed astrology in the wake of the publication of Donald Regan's book *For the Record* and its revelation of Nancy Reagan's regular use of an astrologer for President Reagan's schedule and for the timing of important executive events, such as the signing of treaties.[17] The journalists inherited intellectual sloth from the scientists. Though most of them knew nothing about astrology, they were vehemently against it.[18]

The public's worship of the scientific establishment, and its

---

17. *For the Record* was released to members of the press May 3, 1988. Donald Regan was formerly President Reagan's White House Chief of Staff, from 1985 to 1987. He was pressured to resign from that position, which he did on February 27, 1987, and it was widely rumored that Nancy Reagan lobbied for his departure.

18. Similarly, not having studied the subject but secure in their knowledge that "responsible science" cancels out astrology as a worthwhile discipline, members of the Federation of American Scientists, including five Nobel laureates, questioned then candidate Ronald Reagan during the 1980 Presidential election race "...about reports that he had consulted astrologers in selecting a time for his inauguration as Governor of California" (*N.Y. Newsday*, May 4, 1988, p. 26). They wrote that they were "gravely disturbed" by this. Reagan was too political to let on much, but he did have the time set astrologically. It was at 12:10 AM, evidently a more propitious time on that date than the standard mid-morning announcement. (In early 1984 his announcement that he would seek a second Presidential term was also made untypically, for most politicians, late at night.) Reagan and his wife Nancy consulted various astrologers over the years, including Los Angeles-based Carroll Righter, and more recently San Francisco-based Joan Quigley, via her contacts with Nancy Reagan.

In an "odd" twist of fate that poses a conundrum for strictly rational scientists and their ideas about reality structures and probability patterns, Reagan's former astrologer Carroll Righter died the week of "the Reagan astrology flap," on April 30, 1988, as did Robert Heinlein, the science fiction writer, on May 8, 1988. Heinlein's 1961 science fiction novel, *Stranger in a Strange Land*, is about Earth's chief executive, who makes decisions based on advice from his wife, who in turn regularly consults a San Francisco astrologer.

tendency to follow blindly a perception of reality described and agreed on by scientists, has brought about a prejudice against astrology, at least in the Western hemisphere, confusing even some astrologers about how much they ought to give way to a purely psychological orientation, as those credentials often allow more immediate public access and acceptance.

We need to reexamine what we accept as useful, helpful, "scientific." We must reexamine our prejudices. And finally, we need to reassess the extent to which we have handed over our thinking to scientists and journalists, and for that matter to our educators, doctors, lawyers, bankers, and politicians. (More about this in Chapter 5.) I am not saying we should automatically embrace every alternate form of government, medicine, economy, or education that comes along, but that what we as a civilization have created as the bastions of "reasonable thinking" must be seriously reexamined.

The Scientific Validation of Astrology

The scientific testing of astrology has been conducted numerous times in the 20th century, the most notable of these being the tests and research of 1) Vernon Clark,[19] an American psychologist, 2) the French statisticians Michel and Francoise Gauquelin, and 3) the radio engineer John Nelson, whose work is described more fully in Chapter 2 (pp. 28-29). As a radio engineer Nelson was employed by RCA Communications, where from 1946 to 1971 he conducted systematic investigations of the relationship between the heliocentric configurations of planets and short-wave radio disturbances. His forecasts of such disturbances based on the planetary correlations were accurate 93 percent of the time.

Vernon Clark is among the very few orthodox scientists who has studied the subject of astrology, having obtained a diploma from the British Faculty of Astrological Studies. From 1959 to 1961 he set up three blind trial tests which were given to a total of 50 astrologers from the United States, Britain, Europe, and Australia. The third test was double blind, with data coming from independent physicians and psychologists and the answers unknown to Clark himself. The first test involved matching up ten birth charts with ten descriptions

---

19. A description of the Vernon Clark tests and their results can be found in *Recent Advances in Natal Astrology: A Critical Review*, compiled by Geoffrey Dean, 1977.

of occupations; the second test involved matching ten pairs of charts and ten brief case histories; and the third test involved ten pairs of birth charts in which one was a person of high intelligence (IQ over 140) and the other was a victim of incurable brain damage (cerebral palsy). All three tests were also given to a control group consisting of 20 psychologists and social workers with no knowledge of astrology. The results of all three tests showed that astrologers performed at an extremely high level of significance, whereas the control group performed at exactly chance level. These test results were duplicated in further testing in the 1970s by both Dr. Zipporah Dobyns and Joseph Vidmar. Clark's tests provide a holistic model for testing, as distinguished from the statistical model of the Gauquelins.

Michel and Francoise Gauquelin are veritable pioneers in the statistical investigation of astrology, isolating one or more factors from a complex whole without involving the astrologer's level of competence as a practitioner.[20] Michel Gauquelin holds a Ph.D. in psychology and statistics from the Sorbonne, and Francoise Gauquelin holds a degree in statistics from the University of Paris. For 40 years, since 1949, the Gauquelins have collected birth data of many thousands of people from registrars throughout Europe and studied the planetary positions in the birth charts in relation to various effects in the lives of the people, mainly choice of profession, personality traits, and heredity.

In examining the planetary positions for professionals successful in their fields, the Gauquelins found that sports champions, scientists, and writers all had a diurnal distribution of certain planets following a consistent pattern that differed significantly from chance. The charts of 1,553 sports champions showed the planet Mars either rising or culminating (i.e., just past the horizon or the meridian of the birthplace) with a frequency that would likely occur by chance in a probability rating of 1 in 1,000. Saturn tended to rise or culminate in the charts of prominent scientists, and the Moon tended to rise or culminate for successful writers. When these results continued to be replicated by skeptical

---

20. Results of the Gauquelin studies (including all the birth data) are published in a 23-volume series by their Laboratoire d'Étude des Relations Entre Rythmes Cosmiques et Psychophysiologiques, founded in 1969. In addition, Michel Gauquelin has published widely. Among his best known books available in English are *The Cosmic Clocks* (1967), *The Scientific Basis of Astrology* (1969), *Cosmic Influences on Human Behavior* (1973), and *Birthtimes: A Scientific Investigation of the Secrets of Astrology* (1983).

groups of scientists, including the Belgian scientists from the Committee for the Scientific Investigation of Claims of the Paranormal, it still did not stop French academy member Jean Rostand from saying: "If statistics are used to prove astrology, then I no longer believe in statistics."

Legal Landmarks for Astrology

American astrologer Evangeline Adams came to trial in New York City in 1914 in a legal landmark trial for astrology.[21] She was arrested on a charge of fortune-telling and insisted on standing trial. Here is a description of what happened:

> ...She came to court armed with reference books, expounded the principles of astrology, and illustrated its practice by reading a blind chart that turned out to be that of the judge's son. The judge was so impressed by her character and intelligence that he ruled in her favor, concluding that "the defendant raises astrology to the dignity of an exact science."
>
> Fortune-telling is still illegal in New York, but thanks to Evangeline Adams, astrology is no longer regarded as fortune-telling.[22]

From 1914 to the present, other legal cases have arisen in various parts of the United States. As recently as the spring of 1988 the State of New Jersey had a bill in its legislature which proposed to make astrology and all other "fortune-telling" professions illegal. Currently in the United States astrology is still usually considered under a large umbrella that includes a wide range of burgeoning metaphysical and alternative practitioners. The legal implications of trying to regulate this huge range of practices is not only staggering but alarming, if we remember the Inquisition, which burned astrologers along with any type of witch or perceived troublemaker for the official ecclesiastical point of view.

More recently in Nazi Germany, Hitler rounded up the astrologers and imprisoned them, especially those who were not predicting a German victory! In a more tolerant vein, the

---

21. Evangeline Adams (1868-1932) practiced astrology for over 40 years to a large clientele including such notables as J.P. Morgan, the Prince of Wales, and Enrico Caruso.
22. *Larousse Encyclopedia of Astrology* (English language edition), 1980, p. 21.

British Intelligence Service simultaneously hired astrologer Louis de Wohl to watch the charts of enemy leaders and to second-guess what Hitler's astrologers were telling him. America is also very tolerant of its own political, economic, and weather fore-casters, whose methods are not foolproof. I'm not aware of any who have been imprisoned for making a mistake, or even for daring to make a forecast.

In February 1989 the New Mexico Psychological Association introduced four bills into the New Mexico state legislature. They were intended to regulate those allowed to practice "psychology," "professional counseling" and even "art therapy." The psychologists wanted to protect their profession primarily from those coming in from other states where they were disqualified, and in some cases known for habits of sexual abuse with their clients. Unfortunately, in an attempt to protect their own professional status, especially to maintain insurance coverage (namely third-party payments in the mental health fields), they worded their bills to include the work that most astrologers and many other alternative practitioners do, namely "assessment of personal characteristics... enhancing interpersonal relationships, work and life adjustment, personal effectiveness ...counseling...guidance and human development... developing or changing careers, professions and locations, and the promotion of optimum mental health." A local group calling itself "Concerned Citizens for Metaphysical and Alternative Practitioners" responded with a request for changes to this proposed legislation. They recommended that no law regulate the alternative practitioners, especially if they do not call themselves psychologists, and that, among other things, all the above phrases quoted from Bill #282 be struck from the bill. Similar bills have previously been introduced and killed in Florida and Oregon.

By introducing such a piece of legislation, the question is raised as to whether or not to regulate the wide range of metaphysical and alternative practitioners, including astrologers. It also raises the question of who is a qualified practitioner, and puts astrologers in the uncomfortable position of being assessed alongside psychics, palm readers, channellers, tarot readers, past-life counselors, and so on. Not that any of these other practices may not yield excellent results, but they usually do not involve such a systematized body of knowledge as astrology. Some of these other techniques of predicting probability patterns and interpreting character can be helpful, but they operate on a different level—harder to assess than astrology, and often are much less precise in forecasting actual time and locational frameworks. Nevertheless, all the alternative practitioners should be dealt with on their own merits and by the standards of their own best organizations. (Psychics have a strong organization in Los Angeles and elsewhere in the United States. One such organization is the American Society for Psychical Research.)

In the United States, the NCGR (National Council for Geocosmic Research) is probably the astrological organization with the most thorough and comprehensive educational and testing program for the consulting and/or research astrologer.[23] Attainment of its Level 4 certificate is the equivalent of a full four-year college major program in astrology. This would be a way to qualify astrologers professionally if such legal certification should ever become necessary.

_____

23. Those astrologers who have received the Professional Certificate (i.e. completion of all four levels) from NCGR are listed in the *NCGR Professional Directory*, (The first directory will be available as of October 1991.)

NCGR is a national organization with 28 local chapters in 18 states, chapters in Canada and Mexico, plus 12 special interest groups, as of late 1990. It publishes monthly member letters and a large biannual journal, and holds at least one annual national conference, with numerous local conferences around the United States. The conferences are largely oriented to astrology education and research, with conference tapes available to supplement the educational materials and classes, whether or not the member chooses to test up to Level 4. NCGR Headquarters is at 105 Snyder Ave., Ramsey, NJ 07446; phone (201) 818-2871. For other astrological organizations in the United States and elsewhere, please see Appendix I, pp. 283-284.

If astrologers run into legal problems in their astrological practices, they can go to an organization such as NCGR, and also to AFAN (Association for Astrology Networking), 8306 Wilshire Boulevard, #537, Beverly Hills, CA 90211. AFAN specializes in dealing with any legal issues that may arise for astrologers. It has published a pamphlet entitled *The Law and Astrology* and has a telephone hotline: 1-616-796-3940.

II
Introduction to Some Major
Astrological Tools

Long and Short-Term Cycles: Some of the Big Ones
Western Astrologers Use and How They Work

Among the most important timing cycles that Western astrologers[24] consider are those that run for 29-1/2 years. These include the sidereal period for Saturn (or the length of time it takes for Saturn to make one complete revolution in its orbit around the Sun). Also, the monthly lunar cycle averages 29-1/2 days, which in the secondary progressed system equals 29-1/2 years. The secondary progressed lunar cycle is a key timing tool in terms of your personal timetable, because it always depends on what exact phase of the Moon was occurring when you were born (akin to the Hindu Vimsottari Dasa system, which depends on the exact degree of the Moon at birth). The Saturn cycle, however, occurs for all of us every 29-1/2 years, when we are around 29 years old and later around 58.[25]

---

24. For the most part, Western astrologers are those practicing in Europe, the United States, Canada, Australia, and most parts of the Western hemisphere. "Eastern" astrology is mostly Hindu (Indian) or Chinese. Hindu astrologers also have an excellent system of measuring long and short-term cycles called the Vimsottari Dasa system of prediction. Dasas (pronounced da'shas) can last anywhere from 6 to 20 years, depending on which planetary period prevails. They, in turn, are divided into nine subperiods called Bhuktis (pronounced book'tees). One's Dasa/Bhukti timetable for life is determined by the Moon's degree at the time of birth, which in turn determines the exact part of a Dasa one is born into.

As yet, the structure and techniques of Hindu astrology are largely unknown and unused in the West, and vice versa, but I expect that will change. I personally advocate using both Western (Uranian-based) and Hindu timing and interpretative systems, but there is not space here to delve into the vast intricacies of the Hindu system, which differs considerably from Western astrology. In my experience, using both systems alongside each other deepens and expands the integrity and the accuracy of the astrology.

For those with some astrological knowledge, a few books are being written on the subject especially for Westerners. My favorites so far are James T. Braha's *Ancient Hindu Astrology for the Modern Western Astrologer* (1986) and David Frawley's *The Astrology of the Seers: A Guide to Vedic (Hindu) Astrology* (1990).

25. At these ages, in fact any time between 28 and 30, though averaging at age 29, and any time between 58 and 60, though averaging at age 59, transiting Saturn in the heavens returns to its natal position.

Just as in everyday life, with the lunar cycle acting as one of the most immediate and helpful timers of the type of energy available on the planet, the secondary progressed lunar cycle helps us to determine major new beginnings, peaks, and lows in our personal lives over an expanse of 29-1/2 years.[26] The beginning is at the progressed New Moon, the peak at the Full Moon, and the low from one to two years before the New Moon. The same holds true on a lower scale of eventfulness every month of the calendar year, and has endless variations depending on in which area of the zodiac the New or Full Moon is occurring, whether it coincides with an eclipse, what planetary interrelationships are happening at that time, and in what area of your birth map this occurs. What I have learned working with a number of clients' charts is that the chart for the particular secondary progressed lunar quarter that a person is in is the chart describing much of the type and level of activity for that entire period, averaging around 7-1/2 years (longer or shorter per quarter depending on the orbital speed of the Moon). Thus, the energy of the New Moon is about starting fresh on some new tack in life, whether personally or professionally or often both. There is an experimental feel to this quarter.

When the Second Quarter chart begins (or up to two to three months before it), there is often an abrupt change of tone in terms of being put on the line to take a course of action based on all that you have been developing during the First Quarter Moon. Astrologers often label it the "crisis of action" quarter, not that it is necessarily filled with crises, but that there is some compulsion to make good on the promises of the First Quarter. It is an appropriate time to take chances, spread your wings, branch out—all relative to your chronological age at this time.

When the Full Moon, or Third Quarter chart begins, there are

---

26. If you are not currently working with an astrologer, but would like to determine your own secondary progressed lunar cycle, you can provide your birth data (month, day, year, hour, minute, location of birth) to Astro Communications Services, Inc. (formerly Astro Computing Services, Inc.), P.O. Box 16430, San Diego, CA 92116-0430, or call toll-free 1-800-888-9983. Ask for "Lifetime lunar phases," currently $5.00 (1990).

Established in 1973 by IBM-trained Neil Michelsen, and breaking new ground for all computerized astrological services internationally, Astro Communications Services also produces some of the best and most comprehensive, accurate astrological charts in the United States, as well as a wide choice of natal and timing options. I would highly recommend checking out their annual catalog of available services. The only exception currently is their "Astrolocality" maps (referred to in this book as Astro*Carto*Graphy maps, for which see footnote 27 , p. 26).

often some concrete results from the input of the first two Quarters, if one has put in the effort, although this is not guaranteed. The Full Moon Quarter is a time of fruition, and, especially when it coincides with Saturn transiting the Midheaven of the natal chart, it translates as a time when one can receive open acknowledgement and appreciation for one's efforts—namely, prizes, public appearances, publication, higher sales and/or greater prosperity, etc. If this is not occurring on schedule, you have to look back deeply at the natal chart, and thus your character, and see what you are doing or not doing that is preventing the natural law of your personal timetable from taking place. Perhaps there are further, greater lessons to be learned before you receive rewards or benefits.

The Fourth Quarter is typically one of reorientation and, especially in the last year or two, one of release from much of what preceded this portion of the 29-1/2 year cycle. This is in order to clear the way for new energy that will be seeded at the New Moon of the next cycle. From my experience and from my work with clients, the most dramatic change in energy comes from the last year or so of the Fourth Quarter Moon into the beginning of the new lunar cycle symbolized by the New Moon.

Several years ago I was surprised to find that a client I was about to meet with was on her way to start medical school in a few weeks, in September, although according to her personal 29-1/2 year secondary progressed lunar cycle she was in the last throes of the Fourth Quarter Moon and would not experience the fresh incoming energy of the First Quarter Moon until late February of the following year. Ideally she should have waited another year. However, she was 36 years old starting in her first year of medical school, and there was no question of postponing this lifelong ambition any further.

When I heard from the client some time later, here is how it turned out. The first semester was excruciatingly difficult, and she barely passed all her courses, even with extra time spent with tutors. It was a grueling experience, physically, emotionally, and mentally. When the second semester arrived, she was aware of the change in cycle but scarcely expected things to ease up, perhaps because many people expect medical school to be so trying. In fact, that semester marked a dramatic change in her academic performance. She started to do very well in all her courses, with less study time and no tutor. The abrupt change in energy available to her on all levels was remarkable, because now the flow of energy was with her, not against her. In this case had she not been so smart, so physically strong, and so passionately driven to become a doctor, she would not have lasted through those uphill months from September through January.

As to the issue of decision-making, perhaps on an inner level this woman chose the most difficult time to start medical school in order to prove to herself she could pass any hurdles. There was a tendency in her character to put herself through incredible tests of physical endurance, and my guess is that this may have been the last gargantuan test for herself. After this she may subconsciously or consciously choose coordinates of time and space (timing and location) that make her life easier. I do not mean removing life's challenges and difficulties altogether, but rather moving on to other levels in life, where it is no longer necessary to create situations that prove certain points or honor certain fears and anxieties.

Astro-Mapping

Speaking of coordinates of space, there is a whole realm of astrology that deals with geographical locations very specifically. Called alternately "astro-mapping," "astrolocality maps," and "Astro·Carto·Graphy,"[27] this is a technique in locational astrology

---

27. Currently the best astro-mapping comes from Jim Lewis and any others using his federally registered trademark, Astro·Carto·Graphy. In the United States such maps are available from Astro·Carto·Graphy, c/o Astro Numeric Service, P.O. Box 425, San Pablo, CA 94806; Phone 1-800-MAPPING. In Europe, Astro·Carto·Graphy maps are available in the German language from Claude Weiss, Astrodata AG, Lindenbachstr. 56, CH-8042 Zurich, Switzerland; phone: 01-363-60 60.

In terms of software for personal computers, Quick·Maps (©1991 and endorsed by Jim Lewis) present the patented A·C·G maps in 8-1/2" x 11" format. (Latitude crossing sheets for Quick·Maps are not yet available, as of April 1991, but there are plans to include them.) Quick·Maps are available from Matrix Software; phone 1-800-PLANETS.

There are other types of maps which show not only conjunctions (0°), but also squares (90°), oppositions (180°), sextiles (60°), and trines (120°). While these other aspects are interesting for minor detail, especially the squares, they do not have the forcefulness of a planet conjunct an angle. If we add the latitude factor, especially for sextiles and trines, it makes aspects to the angles other than conjunctions astronomically problematic and thus astrologically suspect. It is also much harder to spot planetary crossings at key latitudes when you have to sort out all the other lines not conjunct the angles. The full size (11" x 17") Astro·Carto·Graphy map makes all this much easier visually, not only because it is large, but also because it always shows only the angular conjunctions as well as the zeniths for the entire world (not just one country or region), and it includes a computer listing of significant world latitudes. A*C*G also produces patented Cyclo*Carto*Graphy maps and booklets, which combine the latest transits and progressions on a transparency which is overlaid on the natal Astro*Carto*Graphy map. (Transits and [secondary] progressions are described on pp. 10-12.) This combines timing directly with the geographical information and works well for a 1-1/2 year period. Both A*C*G and C*C*G maps are extremely useful if geographical location is an issue in any way.

that has been made more widely available since 1976, when Jim Lewis, a California astrologer, developed a computerized system he calls Astro·Carto·Graphy (A·C·G), in which personal (or corporate, national, event or transiting) planetary data is superimposed on a map of the world. (See the A·C·G maps in Chapter 3. Jim Lewis has pioneered the development of techniques for interpreting the maps and continues to teach and train other astrologers how to read natal and mundane A·C·G maps. With Ariel Guttman, he co-authored the first book on the subject, *The Astro·Carto·Graphy Book of Maps*, Llewellyn Publications, 1989.)

The planetary lines on the A·C·G maps reflect geographically where the various planets are angular at any given time. For instance, at your birth time, Jupiter may have been rising in Sydney, Australia, though you were born in New York City. So it's as if you were born on the same date at the same time, only in Sydney. This gives a lifelong resonance for the type of experience you're likely to have in Sydney—in person, or via long distance. With astro-mapping, you can tell what locations are better or worse for you to live at or visit or even be associated with—as the locations work long distance, and you can personally feel the effects of a place without even going there. Once you have an Astro·Carto·Graphy map, you can also consider another tool, the Cyclo·Carto·Graphy map, a transparent overlay which combines the latest transits and progressions in A·C·G format. The transits and progressions shown on the Cyclo·Carto·Graphy map may amplify or even temporarily contradict what is there natally.

In personal terms, the actual birthplace is still the most important, but the astro-mapping reveals geographic locations that shift the emphasis of the natal chart by placing different planets on the angles. If you go to a location where a planet or planets are exactly on the angle, the influence is felt most strongly. It is felt less strongly the farther away you move from the point of exactness. If the midpoint of two planetary lines goes right through a particular location, that is also significant. In addition, the line of latitude that continues from a point where two or more planetary lines cross is considered. These latitudinal planetary crossings should be no further away than 2° north or south of the latitude in question; 1° to exact (0°) is very strong. Out of all this, the influence that is ideal or suitable for you depends on a wide variety of factors based on what is shown in the natal chart. For astro-mapping, it is necessary to work with a fairly certain or exact birth moment. Astro-mapping will be included along with other astrological components in the upcoming chapters.

Hard Aspects: A Key to the Manifestation of Events

Another critical factor (one that derives from the Uranian system of astrology, though now also widely used by astrologers using more traditional systems) is the predominant use of hard aspects, or angular relationships, in determining the likelihood of events or important happenings in our lives.[28] "Hard" aspects are multiples of 45°, or the 360° circle divided by 4, 8, and 16. Thus the square (90°), opposition (180°), and conjunction (0°) are included, as well as the aspects at 22-1/2°, 45°, and 135°[29]—especially any of these planetary contacts to Personal Points (described pp. 29-37). Alfred Witte did experiments with thousands of battle charts during World War I in which he discovered a great deal about the symmetry of the planets in relation to one another. The outcome of all this tended to show a greater effectiveness in using not only hard aspects between planets and angles, but a system very like vector analysis—which will not be considered in this book, but which became central to the Uranian system of astrology in determining character and in analyzing events, present, past, and future.[30]

Though Witte used mainly geocentric astrology, John Nelson, an RCA Communications radio engineer, worked from 1946 to 1971 to investigate systematically the relationship between heliocentric configurations of planets and short-wave radio disturbances. He was able to forecast such disturbances with an accuracy rate of over 93 percent, noting that hard aspects caused heavy static when linked with other aspects, whereas soft aspects (120°, 60°) did not, and at the point of exactness tended to diminish the static caused by

---

28. The Uranian system of astrology was originally called the Hamburg School and was founded in Germany in 1915 by Alfred Witte (1878-1943). Its principles draw together the best of ancient and medieval astrological techniques. Witte had a unique and profound understanding of how astronomical realities apply to astrological principles. He also invented the 360° and 90° dials, now widely used by many astrologers around the world.

29. These are also called fourth, eighth, and sixteenth harmonics, and many consider them the harmonics of manifestation.

30. Although soft aspects (60° and 120°) are much less emphasized here, they do operate in terms of house relationships to one another, and that is how they are used in the Uranian system of astrology and also to some extent in Hindu astrology.

hard aspects. So although Nelson is not saying planetary aspects cause radio disturbances, he has shown that there is a definite correlation between solar atmospheric behavior and certain planetary aspects, specifically the hard aspects, resulting in magnetic storms in the Earth's ionosphere. Similarly, in 1964, when Michel Gauquelin was studying the effect of terrestrial magnetic disturbances on the births of 16,000 children, he found that the planetary effect was stronger when the geomagnetic disturbance increased.

Six Personal Points: The Major Checkpoints of a Chart

> ...It is the essence of any powerful symbol that it says many things to many different levels of the mind, so that any single explanation of its meaning is necessarily a dilution and a distortion.
>
> —Willis Harman and Howard Rhein-gold, *Higher Creativity: Liberating the Unconscious for Breakthrough Insights,* 1984, p. 181.

In terms of the critical astrological components in any chart, we will first look at the planetary influences on six major points, called Personal Points:

1) Aries point or Cardinal Axis
2) Ascendant
3) Moon's Node, or the Lunar Nodal axis
4) Sun
5) Moon
6) Midheaven

In the Uranian system of astrology, it is considered that other than the outer planet cycle returns, squares and oppositions to themselves (See Chapter 4 on "The Seven Year Saturn Quarters" and "Other Big Turning Points for Everyone"), nothing really important can happen in one's life unless it happens along one of these six major points, or Personal Points. In fact, there is even greater likelihood of important events in the life if there is planetary action on more than one Personal Point. This is especially true if the planetary influence is over a longer period of time, such as with the

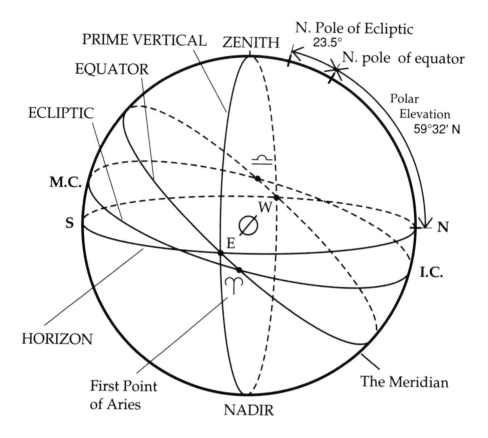

PRIME VERTICAL ZENITH
N. Pole of Ecliptic
23.5°
N. pole of equator
EQUATOR
ECLIPTIC
Polar
Elevation
59°32' N
M.C.
S
W
E
N
I.C.
HORIZON
First Point
of Aries
The Meridian
NADIR

Described for Polar Elevation 51°32'N, the latitude for London

The Five Great Circles
(Reproduced with kind permission of Jeff Mayo.)

outer planets (since they move more slowly in relation to the Earth's orbital speed), if the planet turns either stationary retrograde (SR) or stationary direct (SD) within 1° conjunct or opposite a Personal Point, or if the influence also includes a solar or lunar eclipse within 1° conjunct or opposite a Personal Point.

When looking at the six Personal Points, remember that throughout all astrology the meaning of the planetary positions in relation to each other and in relation to the Earth always has an astronomical basis from which the equivalent to human affairs is translated. (See Law of Correspondences, p. 5.) For instance, the Sun as the center of the solar system is translated in the astrological chart as a primary "luminary" or source of light and energy, the secondary luminary being the Moon, which of course serves as a reflective light-giver. So the Sun further equates to our sense of our own identity, ego, physical body, yang energy, masculine or aggressive energy, and thus the important male figures in our lives—the father, the husband, and so on.

The Moon is the closest body to the Earth, and through its ongoing 29-1/2 day cycles regulates the monthly rhythms of human life, having strong effects on the female reproductive cycle, the flow of the oceans' tides, and, by extension, the ebb and flow of the human emotional cycle. We know that the greatest degree of human excitability comes at the Full Moon, though solar eclipses (at the New Moon) can throw this off slightly, and that crime rates and hospital admissions increase at that time. In astrological charts the Moon then translates as the emotional core of the life, the womb, the home, yin energy, female or receptive energy, and of course the key female figures in our lives: the mother, the wife, and so on. The Moon symbolizes our ability as humans not only to process our own emotions, but to reflect and receive the emotional content of those around us, being aware of it on an intimate level—which in mundane (or world) charts translates as the public, especially that part of the public which is receptive to social, political, and cultural trends, and also that part of the public which nurtures the young and provides the emotional support for a self-regulating group of people, be it a race, nation, or civilization.

Notice that among the six Personal Points, the only two planetary bodies are the Sun and the Moon. (And again, in geocentric astrology, the Sun translates as the Sun/Earth relationship.) That is because the other planets, though each important in its own way, provide only further adjectives as to what is going on in a chart. To get the nouns, or to describe the primary subject matter of the chart, we need the six Personal Points. As for the remaining Personal Points, the Aries point, the Ascendant, the Moon's Node, and the Midheaven, each of these are points in space where two critical astronomical arcs or planes (called Great Circles) intersect or diverge.[31]

In the case of the Aries point (or Cardinal Axis) we have the intersection of the ecliptic and the celestial equator at the Spring and Fall Equinox (creating equal amounts of day and night time); and at the Winter and Summer Solstice, the greatest divergence between the ecliptic and the celestial equator (creating in one hemisphere or another the longest day, or the longest night). In zodiacal terms, the Cardinal Axis is where the Sun, as seen from the Earth, appears to pass through the areas of the heavens labeled 0° Aries, 0° Cancer, 0° Libra, and 0° Capricorn. We have already discussed the relevance of dividing the 360° yearly sequence by four and by eight (and sometimes by sixteen). Thus we see that the points halfway between each of the Cardinal points would also be considered equivalent in chart analysis by eighth harmonic, though not as significant in the calendar year as the original four points.[32]

From ancient times human records show that most of the major spiritual and religious ceremonies throughout the year are timed to coincide with or are dated from either the equinox or solstice. For example, before calendar adjustments were made which put us permanently three days off, Christmas actually coincided with the Winter Solstice. This is how it was in the original Julian calendar. Also, though not on the equinox, Easter is always celebrated on the first Sunday after the first Full Moon occurring on or after the Spring Equinox. The Chinese New Year begins on the second New Moon after the Winter Solstice.

There is something very primordial to all human beings about the solstices and equinoxes, and so too astronomically, the planes of the ecliptic and the equator are fundamental to the Earth's relationship to the Sun and to itself, respectively. The ecliptic is the Earth's orbit around the Sun, as viewed from the Sun, or the apparent path of the Sun around the Earth, as viewed from the Earth. Astrologers use the ecliptic plane to locate the positions of planets, measuring 360° (divided into 30° for each of the 12 zodiacal

31. There are five Great Circles: the ecliptic, the celestial equator, the horizon, the prime vertical, and the celestial meridian. Astrologers measure from central reference points that derive usually from the intersection of two of the Great Circles, and after that measuring north and south of that plane. For instance, lines of latitude are measured north and south of the equator (see diagram p. 30). The apparent path of the Sun around the Earth is called the ecliptic, and the Moon crosses the ecliptic on its lunar nodal axis.

32. The eighth harmonic points to the Cardinal Axis include 15° Taurus, 15° Leo, 15° Scorpio, and 15° Aquarius. In terms of calendar dates, the eighth harmonic points also correspond to the "Fire Festivals" in England: 15° Taurus (May 5-7) is Beltane; 15° Leo (Aug. 6-8) is Lammas; 15° Scorpio (Nov. 5-7) is Samhain, or Halloween, and 15° Aquarius (Feb. 5-7) is Candlemas.

areas), starting from 0° Aries and moving eastward. The Earth's equator, called the celestial equator when projected onto the celestial sphere, is a Great Circle perpendicular to the Earth's axis of rotation. It is also the circle lying halfway between the North and South Poles, thus dividing the Earth into northern and southern hemispheres. Its correspondence as the central belt or plane around the Earth could be said to be to the field of consciousness representing the soul of the Earth, and that of the ecliptic, to the Earth's vital connection to the Sun as life force.[33] In another sense, this tremendously vital connection between Earth and Sun corresponds to the same connection between a human being and planet Earth. Or, to be more specific, this is the key connective point linking up an individual to a much larger public, to a sense of what is happening globally, and to that which makes it possible in social, political, economic, and cultural terms to have a decent existence on Earth. Thus, when a planet is crossing the Cardinal axis or Aries point (again, at 0° Aries, 0° Cancer, 0° Libra, 0° Capricorn, or its eighth harmonic at 15° Taurus, 15° Leo, 15° Scorpio, 15° Aquarius), the more exact—within 1°—the more potent is that planetary energy, and its equivalent in human affairs on a global scale. Likewise in a birth chart of an individual, nation, corporation, or event, when a planet or a Personal Point is located on the Cardinal axis, we have a sense of the type of lens, so to speak, with which that person or group views the world.

The Cardinal axis, the Ascendant, and the Moon's Node are all Personal Points indicating the outer or more external person, whereas the Sun, Moon, and Midheaven are Personal Points representing more of the inner person. Not surprisingly, the Cardinal axis in a global context reflects the generality, whereas the Ascendant is more local, and the Moon's Nodes are more intimate still—in terms of expressing our external interactions in human relationships.

The Ascendant is the eastern point of intersection of the horizon and the ecliptic planes (two of the Great Circles). So at sunrise at any given location, the Sun is on the Ascendant. In the popular lingo, the Ascendant is also the "rising sign," though a planet near the As-

---

33. In his discussion of morphic resonance and morphic fields, biologist Rupert Sheldrake talks about a field which organizes the void, and about organic *and* inorganic things having fields of consciousness.

cendant would definitely outweigh in influence any area of the zodiac per se that happens to be rising at that moment.[34] (In fact the influence of planetary configurations, especially if in close contact, outweighs the influence of zodiacal areas, or "signs" of the zodiac.) The Ascendant describes a great deal about our immediate environment in terms of 1) the places we inhabit, 2) the people we tend to surround ourselves with, and 3) how we are seen by others in a more local way. Also, since our parents are the first people to cross our horizon, sometimes our physical characteristics can be deciphered from the Ascendant, especially if we strongly resemble our parents. But the astronomical correlation is telling us that the Ascendant is very much about place, as in the place where we live and the place where we connect with people.[35]

Astronomically also, nodes are pairs of points where two planetary orbits intersect. Astrologers are most interested in where various planetary orbits cross the Earth's orbit, but especially where the Earth's orbit crosses that of the Moon, since the Moon is the closest planetary body to the Earth and thus represents a sense of intimacy with the Earth.[36] Following the Law of Correspondences, we would then consider the Moon's Nodes to represent that place in our lives where we connect with others more intimately. This would include our mate, close family members and friends—emotionally speaking, that very inner circle.

I have already described the Sun and Moon as Personal Points. Together with the Midheaven, they are considered more evocative of the inner person, though of these three the Sun—as a manifestation of the physical body—can give us the most direct and outward clues as to the nature of the inner person. In terms of gradation, the Moon and the Midheaven, respectively, are increasingly symbolic of the inner life and a key to the soul identity.

34. The Earth's diurnal movement is such that the Ascendant passes through an entire zodiacal sign (30°) in an average of two hours, though depending on latitude and time of year it could take less than half an hour and up to over three hours per zodiacal sign.

35. A key factor in denoting place on the planet, the Ascendant is always 90° from the zenith, which is the point of the celestial sphere that is always directly overhead at any location on the surface of the Earth. The zenith, not to be confused with the Midheaven, is where the upper Meridian intersects the prime vertical. (See the diagram of the five Great Circles, p. 30.)

36. The Moon's Node is measured two different ways, which are usually no more than 1° apart. One measurement is called the true node, the other the mean node. I prefer the latter, and use it in the charts in this book, though the Astro*Carto*Graphy maps do not include the Moon's Node.

In discussing the Midheaven, we find a paradox of sorts. Although the most elevated point in the chart, and the most indicative of our higher aims in life (often equated with career goals and achievements), the Midheaven is still the hardest to pin down in terms of identifying the individual.[37] Perhaps that is because the seat of our consciousness is symbolically located there, and whether we are aware of it or not, we are constantly in the process of either stretching or awakening our capacity for higher consciousness. Think of what the Midheaven is in astronomical terms: it is the point where the upper Meridian intersects the ecliptic, or the point where the Sun can be seen at local apparent noon time. At that time of day, the Sun has reached its highest altitude in relation to Earth (that altitude dependent on the time of year, of course), and so with human beings there is something about the Midheaven that is deeply symbolic of our highest aspirations. But just to complicate matters, astrologers also identify parents with the Midheaven axis. And so we see that, as in life, to separate out and identify our own aspirations as distinguishable from those of our parents becomes part of the process of reaching toward our own higher consciousness and our own higher purpose as to what we're doing with our lives.

In the upcoming chapters all of these six Personal Points will be used as a basic vocabulary in dealing with issues of decision-making—expanding on that basic framework using the language of the other planets, mainly Mercury, Venus, Mars, Jupiter, Saturn, Uranus, Neptune and Pluto. I say "mainly" because there are thousands of other planetary bodies that could be considered if asteroids, planetoids, fixed stars, comets, etc. are taken into account.

Again, a reminder that when we study the effects of the planets in matters of decision-making, we are dealing with planetary energies (other than the Sun and Moon) as *adjectives* in describing what is affecting the six Personal Points, the *nouns*. The six Personal Points can be called the nouns, because unless the planets are operating in close hard contact to certain points in space (which have already been identified as the interrelationships of the five Great Circles), they are not affecting the individual or collective as

---

37. The Midheaven is also the point in the chart that is changing the most quickly (1° every four minutes), so that to be able to analyze this axis accurately demands the most precision in locating the correct space and time coordinates.

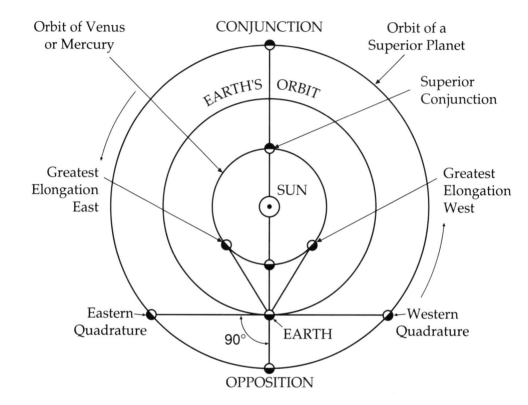

The Principle of Astronomical Conjunction
(Reproduced with kind permission of Jeff Mayo.)

radically. Their potential effect is always there, but not as decisive in human terms as when they are making hard contact with one or more of the Personal Points, or in the case of the outer planets, when they are making hard contact by transit to their natal positions. As you might imagine, some of life's biggest turning points are more affected by the slower-moving planets (which include Jupiter, Saturn, Uranus, Neptune, and Pluto), and their hard contacts to Personal Points. Not that the inner, more quickly-moving planets

(Mercury, Venus, and Mars) are unimportant, but more often they affect the momentum of our daily lives. They serve as triggers to larger events, unless they make close hard contacts to the outer planets, in which case they serve as *secondary adjectives* in describing the major event.

In terms of larger cycles, we will also be looking at the synodic cycles of planets, which in this context are nouns in themselves.[38] But again, when they occur on a personal, corporate, or national Personal Point, especially the Cardinal axis, affecting us all, they are extremely important in describing various social, economic, and political patterns in history.

The Other Planets:
Their Connection to Human Life and Human Affairs

Many people have asked me how astrologers *know* what the various planets mean in terms of human lives and human events. It is easy enough to find books which describe what they mean in human terms.[39] But how do we come about those descriptions? Chiefly through the Law of Correspondences, which is refined somewhat to fit each major new period of civilization, not to mention the many cultures coexisting within a civilization. But again, we should remember that even without fancy telescopes, people inhabiting the Earth in ancient times had a sense of the nature of the planets they knew about, and these seem intrinsically consistent with the meanings we use today. In fact, for the ancients, the most remote planet they probably knew about was Saturn. (Uranus was not officially discovered until March 13, 1781; Neptune on September 23, 1846; and Pluto on February 18, 1930.)

It is not the purpose of this book to delve deeply into the descriptions of the planets and the signs of the zodiac, but in order to provide the reader with the basics of the astrological vocabulary in one book, we will proceed with brief descriptions of the planets Mercury through Pluto, especially with reference to the Law of

---

38. A synodic cycle is the interval between two successive conjunctions of any two planets. For example, Jupiter and Saturn conjunct once every 19.859 years, Uranus and Neptune conjunct once every 171.403 years, and so on. A conjunction (0°), in turn, is an extremely important planetary contact, where two or more planets occupy the same degree of celestial longitude. (See diagram on p. 36.)

39. For this purpose I particularly recommend Robert Hand's *Horoscope Symbols*, 1981, and *Alan Oken's Complete Astrology*, revised edition, 1988.

Correspondences as it connects these planets astronomically to human life and human affairs.

Mercury ☿

Mercury is the planet closest to the Sun, and, seen from the Earth, is never more than 28° away from the Sun. It takes Mercury only 88 days to make a complete orbit around the Sun, traveling at a tremendous speed of around 108,000 miles per hour. So it is the fastest, closest, and, not surprisingly, the hottest of all the planets orbiting around the Sun, with a mean daytime temperature of 760°F.

Without straying too deeply into the territory of mythical symbols, which is not the subject of this book, suffice it to say that Mercury and all the remaining planets are amazingly aptly named. Some would say this is no coincidence. Because Mercury is related to the quick movements through the nervous system and the brain outward to the limbs of the body, it represents not only our ability to think and communicate, but also our ability to get that message transmitted in a broader way. Thus it is said to rule over all manner of travel and communications on a wide scale. Also, perhaps because of the correlation to its small size and speed of movement, Mercury is associated with children and young people.

One last word about Mercury: its rulership over the brain has to do with logical thinking, cleverness, wit, and verbal skills. How it links up to other points and the outermost planets in the chart tells us more about the higher mind, and the deeper intellectual capacities, over and above the use of a fast-paced ability to keep functioning in the world.

Mercury is the planetary ruler of the areas of the zodiac known as Gemini and Virgo.

Venus ♀

Though Venus is the brightest object in the sky, as seen from Earth (not counting our Sun and Moon), it has simultaneously one of the most mysterious appearances of all the planets and also one of the most unusual and ferocious environments. Venus is quite close to the Earth in size, mass, and density. It is also our nearest planetary neighbor (other than the Earth's Moon). Venus is 30 percent closer to the Sun than the Earth is, with surface temperatures as high as 860°F, and its volcanic gases (with carbon dioxide in the greatest abundance) are accumulated in its atmosphere rather than into the oceans, as on Earth. (There are no oceans on Venus.) So this very heavy and dense gaseous atmosphere, with excessive carbon dioxide and a crushing air pressure 90 times that of Earth, serves to trap infrared radiation from the Sun. Together with the shimmer of heat waves and the effect of refracted light, it is difficult to see what the surface of Venus is really like. Venus looks mysterious through a thick blanket of opaque clouds, which have a slightly creamy color because of the large quantities of sulfuric acid.

Compared to an Earth day of 24 hours, a day on Venus equals 5,832 hours, or 243 Earth days. That is a lot of continuous daytime! Add up the factors of 1) excessive heating of a dense carbon dioxide atmosphere, "the greenhouse effect"; 2) clouds so thick with sulfuric acid (acid-rain producing) that they have corroded American and Russian space probes; and 3) perpetual lightning and thunder from the combined effects of light, heat, gas, and electrical components, and you have a planet representing all of the things astrologers associate with Venus in human terms: mystery, allure (with the promise of fire underneath), sensuality, attractability (the brightest star), female sexuality and beauty, pleasure, and by extension, money, creature comforts, charm, affection, and, on a higher level, harmony and love.

Is it ironic that Earth's atmosphere is starting to resemble that of Venus, with the acid rain and possibly the "greenhouse effect"? Perhaps it is only a reflection of the principle of Venus as an astrological symbol, where an excess of money or creature comforts, or both, as evidenced by overindustrialization on Earth, causes the bright object with the mysterious veil to be stripped away to reveal what is potentially underneath—a gaseous inferno. Because planet Venus is so close in size and proximity to the Earth, the correlation is often made astrologically that it's something comfortable and familiar to us all. In fact, it is never beyond our visible reach in the morning or evening skies (and never more than 48° from the Sun, as seen from the Earth). Unfortunately it is also easy to misuse and miscalculate when dealing with familiar objects that are bright, shiny, and enticing, but up close appear to be more veiled and less accessible.

Venus is the planetary ruler of the areas of the zodiac known as Taurus and Libra.

Mars ♂

Mars is about half the size of the Earth. It has two moons, takes 1.88 years to orbit the Sun, and has days equaling 24 hours 37 minutes. Its atmosphere is dry and thin and contains only carbon dioxide. It absorbs a lot of ultraviolet sunlight, since there is no protective upper atmosphere to shield the surface from damaging radiation (such as the Earth's ozone layer). Like every planet, the atmosphere and surface of Mars has gone through numerous changes; but even so, with its slight amount of gravity and thin atmosphere, it has probably been millions of years since liquid water ever existed long enough in any one place on Mars for living organisms to evolve. Liquid water evaporates almost immediately there. (No organic matter was found on Mars by probes from Viking 1 and 2 in July and September 1976, respectively.)

Mars is a dynamic planet with a great deal of geological activity. It is notable for having the largest volcano in our entire solar system, called Olympus Mons, formed within the last billion years and probably still active. Olympus Mons is ten miles (15 km) higher than Mount Everest. The state of Rhode Island would fit inside its crater, and the mountain itself would contain the state of Missouri. Geothermal activity is associated with Mars's huge volcanoes and possibly accounts for its ancient river beds, called "channels" or *canali* by the Italian astronomer Schiaparelli (late 1800s).

Mars also has the largest canyon known in our solar system. Called Valles Marineris, it is 3100 miles (5000 km) long, as compared to the Grand Canyon, which is 280 miles (450 km) long. Through this 3100-mile canyon, equaling the width of the United States, howl incredible winds up to 124 mph (200 km/hour). These winds also stir up astonishing dust storms which can envelop an entire hemisphere for several weeks at a time. The unusual feature of this dust is that it is red or rust-like in color. This is due to the fact that what oxygen Mars had at one time was locked into its soil and caused iron-rich compounds to oxidize. This soil rich in ferrous oxide appears as a reddish landscape and causes Mars to be called "the Red Planet."

Not surprisingly, the astrological correlations for Mars include physical energy, aggressive action, initiative, courage, violence, and by extension, heat and male sexuality. There is an extraordinary amount of wind and dynamic volcanic action on this planet, which, whether current or not, still account for the largest volcano and the largest "grand canyon" in our solar system. Mars has a maximum surface temperature of 86° F and dips down to temperatures so cold as to cause cloud layers of carbon dioxide mist, or "dry ice."

Heatwise, of course, all the other planets closer to the Sun are hotter, especially Mercury, but unlike Mercury, Mars still has a lot of geological, geothermal activity and so is more associated with hot temperatures; whereas, if Mercury is considered at all hot in astrological terms, it is more a question of things "heating up" via the speed of motion and communication.

Mars is also the next planet farther out from the Earth away from the Sun. Its position vis-à-vis the Earth thus lends itself to connotations of a pioneering spirit apropos physical energy and aggressive action. (Remember the large numbers of sports champions in the Gauquelin research whose natal charts showed Mars prominently. See p. 19.) And, lastly, what more perfect color to symbolize physical energy or the warrior in action than red?

Mars is the planetary ruler of Aries and (jointly with Pluto) Scorpio.

Jupiter ♃

Jupiter is the giant planet in our solar system, with a mass 318 times larger than the Earth's. In fact, Jupiter's mass is 2-1/2 times larger than all the other planets combined—which gives it the strongest gravitational pull (2-1/2 times stronger than Earth's surface gravity). There is also a strong magnetic field around Jupiter, extending about 270,000 miles out to its nearest satellite. And in terms of satellites, Jupiter has 16 moons (four of the outermost moons travel in retrograde motion) and a single ring composed of fine microscopic dust. Among its satellites are those larger than some of the other planets. Ganymede, for example, is larger than Mercury.

After Venus, Jupiter is the next brightest object we see in our night skies on Earth. And like Venus, Jupiter's atmosphere is so dense that its surface cannot be seen through telescopes. We do know, however, that its surface probably consists of liquid hydrogen, and we know its atmosphere consists of hydrogen, helium, ammonia, and methane. This accounts for such a largely gaseous composition that Jupiter's density is less than a fourth that of the Earth. Another notable feature is that Jupiter has many brightly colored belts parallel to its equator which, while constantly changing colors—including yellow, gray, pink, red, orange, blue-green, and tan—also rotate at different speeds. Jupiter has the shortest day of all the planets, at 9 hours 55 minutes, so its rotational dynamics emphasize the shift in the bands of colors.

Another unusual feature about Jupiter, especially with regard to the Law of Correspondences, is the fact that it radiates 2-1/2 times more heat than it receives from the Sun (a 1965 discovery). This extra energy must be coming from its interior, from some kind of ongoing storage and regeneration process, which also may account for some of Jupiter's huge storm systems. One such system, which may be an oval hurricane, is a disturbance that has been in existence for at least several centuries and is called the "Great Red Spot." This cloud system, brick-red in color, is larger in diameter than the Earth.

In ancient and classical astrology Jupiter was named the Greater Benefic (or Greater Fortune) and Venus the Lesser Benefic (or Lesser Fortune). Nowadays there is still some resonance for those ancient labels in that Venus and Jupiter *are* the brightest objects in our heavens (after our Sun and Moon) and thus are the chief factors we look at in a chart for attractability—Venus more in the sexual sense (though it includes money), Jupiter more in the financial sense (though it includes personal happiness and success). Because Jupiter is the largest planet in our solar system, it is and has always been associated with growth and expansion and therefore, potentially, extravagances and anything in excess. However, it has also been associated with expansion of the emotional being—joy, optimism, humor, and generosity. (For generosity and attractability, remember the strong magnetic field and the heat that is stored and radiated out from Jupiter, 2-1/2 times more than it receives from the Sun; for joy and optimism, remember the bright multicolored bands around its equator.)

Jupiter is the first of the truly outer planets, as seen from the Earth. Earth is 93 million miles from the Sun, which, if we call this distance one Astronomical Unit (AU), compares to Mars's 1.52 AU and Jupiter's 5.2 AU in their respective distances from the Sun. (See diagram, p. 47.) It takes Jupiter 11.9 years to orbit the Sun. The astrological correlation in terms of being the first outer planet, and also a big and buoyant one, is to larger systems of thought, larger than those needed for simple everyday living. Thus it includes those ideas and levels of idealism and honor which enable us to rise above and beyond the everyday needs and chores, such as religion, philosophy, law, foreign trade and exchange, and politics—in fact, higher education in general, especially with regard to the use of the higher mind. When we put this together with the exuberance and optimism associated with Jupiter, we can understand why the Gauquelin statistical research of thousands of groups of professionals showed Jupiter to be most prominent in the birth charts of actors, soldiers, and writers.

Jupiter is the planetary ruler of Sagittarius, and (jointly with Neptune) Pisces.

Saturn ♄

Saturn has many similarities to Jupiter in being the planet that is second largest in size. (Saturn has a mean diameter of 72,000 miles, or 120,000 km, as compared to Jupiter's mean diameter of 87,000 miles, or 143,200 km) It has nearly the same length of day (10-1/2 hours compared to Jupiter's 9 hours 55 minutes), the same atmosphere (hydrogen, helium, ammonia, and methane), and same probable surface material (liquid hydrogen). Like Jupiter, Saturn has many moons, 20+ to Jupiter's 16, with one—Titan—nearly the size of Mercury and the only satellite in the solar system other than Neptune's satellite Triton to have an atmosphere. Saturn also radiates more heat from its interior than it receives from the Sun, though this phenomenon is less pronounced than in the case of Jupiter. From there the differences abound. Whereas Jupiter is brightly colored, Saturn has color tones that are much duller (yellowish-tan), though still beautiful; Saturn is colder, with temperatures around –250°F compared to Jupiter's maximum surface temperature of –216°; and it has a longer orbital period: 29-1/2 years—a pivotal time span in astrological timing.

By far the most distinguished and magical feature about Saturn is its series of rings, which is the largest ring system of all the planets in our solar system. They can be seen prominently from Earth through small telescopes and measure 171,000 miles from one outer edge to the other. They look like a wide, flat, thin disk surrounding the planet at its equator, and they are composed of particles ranging in size from marbles to basketballs. There are even some larger particles called moonlets, which are as big as 0.6 to 60 miles (1 to 100 km) in diameter.

Given that Saturn's mass is 95 times that of Earth, with gravity almost the same as Earth's, it is extraordinary to consider that Saturn is the least dense planet in the solar system. Its density is less than that of water. Saturn is also 9.5 AU away from the Sun (by comparison to Jupiter's 5.2 AU and Earth's 1AU), and as such, represents the outermost planet about which we have written records from the ancients.

In ancient and classical astrology Saturn was called the Greater Malefic (or Greater Infortune) and Mars the Lesser Malefic (or Lesser Infortune). The reasons for this will be explored, but suffice it to say most modern astrologers do not consider Jupiter and Venus automatic advantages and guarantees of success and happiness in the chart, because they can be dangerous in their excesses. Similarly, Saturn and Mars, while they can be difficult in what they represent symbolically, they are also balancing factors for the meanings inherent in Jupiter and Venus, respectively.

So what is there about Saturn that is often seen as difficult and challenging? And how does it correlate to the astronomical reality of Saturn? Well, the fact that Saturn is the outermost planet that can be seen with the naked eye, and that it appears as a rather dull, slow-moving object in the heavens (no brighter than Mercury), sets up a series of correlations to human life and human events which are still relevant today. Saturn was from ancient times aligned with concepts of contraction, containment, order, structure, and form, and thus also discipline, responsibility, and at times the limitation, overcautiousness, and restriction which can go along with those. The awesome structure of the rings around Saturn, extending its width beyond that of giant Jupiter, was probably not known before Galileo spotted them with his telescope in the 17th century. However, this gigantic ring system also magnifies and confirms, through the Law of Correspondences, the initial meanings assigned to Saturn. Beyond those listed above, they include rulership over the laws of time and space, the concept of crystallization (and thus the material plane), and also government and science, in the sense that we assign concepts of order, structure, and limitation to these areas. For better or worse, what are our political rights and boundaries? And who establishes them? What are our boundaries in terms of what we know? And who most often decides that?

When the Gauquelins were researching groups of professionals, they found Saturn to be most prominent in the charts of doctors and scientists, and furthermore, whether or not they belonged to those professions, strongly Saturnian people were found to be reserved, modest, conscientious, and taciturn.

As for the larger cycles in human terms, Jupiter and Saturn together represent the concept of economic realities and social structures, both national and corporate. The synodic Jupiter/Saturn cycle (i.e., from one conjunction to the next) is 19.859 years, and in the various interactions of Jupiter and Saturn throughout that time we observe how the expansionary idealism of Jupiter coincides or does not coincide with the more conservative (yet often practical) reality structure of Saturn. Together they operate as a team, seemingly alike, as in the heavens, and yet very different, balancing each other's best and worst qualities.

Saturn is the planetary ruler of Capricorn, and (jointly with Uranus) Aquarius.

Uranus ♅ or ♅

All the planets discussed thus far were discovered so many millennia ago that they have to be dated prehistorically. The cosmological and astrological systems developed by ancient astronomer-astrologers included planets only out to Saturn, although most likely some of the initiated astrologer-priests of Egypt, Israel, Babylon, and Greece knew there had to be other planets that symbolized characteristics of the human being and the human races not attributable to the seven known planets.

Uranus was discovered by astronomer William Herschel with the aid of a telescope on March 13, 1781. Neptune's discovery was to follow in 1846 and Pluto's in 1930. Astrologers often say that the astrological essence of a planet and its effect and influence on human affairs is not conscious for human beings until around the time of that planet's discovery and afterwards. We shall soon see how this applies to Uranus.

Remember that Saturn's distance from the Sun is 9.5 astronomical units (AU). By comparison, Uranus is 19.16 AU from the Sun. Uranus is the third largest planet in the solar system, with a mass 14.7 times that of the Earth and a mean diameter of 29,500 miles (or 47,466 km), a little over a third the diameter of Jupiter. The atmosphere of Uranus consists of hydrogen, helium, and methane at temperatures probably around –300°F. Its surface material is unknown to date (1990). It takes Uranus 84 years to orbit the Sun (seven years per zodiac area, or "sign"), and the length of its day is around 10-1/2 hours.

Similar to those of Jupiter and Saturn, the poles of Uranus are flattened by the speed of its axial rotation. Through a telescope Uranus looks like a sea-green disk flattened at the poles, with 15 moons (probably composed mainly of ice) and 10 rings around it. Circling its equator, the narrow rings are the color of powdered coal.

By far the most interesting astronomical factor about Uranus is the tilt of its axis at 98° to the plane of its orbit. The other planets tilt between 3° and 32°, as illustrated on p. 47 for the planets Mercury through Pluto. The tilt of the Earth's axis at 23°27', for example, accounts for our seasons—during the summer, the northern hemisphere gets more direct sunlight as it tilts towards the Sun; six months later it gets less sunlight as it tilts away from the Sun, creating winter. By contrast, the pole of Uranus lies almost exactly along the plane of the solar system: Uranus therefore has quite extraordinary seasons. For much of each hemisphere, but especially the north and south polar areas, there are 42 years of sunlight followed by 42 years of darkness, during which the other hemisphere gets all the sunlight.

This factor of the 98° axis tilt is perhaps *the* main factor around which so many of the astrological correlations have developed. By comparison to what is considered to be more normal (i.e., from 3° to 32°), Uranus's axial tilt is downright topsy-turvy and unlike anything we are familiar with in planetary behavior. Thus the correspondence in human terms is to deviating, eccentric, non-conforming, unconventional, iconoclastic, and sometimes amoral behavior, but also to uniqueness, individuality, originality, and innovation. Being sideways like that gives a whole new perspective, keeps us from stagnating, and so liberates us to make big changes, to be more independent from the social, political, and philosophical structures that preceded. Thus Uranus is associated with sudden or revolutionary change, at times with rebelliousness, and also, by extension, with innovation and the inventive thinking that leads to the harnessing of a particular kind of insight, those sudden intuitive flashes which can rapidly bring scientific inventions to the fore. So

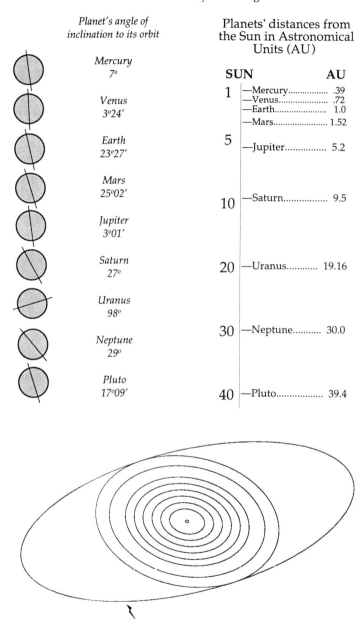

Planet's angle of inclination to its orbit	Planets' distances from the Sun in Astronomical Units (AU)	
	SUN	**AU**
Mercury 7°	1	—Mercury................. .39
		—Venus...................... .72
Venus 3°24'		—Earth....................... 1.0
		—Mars....................... 1.52
Earth 23°27'	5	—Jupiter................ 5.2
Mars 25°02'		
	10	—Saturn.................. 9.5
Jupiter 3°01'		
Saturn 27°	20	—Uranus............ 19.16
Uranus 98°		
Neptune 29°	30	—Neptune........... 30.0
Pluto 17°09'	40	—Pluto.................. 39.4

Pluto's Orbit

Planetary orbits, angles of inclination to their obits, and distances from the Sun in astronomical units by extension also, Uranus is associated with electricity, aviation, electronics, computers, astrology, and that more rare part of science which thinks intuitively and adventurously, continually breaking new boundaries and unafraid to buck the tide.

In terms of sexual mores, there has been an observed 84-year pattern, coinciding with Uranus's 84-year orbital period, in which male and female behavior and prominence respectively are polarized every 42 years. We can make a correspondence here between the positive and negative poles of planets and concepts of masculinity and femininity, evidenced here through fashions in clothing and various modes of behavior.

Remember too that Uranus's discovery in 1781 was preceded and succeeded closely by the American and French Revolutions, also by the harnessing of electricity and numerous inventions stretching through the Industrial Revolution and beyond.

Uranus was assigned to be the planetary ruler of Aquarius (jointly with Saturn).

Neptune ♆

Neptune was discovered September 23, 1846, by the German astronomer Johann Galle, though his discovery resulted from previous work by English astronomer John C. Adams in 1841 as well as that of French astronomer Urbain Leverrier. They observed that the orbit of Uranus was disturbed by something that probably was a further outlying planet. (In fact, the orbits of most planets are affected by other nearby planets. For example, Venus and Mars influence or cause a perturbation in the Earth's motion, as Jupiter causes perturbations of Saturn and the asteroids—most of which lie between the orbits of Mars and Jupiter.)

Although Uranus is almost impossible to detect with the naked eye, Neptune and Pluto are both quite undetectable without a powerful telescope. Neptune orbits 30.0 AU away from the Sun as compared to Uranus's 19.16 AU. Neptune is the fourth largest planet—after Jupiter, Saturn, and Uranus—making it the fourth of the giants of our solar system. Its color is a striking baby-blue, resulting from light being filtered through a veil of methane. With an orbital period of 164.8 years and a day lasting about 15 hours 45 minutes, Neptune stays in the same zodiacal sign for approximately 13 years (compared to Uranus's seven years in a sign), and as such correlates with an influence that is usually more obvious on an entire generation than on a single individual. Neptune has eight moons and five rings. One of the moons (Triton) is very unusual in that it is the only large satellite in our solar system that orbits in retrograde motion, i.e. east to west. Like Uranus, Neptune's atmosphere contains hydrogen, helium, and methane, and its surface material is unknown. Neptune is the densest of all the outer planets, including Jupiter and Saturn (though Neptune's density is only 40 percent of Earth's); it has a mass 17.2 times that of Earth, and a diameter of approximately 30,759 miles (or 49,500 km). Its temperature is about $-330°F$.

The Law of Correspondences that unites planet Neptune astronomically with human events is more mysterious than for the other planets closer to the Sun in our solar system. (The same holds true to some extent for Pluto, although Pluto gives us some obvious clues.) However, as we do eventually find out more about Neptune from our space probes, I would expect those descriptions to connect closely with the meanings assigned to this planet in human terms. So far astrologers have based the correlations almost entirely on world events and cultural trends closely preceding and following the discovery of Neptune in the fall of 1846.

As it also happens, in late August 1989 the unmanned American spacecraft Voyager 2 made its closest approach ever to observe and photograph Neptune. Eventwise, it is significant that during that same exact week the biggest news on earth in human terms was the outbreak of violent war between the government of Colombia, backed by the United States, and the billion-dollar Colombian Medellin cartel, the largest single drug operation in the world. (Neptune's correlation to drugs had already been established.)

In general, Neptune is related to changing one's perception of everyday reality, and as such, there is a long list of all the things included in such a necessarily amorphous category. General anesthesia was first used in surgical procedures in the 1840s. In the latter part of the 19th century also came hypnotism and psychoanalysis, with the pioneering work of Freud with the unconscious mind and of Jung with the collective unconscious mind. This process of breaking down ordinary states of perception applies to: 1) science, with Einstein's Theory of Relativity (1905) and Max Planck's quantum theory (his first theory in 1900); 2) motion pictures, which started developing in the 1880s; 3) the arts in general, where "romanticism" in literature, music and painting exalted the senses and the emotions over reason and the intellect, and where, later, in the late 19th and early 20th centuries, "impressionism" pervaded in depicting transitory visual or auditory impressions; and 4) political-social realities, which after the mid-19th century could no longer assume that slavery or serfdom was a normal state of affairs, or that nation-states were not linked within a very real international entity (more blurring of boundaries).

On a higher level, Neptune corresponds to spirituality, refined sensitivity, spiritually inspired artistic endeavors, and dissolving the boundaries of mundane reality. On a lower level, Neptune is related to a dissolving action that can take one over into states of confusion, illusion, or intoxication. Often issues of obligation are bound up with Neptune, and if not well-supported in an astrological chart, Neptune's influence in our lives can carry us into personal grand schemes as self-styled martyrs or saviors. In exploring an influence which has to do with dissolving the artificial barriers of time and space, it is easy to sink into the lower levels before reaching for the higher. Music, film, dance, photography, all of these Neptunian professions are filled with those who tend to struggle with drugs, alcohol, or other forms of chemical dependency in the process of mastering the art of moving in and out of the everyday boundaries of reality. So understandably, Neptune can also be ego-denying, and represents the various states of water—steam, fog, vapor, clouds, rain, or oceans, which transport us into a greater sense of oneness and flow with Nature.

> Under heaven nothing is more soft and yielding than water. Yet for attacking the solid and strong, nothing is better; it has no equal.
>
> Lao Tsu, *Tao Te Ching*, translated by Gia-Fu Feng and Jane English, Vintage Books Edition (Random House), 1972, Verse 78.

Astrologers assigned Neptune as the planetary ruler of Pisces (jointly with Jupiter).

Pluto ♇ or ♇

As early as the 1870s, astronomers at the U.S. Naval Observatory in Washington, D.C. were systematically searching for a planet believed to be beyond Neptune's orbit, chiefly due to factors in the behavior of Uranus's orbit that could not be explained by Neptune alone. From 1903 until his death in 1916, American astronomer Percival Lowell searched for what he called "Planet X." He was correct in several of his predictions. He said the planet would be small, would orbit the Sun in 282 years (it is actually 248.4 years), and be about 4 billion miles from the Sun. Astronomer Clyde Tombaugh conclusively sighted Pluto February 18, 1930 in Flagstaff, Arizona.

Pluto is nearly 40 times as far from the Sun as the Earth, at 39.4 AU. It looks like a small yellowish disk, and has a day lasting six Earth days and nine hours. Its probable atmosphere is thin methane gas. Methane freezes only in the outermost reaches of the solar system, so we have a planet of very low density, consisting of mostly methane ices at temperatures around –350° F, and a gravity 5 percent of that of the Earth.

Considering that it affects the orbits of Uranus and Neptune so strongly, it is surprising that Pluto is so small. In fact, it is the smallest planet in our solar system, about the size of Earth's Moon, and just over three times the size of the largest asteroid, Ceres. (Pluto's diameter is between 1860 and 2480 miles—3000 to 4000 km.) In the contest for planetary status, this naturally raises the question of whether Pluto deserves to be ranked as a planet at all, and lately astronomers have discussed demoting Pluto to planetoid or asteroid status. Even with its one satellite, Pluto is not unlike some asteroids, which, according to recent evidence, have satellites as well (although they are tiny).

But, all told, Pluto has several extraordinary features. First, its moon, called Charon (discovered in 1978) is half the size of Pluto itself. This is a much larger size ratio than any other planet-satellite pair. Also, Pluto's orbit is unusual in its eccentricity. Sometimes it lies within Neptune's orbit, as during the 1980s and early '90s when Pluto was closer to the Sun than Neptune. Only the asteroid Chiron (discovered in 1977 and located between the orbits of Saturn and Uranus) is also known to cross over the orbit of another planet. In Pluto's case, its orbit is so irregular that it can take anywhere from 12 to 32 years to pass through a zodiacal area or sign. In later chapters we shall see how this factor affects the so-called "generation gap," as Pluto ideologically united a whole generation from 1913 to 1939. Since that time, however, Pluto's period in a sign has become shorter and shorter. It remains in Scorpio, for instance, just under 12 years, from 1984 to 1995.

For Pluto, as with Uranus and Neptune, there were no astrological traditions from ancient times. And, also as with Neptune, most of the correspondences had to be determined from prevailing trends around the time of Pluto's discovery in 1930. Coming as it did just months after the October 1929 stock market crash and preceding the depression of the 1930s, Pluto was observed to relate closely to collective and shared financial resources, the masses, and the drastic and absolute effects of control and power, its uses and/or misuses. Certainly the unrelenting misuse of power brought the rise of Nazism and fascism in Europe during the 1930s.

Pluto came to be associated closely with radical transformations that tend to occur through elimination and renewal, as if a total breakdown must happen before a building process can occur. In psychology, this is related to deep probing and analysis in order to destroy the old behavior pattern and create a new one. In medicine, it is related to generational illnesses such as tuberculosis, syphilis, and cancer, which work a long time below the surface before being diagnosed. (In the 1930s, there was also a sudden prevalence of cancer.) In science and politics, it is related to plutonium, the most dangerous and poisonous substance known to man, and a radioactive element first artificially produced in 1940. It is now used as a fission fuel for nuclear reactors and weapons. "Success" with nuclear fission led to the first atomic bomb explosion July 16, 1945, which preceded the American bombing of Hiroshima and Nagasaki three weeks later.

Clearly Plutonian elements, like radioactivity, have no political or geographical boundaries, but, unlike Neptune, the boundaries are often blurred through blatantly coercive or violent means, as if Pluto also represents those hidden volcanic forces which erupt and affect masses of people. This is reflected in the rise of the Mafia, the dramatic increase in terrorism, and the increased power of the mass media to make us aware of those underground forces and give them more (probably too much) publicity and attention.

Civilization is still reeling from the emergence of Plutonian realities. There are no soft edges here, but then the most radical transformations of all—birth, death, rebirth, regeneration, and sexuality—are not known for their soft edges or painlessness. These too are very Plutonian, and as Pluto transits its strongest placement in Scorpio (1984-1995), we are witnessing a public acknowledgement of the death process, particularly with AIDS—if not with actual physical death, then in the larger sense, the death process of a way of life that is no longer tenable for our planet. Because, just as it rules over birth *and* death, Pluto also rules over pollution *and* purification. It does seem we are witnessing a process whereby Pluto signals the acceleration and the magnitude of Earth's pollution, so that we can get on with the cleanup.

Eventually, when we learn more about Pluto astronomically, I expect to see many more correspondences to human affairs; but as it stands, Pluto's unusual eccentric orbit and its strong effect on distant planets much larger than itself tends to correlate to atomic or nuclear energy, which, when released, has an impact on an environment far more huge than that in which it began. Also, there is something fascinating about Pluto's enormous moon, traveling close to it and engaged with it in an endless lugubrious shadow dance. It's as if this dance represents the self-realization process which, unpleasant though it can sometimes be, is an inescapable part of the life and death process.

Pluto is the planetary ruler of Scorpio (jointly with Mars).

The 12 Houses of the Horoscope

The 12 houses of the horoscope are among further key adjectives describing how the planetary energies manifest. In an astronomical sense, there are many differing ways to divide the 360° of the ecliptic into 12 sectors, called "houses" in astrology. All of them have their theoretical and empirical rationales, and though one astrological software company offers up to 39 house systems, currently in the United States one tends to see only a dozen or so of these in regular use. Some of the most popular house systems, like many things which become popular, have numerous faults and no real reason for being in such widespread use other than a history of widespread availability.

My personal preference, and the house system of choice among the developers of Uranian astrology, is the Meridian system, which is not common around the world but which solves many astronomical and astrological problems, works extremely well for timing, and appears in the astrological charts in this book. The houses are almost equal as measured from the Midheaven. (See the

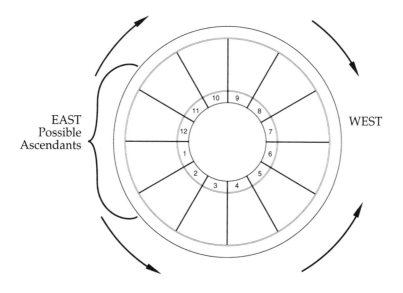

The 12 Houses of the Horoscope

The arrows reflect the astronomical reality of the two sets of motion that we experience on earth: 1) clockwise, reflecting the Earth's rotation on its axis from west to east, and how the planets (and the Sun and Moon) rise daily on the eastern horizon and set on the western horizon, and 2) counterclockwise, reflecting the Earth's orbital revolution around the Sun in an eastward direction through the sequence of the constellations, or zodiac, like all the other planets, though in the case of the Earth taking one year. So in one chart, as with so much in astrology, a 24-hour period and a 12-month period become a whole integrated entity expressing the planets in the context of both a day and a year. Notice the parallel to the concept of secondary progressions, where a day equals one year.

Meridian house tables in the Appendix.) If you are used to seeing other types of astrological charts, the Meridian system looks strange at first only because the first Meridian house is not also, as in most other house systems, the Ascendant (again, the meeting point of the horizon and the ecliptic). It is an Equatorial Ascendant, also called the East Point, where your Ascendant (or "rising sign" in the popular lingo) would be if you were born at the equator, always an important reference point and one of the five Great Circles. (Astronomically, the Equatorial Ascendant is where the eastern horizon crosses the prime vertical and the celestial equator. See diagram on p. 30.) So , in a sense, you have two Ascendants in this system, but the major point where we derive the "rising sign" is the Ascendant that is the intersection of the horizon and the ecliptic. In the Meridian house system, depending on the latitude and time of year, the Ascendant can be as far up as into the 11th house and as far down as into the 2nd house. More commonly it is in the 12th or the 1st house. At the equator, or with early degrees of either Cancer or Capricorn on the Midheaven, the Equatorial Ascendant and the regular Ascendant are equal or very close to each other. This translates in human terms as others seeing us as we see ourselves, without much discrepancy.

So much for dividing up the 360° circle. It is one of the areas where astrologers tend to disagree the most, though they do not disagree much on the meanings assigned to the 12 houses[40] nor with the concept that a planet's energy and meaning is colored by where it is located in the chart. For instance, Mars in a certain house lends extra energy and movement to that particular arena of life, and is further modified by its aspects to other planets, its position by zodiacal sign, and whether it is in retrograde or direct motion (geocentrically speaking). If there are no planets in a given house, it does not mean that nothing is happening in that arena. One looks to the planetary ruler of the zodiacal sign on the house cusp to see how it is acting in the chart.

The meanings of the 12 houses in the horoscope have to do with life's major arenas, and have been more or less in effect—with a few historical and cultural variations—for thousands of years. Here are some of their basic meanings in Western astrology, which apply chiefly to the horoscopes of individuals, though some of the same meanings apply in national, corporate, or event charts. Notice that the houses operate in pairs of opposites. Whatever happens in the 1st house is inextricably linked to the 7th house, the 2nd to the 8th, and so on around the chart.

FIRST HOUSE— Inherited tendencies which influence the look of the physical body as well as the character and personality that can be seen by others. (The Uranian system includes other persons here, particularly one's parents and ancestors, because this is where

---

40. An exception to this is that while Western astrologers are in basic accord about the meanings of the 12 houses, Hindu astrologers have some important variations from these and use them consistently within the Hindu system of astrology.

others first enter our lives at our birth, our own sunrise of life.)

SECOND HOUSE—One's financial affairs, including earning capacity, movable personal possessions, losses, gains, and what is most deeply valued.

THIRD HOUSE—Communications and relations on a direct and immediate level, including visits, letters, phone calls, contracts, unsigned agreements. Also, brothers and sisters, neighbors, short trips. Primary and secondary education.

FOURTH HOUSE—One's home, residence, and real estate in general. Also, one's origins, ancestry, and foundation, as well as the end of life. (Opinions differ on whether the mother is found here or in the 10th house, and the same for the father. In any case, matters relating to the parents appear on the MC/IC axis, i.e. on the 10th-house/4th-house axis.)

FIFTH HOUSE—Artistic creativity and creative self-expression. Love affairs, romance. Children. Art, pleasure, recreation, entertainment, sport, gambling, and speculation.

SIXTH HOUSE—Work, especially the everyday routine of work. The working efficiency of the body, i.e. health matters, including illness, diet, nutrition. Matters of service to others.

SEVENTH HOUSE—One's counterpart. Having come from the Ascendant, one now meets the other, the mate. Thus the marriage partner is here and also the business partner. One's adversaries are here as well.

EIGHTH HOUSE—All of life's most radically transformative experiences: sex, death, birth, rebirth, and healing, especially from severe illness. Shared finances and other people's financial resources, including legacies, inheritances.

NINTH HOUSE—Long trips, especially to foreign countries. Higher education. Universities. The higher intellect and one's view of the universe. Thus, large systems of thought such as philosophy, religion, law, and science.

TENTH HOUSE—High point of the day and the year (i.e. the most light and heat), and thus the point of greatest visibility in terms of one's station in life or one's career. Public image, social position, reputation. Also, that to which one aspires. (See 4th house description regarding mother and father.)

ELEVENTH HOUSE—Large groups and organizations, especially related to one's career hopes and wishes. Friendships and acquaintances on a more impersonal level. Labor unions, political parties.

TWELFTH HOUSE—All enclosed places, especially those involving confinement, such as prisons and hospitals. That which is hidden in deepest consciousness, even from ourselves, until it is made conscious and usable in our lives. Thus self-undoing, self-sacrifice, and also research, meditation, and any behind-the-scene activities. (In the Meridian house system, if the Ascendant is located in the 12th house, it is often difficult for that person to perceive clearly both what it is he or she is projecting, in terms of body image and personality, and who it is that is crossing his or her horizons, i.e. who is being attracted.)

The Three Modes = The Three States of Matter = Energy

Each of the 12 signs of the zodiac is assigned a "quality" or "mode," which can be described as a quality of being and/or a mode of operating. Essentially this is the same as the three states of matter, which consist of solid, liquid, and gas. The solid state of matter is equivalent to Fixity, or a state of being static, and corresponds to the *Fixed* mode in astrology. Liquid is equivalent to oscillating or wave-like motion and corresponds to the *Mutable* mode; and gas corresponds to action and straightforward motion (aligned to the molecular action of gas, which is energetic enough to escape the liquid state) and to the *Cardinal* mode in astrology. Without introducing the more technical aspects of modern physics, we also know that mass is considered essentially equivalent and transmutable to energy. This concept is central to Einstein's Theory of Relativity, first proposed in 1905, and is implied and in some cases explicitly stated in the writings of some of the ancient mystics. In human terms all of these qualities or modes have their positive

ZODIAC SIGNS IN SEQUENCE	GLYPH	SYMBOL	TIME OF YEAR (cusp dates vary yr. to yr.)	PLANETARY RULER(S)	ELEMENT	QUALITY OR MODE	OPPOSITE SIGN	PARTS OF THE BODY
ARIES	♈	RAM	3/20 to 4/19	Mars	Fire	Cardinal	Libra	Head and Face
TAURUS	♉	BULL	4/20 to 5/20	Venus	Earth	Fixed	Scorpio	Neck and Throat
GEMINI	♊	TWINS	5/21 to 6/20	Mercury	Air	Mutable	Sagittarius	Hands, Arms, Lungs
CANCER	♋	CRAB	6/21 to 7/22	Moon	Water	Cardinal	Capricorn	Stomach, Breast
LEO	♌	LION	7/23 to 8/22	Sun	Fire	Fixed	Aquarius	Heart, Upper Spine
VIRGO	♍	VIRGIN	8/23 to 9/22	Mercury	Earth	Mutable	Pisces	Intestines
LIBRA	♎	SCALES	9/23 to 10/22	Venus	Air	Cardinal	Aries	Kidneys, Lower Spine
SCORPIO	♏	SCORPION (eagle, dove, phoenix)	10/23 to 11/21	Mars Pluto	Water	Fixed	Taurus	Sex Organs, Bladder, Anus
SAGITTARIUS	♐	ARCHER	11/22 to 12/20	Jupiter	Fire	Mutable	Gemini	Thighs, Liver
CAPRICORN	♑	MOUNTAIN GOAT	12/21 to 1/19	Saturn	Earth	Cardinal	Cancer	Knees, Skin
AQUARIUS	♒	WATER BEARER	1/20 to 2/18	Saturn Uranus	Air	Fixed	Leo	Calves and Ankles
PISCES	♓	FISH	2/19 to 3/19	Jupiter Neptune	Water	Mutable	Virgo	Feet

PLANETS AND POINTS IN SPACE	GLYPH	DAY OF THE WEEK	ZODIAC SIGNS RULED BY THIS PLANET		TIME OF YEAR (cusp dates vary from year to year)
SUN	☉	SUNDAY	LEO	♌	7/23 to 8/22
MOON	☽	MONDAY	CANCER	♋	6/21 to 7/22
MIDHEAVERN	MC				
ASCENDANT	ASC				
MOON'S NODE	☊				
MERCURY	☿	WEDNESDAY	GEMINI AND VIRGO	♊ ♍	5/21 to 6/20 8/23 to 9/22
VENUS	♀	FRIDAY	TAURUS AND LIBRA	♉ ♎	4/20 to 5/20 9/23 to 10/22
MARS	♂	TUESDAY	ARIES AND SCORPIO	♈ ♏	3/20 to 4/19 10/23 to 11/21
JUPITER	♃	THURSDAY	SAGITTARIUS AND PISCES	♐ ♓	11/22 to 12/20 2/19 to 3/19
SATURN	♄	SATURDAY	CAPRICORN AND AQUARIUS	♑ ♒	12/21 to 1/19 1/20 to 2/18
URANUS	♅		AQUARIUS	♒	1/20 to 2/18
NEPTUNE	♆		PISCES	♓	2/19 to 3/19
PLUTO	♇		SCORPIO	♏	10/23 to 11/21

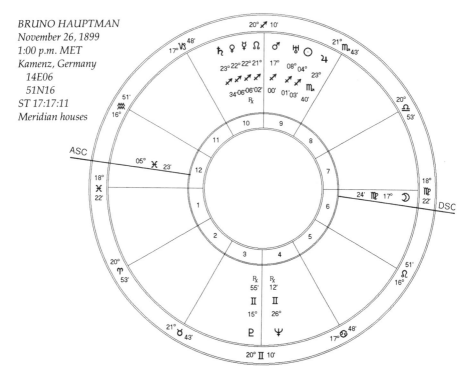

Example of a Mutable Mode Overload
Natal Horoscope of Bruno Hauptman

and negative sides, and they are important in their interaction with one another. Ideally, one wants a balance of all three modes, and one is very aware of compensating when one or more modes is lacking, partially or altogether. When there is an overabundance of one mode, especially when it affects the personal planets (Sun, Moon, Mercury, Venus, and Mars), or a total lack of one mode, a person can become obsessed with that mode of action. (See the example above of a chart with Mutable mode overload: Bruno Hauptman, the criminal convicted and executed in the infamous Lindbergh baby kidnapping. [For more on Hauptman, see pp. 141-143.])

Fixity connotes steadfastness of purpose, tenacity, loyalty, patience, and perseverance, but can also deteriorate into stubbornness or adherence to a way of thinking and acting long after it has ceased to be useful or even rational. **Mutability** connotes adaptability, diplomacy, and openness to change. In the extreme, or when unevolved or undeveloped, it can easily lapse into fickleness, changeability, undependability, and being overly susceptible to the passage of events and the opinions of others. **Cardinality** connotes action, initiative, boldness, courage, and confidence. This can easily move into the territory of recklessness, a commitment to action for action's sake, over-confidence in one's abilities and physical stamina, and a distinct dislike if not disdain for finishing projects one has boldly begun.

The Four Elements

In Western astrology, four elements are used and are dispersed throughout the zodiac three times from Aries through Pisces, occuring in this order: Fire, Earth, Air, and Water. As with the three modes, one ideally wants a good balance and interaction among all four elements. Sometimes this is supplied when natal planets change elements, especially the Sun, when it changes zodiacal sign in the secondary progressed system of timing. If your natal sign is at 0° of one sign, however, and with a day equalling a year in this system, you will have to wait 30 years for such a change. And while this will be a good rebalancing, there are other ways to do it much sooner, most of which boil down to one word: self-awareness.

Here's how the elements work: **Fire** has a great deal in common with Cardinality. It relates to action, especially physical action, but also to sexual action and the ability to take initiatives in life and seize the moment with passion and inspiration. You begin to see how the language of astrology works when you consider that Mars is the planetary ruler of Aries, which as a Cardinal Fire sign embodies all of these concepts in the strongest way and yet also has the greatest chance of manifesting its worst pitfalls—rashness, recklessness, and an inability to finish what is started (since so much zeal goes exclusively into the beginning of an enterprise). In any case, Mars can do very well in Aries, but it is far better in Capricorn, where the action is tempered by Saturnian circumspection. Bear in mind, however, that planetary contacts to one another always outweigh the zodiacal sign. For instance, you may be very pleased with your Mars in Capricorn, but if it is closely conjunct or in any hard contact with Neptune, then you have an altogether different Mars operating, one that is both more sensitive, and more susceptible to human frailties, especially to drugs and alcohol. Neptune slows down and modifies the naturally fiery quality of Mars.

Earth has much in common with Fixity. It is concerned with steadfastness and stability in life, especially as regards material and financial security. Here the arena of sensual and sexual pleasures is important, but, unlike Cardinal and Fire, which can get caught up with the aspect of the sexual pursuit and adventure, Earth needs to know that there will be plenty of food available to eat and that everything in the domestic surroundings is cozy and comfortable. Unless these requirements are met, not to mention the reality, or at least the promise of steady money in the bank, Earth cannot rest easily or enjoy the situation that completely. This is why Venus is considered to rule over the Fixed Earth sign Taurus, where it does well, though it can get stuck there in its material and sensual ways. It is considered to do its most elevated work in Pisces, where the love and good will of Venus is tempered with the compassion and sensitivity of Neptune (the planetary ruler of Pisces).

Air does not fit neatly into comparison with one of the three modes, as it can vary so quickly in its consistency and its movement. Certainly it is an elastic and invisible mixture of gases, and as such should have something in common with Cardinality. In the sense of the speed of the airwaves, Air definitely does like action, but not necessarily physical action per se as much as mental, verbal, intellectual, communicative action. Planets operating in an Air sign are much more oriented towards this arena, and therefore it is easier for the individual or the collective to express that energy verbally and to share it with others verbally. Not surprisingly, a good amount of Air in an individual's chart can make the business of education and processing information (via books, newspapers, television, films, video, computer modems, etc.) a relatively painless and even quite enjoyable area of life. I have also found that persons having a chart with no Air are often comfortable with communicating, and persistently seek out this arena of life as a means of direct compensation for the very lack of it.

Mercury is comfortable in the Air element, especially in Gemini, but like any excessive amount of Air, there can be too much talking, too much gathering of information and verbal exchange without any real depth. There is danger of excess in burning out on the sheer excitement of gratifying one's constant intellectual appetite, of talking without thinking or centering enough in other ways, especially through the emotions (Water) or practicality (Earth). That is why Mercury is considered to do even better in Virgo or Aquarius, its so-called "exalted" signs. In Virgo, Mercury is tempered by Earth, though still adaptable in the Mutable mode. In Aquarius, there is still Air, the most natural medium for communications, though Fixity stabilizes and focuses it.

Water has a lot in common with the Mutable mode, but, as with Air, we start to find many variations in the connections. That is why we have both modes and elements in astrology. The Water element concerns the emotional, feeling contacts in life. In the positive sense, it has to do with the ability to connect with other people on an emotionally intimate or at least sensitive level, and thus has much to do with not only families and close friends, but also how large groups of people can be swayed emotionally, almost as if they were a single unit. (Politics and advertising come to mind, of course.) In the negative sense, Water is about being overly sensitive to our environments, taking on the problems and ailments of others, and being too attached emotionally to certain people and emotional states.

Even though the Earth element traditionally has the most to do with the accumulation of material wealth and security, Water also is closely associated with wealth due to its capacity to absorb and to extend its boundaries. In the ancient Chinese system of Feng Shui, water is the most revered symbol for both wealth and health.

With the Water element, I have observed that, unlike Air, when if it's absent in a chart, it can be learned from the outside world and assimilated almost as if there were no absence, it is much harder for individuals who have a total lack of Water in their natal charts. The emotions have to be learned from the inside out, and must make that oftentimes difficult progression from the emotional reality of a child to that of an adult. That is why, even though the Moon rules over the Water sign Cancer and does reasonably well there, it can also get caught in the attachments and self-absorptions of childhood in this sign. The Moon is considered the most strengthened or "exalted" in Taurus, where its natural fluidity and sensitivity is grounded with the unwavering practicality of a Fixed Earth sign.

Reading the Chart: The Music of It

Coming from a strongly musical background myself, I always see the parallel between reading a sheet of music and reading an astrological chart. There are many symbols to make sense of and pull together. Are you reading the bass clef or the treble clef line? What key are you in? Are there any accidentals? What is the time signature? Are there any octave changes? What are the expression marks? You get your bearings straightaway.

This last section of the chapter is about putting the pieces together, much like a music sight-reading class, though of course we all know a great deal goes into being able to play or sing music with distinction. The same is true in astrology, and so no easy route to mastery is assumed here, but rather a description is presented for the layperson of how the astrologer goes about reading or interpreting a chart.

First, there is an intrinsic understanding of the meaning of the shape of the chart and how it is organized, as well as the meaning of the six Personal Points (Aries point, Ascendant, Moon's Node, Sun, Moon, Midheaven) and all the planets. Next, there is an under-standing of how those planetary meanings are colored by: 1) being in close hard aspect, or angular relationship, to a Personal Point, especially the angles of the chart; 2) being in close hard aspect to another planet; and lastly 3) which zodiacal sign; and 4) in which house the planet is located. Please note that the zodiacal sign and house placement are listed last, not because they lack importance, but because the first two factors will always yield potent information no matter which house system or which zodiac you use.[41] These factors will also yield the consistency that crosses all theoretical boundaries in astrological thought and practice around the world.

Although house systems and zodiacs should not be mixed at random, it is also true that working consistently within the house system and/or zodiac of choice can yield excellent results, regard-less of the fact that somewhere there may be a better choice of house system or zodiac. It's like the idea of vantage point in physics. Everything is changed by the observer and his or her point of view, but if the observer remains true to just one set of measuring devices,

---

41. Remember that there are more than 20 house systems in use by astrologers, though many fall close to one another, and that most Western astrologers use the tropical zodiac, whereas all Hindu (and some Western) astrologers use the sidereal zodiac. The sidereal zodiac uses the fixed stars as reference points, whereas the tropical zodiac is based on the seasons and divides the ecliptic and year beginning at the Spring Equinox into 12 equal zodiacal areas, or signs of 30° each. Currently, due to a factor called the precession of the equinoxes, the two zodiacs are about 24° apart. This numerical differerence (called *ayanamsha*) increases yearly by 1', or 1/60 of a degree.

he or she will probably come up with some worthwhile results. Nonetheless, the results should be consistent in their basic content to another interpretation, as the object being studied and observed, in this case the astrological chart, has a clear existence of its own (assuming that the data is confirmed and accurate). The parallel to music is that we're all playing the same set of notes. They are recognizable as such. And yet the scope and variety of interpretation is endless, depending upon the skill and level of artistry of the performer.

Also like music, an astrological chart is never frozen in time and space. One brings an old piece of music to life and endows it with a contemporary spirit and sound. A horoscope, even if it's the chart of a wedding or the launching of any major venture in life, business or personal, is always being affected by the ongoing planetary movements and cycles in time and in space (i.e. geographically). Especially if there is a timing question or consideration, the astrologer looks at a chart to see how it is being affected by timing or cyclical factors. The geographic material is less easy to see without the aid of a 360° dial or an Astro∗Carto∗Graphy map, which is necessary in particular to see the latitude crossings.

The astrological art is similar to the art of music in terms of the quest to bring some sense of wholeness, inspiration, understanding, wisdom, and joy to a large array of symbols and numbers, some right in front of our eyes, some captured in memory. Astrology is necessarily a verbal art, and yet the symbols on the page hold the key to a great deal about a given human existence. By themselves, they may not tell us the exact level of consciousness of that individual or collective, but they will give us every other possible clue.

The Issues of Autonomy and the Limits of Human Creative Capacity

In Zen Buddhism there is great emphasis placed on how the self is one's greatest teacher; that in fact the more one distracts oneself with the opinions and actions of others, the longer it takes to reach enlightenment, which is considered to be a state of intense (some might say divine, or ecstatic) self-awareness and at-oneness with the universe. They talk about the advantages of a teacher to poke and prod one onto the right path, but that ultimately one's greatest guidance comes from the Inner Guide, which, if it is wise, has a sense of the awesome wholeness of the universe and of the basic harmony and interconnectedness of all things. This idea is common to all the great religious and spiritual teachings, no matter what name you assign to the great Inner Guide.

The point here is that the birth chart is the map of your personal universe, at least in terms of the solar system, which is plenty to come to grips with, and far more than can be seen with the naked eye. It is the map of your interior and exterior universe, and as such is an extremely important message *from* yourself *to* yourself. The challenge is to voluntarily choose what you must do, with the best possible help from your Inner Guide. Only then do you experience free will.

As to the planets actually controlling us, the point has already been made (in the discussion of the Law of Correspondences in Chapter 1) that they only mirror what is going on in human terms, and that we can choose at what level those symbolic meanings operate. The great Italian philosopher and theologian St. Thomas Aquinas (1225?-1274) expressed this issue well in his discourse called *Summa Theologica:*

> Are the celestial bodies the cause of human action?...
> Most men follow their corporal passions; their actions
> therefore for most of the time are subject to the influences
> of the celestial bodies. There are but a few wise men alone
> who moderate these influences by their reason. This is
> why in many cases astrologers announce true things,
> especially for events which depend on humans in
> groups.[42]

The astrologer is trained in the vast complexities of the chart in order to translate to the individual or collective what he (or she or they) have chosen for their character and their destiny. In no way is the astrologer's personal philosophical framework a substitute for the content of the chart, but if the individual wants to learn astrology in order to read the chart for himself, that is fine too. Just be aware that it is not confined to the "Daily Horoscope" section of the newspaper. Astrology is a lifetime study.

Meanwhile, going to an astrologer to interpret and read one's

---

42. *Larousse Encyclopedia of Astrology* (English language edition), 1980, pp. 10-11.

chart should never be perceived as an exercise in losing one's autonomy. Presuming the astrologer is professionally exemplary, he or she is only like a teacher doing the occasional poking and prodding towards the process of ultimate self-awareness, as in the Zen example above. The astrologer is in touch with and trained to read the road signs that most of us can no longer read accurately for ourselves, unless we are never distracted and are always perfectly attuned to the vibrations of the universe. Quite a feat!

What about the limits of human creative capacity? Are we limiting ourselves by defining ourselves? No, just the opposite, I believe. By knowing more deeply who we are and our likely strengths and weaknesses, we liberate ourselves from false perceptions, not only about whom others think we are, but about who we think we should be. The birth chart gives us clues as to our innate abilities and talents and our unique ways of approaching life. When we go with that and modify the likely excesses, tone down the likely weaknesses, and amplify the likely strengths, we are working within limits—yet we have no limitations within the limits. If we pay no attention to those limits, we are much like Icarus, who, in Greek mythology, was freed from the Minotaur's labyrinth when his father Daedalus made wings of wax and feather so they could fly away. But whereas Daedalus escaped to Sicily, Icarus flew too close to the Sun, his wings melted, and he fell to Earth to his death. Paying no attention to the limitations within the limits of our creative capacities will cause us to fall; and though it may not be to our death, as with Icarus, it may feel like a form of death in life.

III
Where on Earth?

What On Earth = Where + When

When you're awake, the things you think
   come from the dreams you dream.
Thought has wings and lots of things are
   seldom what they seem.
Sometimes you think you've lived before
   all that you live today.
Things you do come back to you as
   though they knew the way.
Oh, the tricks your mind can play.

Refrain:
It seems we stood and talked like this
   before.
We looked at each other in the same way
   then,
But I can't remember where or when.
The clothes you're wearing are the
   clothes you wore.
The smile you are smiling you were
   smiling then,
But I can't remember where or when.

Some things that happen for the first time
Seem to be happening again.
And so it seems that we have met before
And laughed before
And loved before
But who knows where or when?
> —Rodgers and Hart, "Where or When,"
> from *Babes in Arms.* 1937.

In astrology, the sum of your being is derived from the where and when of your birth. No astrologer can pretend to unearth every secret of your being from that chart, but it is there nonetheless,

69

waiting to be unlocked, and all stemming from the time and place of your birth. Not surprisingly then, *who* you are and *what* you are doing is always inextricable from *when* and *where* you are doing it. How you will react to a given situation in time and space is dependent upon not only what is given in the natal chart, but also how you have evolved over time with that chart. That is why certain situations are very predictable and others less so—especially if you have modified your thoughts and actions to fit the new situation, and you've developed your natural mode of expressing yourself to flow with the new set of circumstances, no matter what it may be.

As you might imagine, there are as many complexities and varieties of natal charts as there are varieties of people on the Earth. So, while this book will not deal with that vast subject area in its entirety, some examples will be touched upon of how a person's cosmic inheritance (and a self-awareness of it), in combination with factors of time, place, and relationship, accounts for the method and type of decision one is likely to make.

Home As a Mobile Concept

The geographic location of the domestic establishment is not necessarily where the heart grows fonder, nor is it necessarily a place one has chosen voluntarily. It may be ideal for one's growth and development, or it may be one of the worst or most dangerous places you could possibly live. Also, of course, you may find yourself living comfortably in several different locations, or in transit most of the time. When the latter occurs, we would definitely expect to see one or more of the following items in the natal chart. The greater the number of these factors, the more likely one is to have a large amount of travel in one's life.

1. Ascendant/Descendant and Midheaven/IC axes at or near Cardinal degrees (0° Aries, 0° Libra, 0° Cancer, and 0° Capricorn).[43]
2. Planets scattered in eight to ten different signs or houses.[44]

---

43. For examples, see the natal charts of Shirley MacLaine and Robert Redford, p. 88.

44. Leon Trotsky had planets in eight different signs and eight different houses. Through his life he lived during various periods in Leningrad, Siberia, London, Turkey, France, Vienna, New York City, Norway and Mexico City. (See pp. 124-126 and natal chart on next page.) Also, the ruler of Trotsky's 4th house, Venus, is located in the 3rd house—as per item 9 on the next page.

Planets so spread out can also indicate an individual with decidedly broad interests, or, on the negative side, an individual who can get too scattered and spread himself or herself too thin. This is obviously a potential pitfall for any of the big travelers.

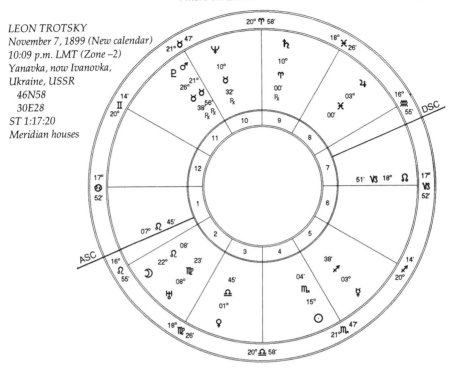

LEON TROTSKY
November 7, 1899 (New calendar)
10:09 p.m. LMT (Zone –2)
Yanavka, now Ivanovka,
Ukraine, USSR
46N58
30E28
ST 1:17:20
Meridian houses

Natal Horoscrope for Leon Trotsky

3. Jupiter angular, especially conjunct Ascendant or Midheaven.

4. Natal Moon in close hard contact (again, any of the 45° multiples) to Jupiter or Uranus.

5. Natal Moon in the sign of Gemini (♊), Sagittarius (♐), or Aquarius (♒).

6. Natal Moon in the 3rd or 9th house.

7. Concentration of planets in the 3rd or 9th houses, especially the Sun, Moon, Mercury and/or Mars.

8. Concentration of planets in Gemini (♊) or Sagittarius (♐).

9. Planetary ruler of the 4th house (the physical or emotional house) located in the 3rd or 9th house, or in Gemini (♊) or Sagittarius (♐).

When there is so much travel or mobility indicated, the warmth and security of home at best becomes a very mobile and possibly multicultural concept. At worst, it becomes a scattering force on the focus of attention for family and basic domestic concerns.

So a big traveler has a different concept of home to begin with, the home being oftentimes "where you hang your hat." There is a lot of personal flexibility here, but even so, astro-mapping will give us the big picture—whether or not there is a great deal of travel in the life.

Where Your Career and/or Relationships Thrive More, or Less

A planet or planets on the MC/IC axis tend to operate through one's profession, career, and position in society as well as through one's home and family.[45] Since the Midheaven (MC) is above the horizon, the manifestations of the planet(s) here are more outward, visible, and accessible to other people. Planet(s) on the IC are below the horizon and are more likely to describe the personal, inward, and at times inherited tendencies of behavior and emotional inclinations. Family roots and the foundations for inner strength set the tone for the type of domesticity that will be experienced. In some ways, it is your concept of yourself in this location.

A planet or planets on the ASC/DSC axis describe the relationships one attracts through the force of one's personality and thus the relationships attracted into the home environment. The Ascendant is often said to describe what you are projecting in terms of your personality, and the Descendant what you are likely to receive, and in fact what you *expect* to receive in terms of relationships, based on what you have projected.

What I have found is that the Ascendant and Descendant are almost interchangeable, and that the only way the Descendant starts representing other people exclusively is if you have totally repressed that planetary energy and continue to let other people act it out for you.

Astro-mapping is a critical tool in helping the astrologer to establish where on Earth you do better, or worse, as the case may be. For more detailed information on geographical locations, the astrologer also uses a Cyclo·Carto·Graphy (C·C·G) map to add the timing element. This may amplify or even temporarily contradict what is there natally. (As they are plastic overlays and hard to reproduce well in book form over the Astro·Carto·Graphy [A·C·G] maps, they will not be shown in this book, although in the "Geographical Clues" section there are periodic references to C·C·G indicators that have been researched. The C·C·G work has not been done in every instance.)

---

45. See Appendix A, p. 248, for a diagram showing the angles of the chart: MC/IC and ASC/DSC.

An A·C·G map shows planetary lines projected over a map of the world. The equator becomes extremely important here, and any planetary crossings or planets at their zenith on the equator, marked on the map, affect the entire life at all locations. Throughout, the strongest signals and the most important information come from planets conjunct any of the four angles (the MC, IC, ASC, or DSC), especially when two or more planets cross the angles simultaneously, called a "paran" in astrology.[46] In a paran, the planets cross either the same angle or two different angles in a birth chart, and not necessarily at the exact time of birth, though usually within a few hours before or after. (Parans are easy to spot in a natal chart using computer software capabilities, especially Astrolabe's Chartwheels II program.) The two planets may or may not be in aspect in terms of zodiacal longitude, but, if they are crossing angles at the same time, they are extremely important in defining significant locations (favorable and unfavorable) for the individual, nation, or corporation. The meaning will of course depend on which planets are in paran. This is also true for any locations along the same line of latitude within 1°-2° of those crossings anywhere else in the world, though the actual location of the paran gives the strongest effect.

The MC/IC and/or ASC/DSC axes may contain one or more midpoints, acting like a vector, and certain midpoint combinations on these angles would designate a desirable location.[47] Again, the strongest positions for planetary influence are probably those conjunct the ASC or MC. Here are some lines to look for on the

---

46. Birth charts of persons born at moderate latitudes (between 45° South and 45° North), with planets anywhere between 27° and 30° Gemini or Sagittarius and 0°-3° Cancer or Capricorn, will always have those planets conjunct one angle while square the other. At latitudes higher or lower than 45° North or 45° South, respectively, this is only true if the planet is located at 0°-3° Cancer or Capricorn. The consequence is that this brings in a whole double-edged effect, when one might have thought there was a clear-cut advantage. For example, when a location shows Sun conjunct Midheaven (SU MH), *and* the natal Sun happens to be at 0° Cancer or Capricorn, then it means it is great for career visibility and prominence but tends to create problems for success and harmony in relationships due to Sun square ASC. The reverse situation is true for Sun conjunct ASC and square the MC. It is wise to know this in advance as a given, as it is the only situation where there is an automatic square to the angles. The patented Astro·Carto·Graphy map shows you only planetary lines conjunct the angles, as those are generally the most powerful.

47. A midpoint is a point on the zodiac located halfway between two planets or points in space, as measured by their distance in celestial longitude, and is a sensitive point combining the influences of both planets or points. In a 360° circle, a midpoint can be direct or inverse, and, if a third planet is making a hard contact to the midpoint, it is called an indirect midpoint. Used by 13th-century astrologers and probably earlier, midpoints were brought back into use by the German astrologer Alfred Witte (1878-1943).

A·C·G map.[48]

What to seek out: Sun, Mercury, Venus, or Jupiter conjunct MC, ASC, IC, or DSC.

What to avoid: Mars, Saturn, Uranus, Neptune, or Pluto conjunct MC, ASC, IC, or DSC

Depending in each case on whether that planet is strongly placed in the natal chart, here, briefly, are reasons why you would want to seek out the following:

1. **The Sun line** can enhance one's sense of ego, identity, achievement, and, if a male, masculinity. For a woman, it can be a jolt in making her aware of her ego, acting somewhat like a Mars line. A good place for success unless there are problems with ego-inflation.

2. **The Mercury line** can increase the number of communications one has in a certain location and the extent to which one's verbal and written communications are more effective. One's contact with children and young people is also increased.

3. **The Venus line** can increase the love, beauty, artistic sensibility, and sense of pleasure and well-being in relationships and in regard to financial security. It can soften the blows in an otherwise difficult chart, or it can cause too much pleasure-seeking in a chart of someone who lacks a sense of purpose or self-discipline.

4. **The Jupiter line** can bring financial good fortune and career success with the MC/IC axis, or relationship success with the ASC/DSC axis. One's horizons are expanded through travel, education and reading, contact with other cultures, religions, and civic systems—especially their laws or ethics. Like Venus, the negative side of Jupiter along this line is overindulgence, and in addition, overconfidence and/or intolerance of other points of view.

If you have located one of the above lines but it is significantly close to a Mars, Saturn, Uranus, Neptune, or Pluto line (within 10° or 700 miles either side of the A·C·G line), you need to reassess the situation. The benefits of being at that location will be outweighed by some other influences that will probably negate the positive

---

48. There are always some exceptions for certain people, depending on their natal charts, what they need in their lives, and how they're experiencing a particular planetary energy at a given time. Some of these exceptions are noted in the upcoming sections.

influence of the Sun, Mercury, Venus, or Jupiter line. The exceptions are combinations involving Sun or Moon with Jupiter, Jupiter/Uranus, Jupiter/Pluto, or Jupiter/Uranus/Pluto, which can be quite fortunate in terms of money and/or career.

The Moon line is a special case, because it can easily reflect any other influence. As an odd paradox, for instance, even though it naturally represents the home, the Moon is not comfortable exactly at the angles, especially conjunct the IC. There it becomes too emotional a place, with too many fluctuations in one's emotional stability, too many overwhelming and potentially obsessive ties to home, mother, and any other important female friends and relatives. The exceptions are the combinations listed above. However, it is somewhat easier for a woman along her Moon lines than a man.

The following are generally lines to avoid. Exceptions occur when the planet is well-placed natally and there are certain other combinations, to be discussed momentarily.

1. **The Mars line** can be terrific if you are chiefly involved in athletic or highly physical activities or work, or if you lack drive or physical energy or the ability to identify what your life's work is. Otherwise, the outright aggression of the Mars line is not desirable for interpersonal harmony. It wants too much to have its own way, and thus can attract fights, war, violence of various kinds, surgery, and accidents, although accidents are especially associated with Mars/Uranus.

2. **The Saturn line** can represent commitment, discipline, and longevity in career and relationships—or, on the negative side, resistance to change, stagnation, delays, restriction, and hard times. Saturn conjunct IC (SA IC), for instance, is not recommended for a retirement location, because the home base is given the extra weight of duty and restriction just at a time in life when one might enjoy some freedom. Conversely, if you have never had enough responsibility or duty in your life, you might choose such a location to bring that needed balance. SA MC line is the best and easiest of the lines, in that it can bring a sense of well-earned respect and dignity to your career image. A corporation would want to test a product on a Saturn line, and ideally sell it on a Jupiter or even a Mercury line.

3. **The Uranus line** brings a sense of electric excitement, surprises, sudden changes, and even innovation in the life. That is, the creative abilities may find new wellsprings of inspiration here, though the going is definitely not slow and easy. That is why living on the Uranus line is generally not recommended for long periods of time, because the intensity level of the ongoing excitement and endless changes of plans can cause burnout and/or identity crises. For home and career stability, Uranus is most difficult conjunct IC or MC. For relationship stability, Uranus is most difficult conjunct ASC or DSC.

4. **The Neptune line** inspires in a slower, more watery and idealistic way. On the highest level, Neptune concerns spiritual striving and perfection, and many people find their Neptune lines running through India, Tibet, and other places closely associated with seeking after spiritual wisdom. On the negative side, living permanently on one's Neptune line can be a shifty experience, especially as regards real estate. (This applies mostly to Neptune conjunct IC [NE IC] or MC [NE MC], but especially NE IC.) It implies that you cannot be totally sure of the ground beneath your feet and had best not try to own it, but rather rent it, as there are strong ego-denying qualities associated with Neptune that do not coincide with strict concepts of individual ownership. On the other hand, communism and concepts of communal property do fit under Neptune. In regard to Neptune conjunct ASC (NE ASC) or DSC (NE DSC), Neptune bestows its ego-denying qualities on relationships. You may think you know who you're involved with, but it is easy to deceive oneself with unrealistic and glamorized ideals in such a location. At best, one is dealing in relationship with people who are attuned to the higher Neptunian vibrations through spiritual practice or the arts (especially music, dance, film, and photography), and here also one could be called upon to work with alcoholics, drug addicts, and a wide variety of martyr/savior types. If it is your profession to work with alcoholics and drug addicts, then you still have to consider that the more negative aspects of Neptune may adversely affect your personal relations at this location.

5. **The Pluto line** is extremely forceful in a relentless, obsessive, and hidden or potentially underhanded way in helping to manifest deep and irrevocable changes in one's life. If you need someone to

force you to change your ways, your psyche, your health, career or relationship patterns, go to your Pluto line and see the best counselor you can find. He or she will have the x-ray vision, if you don't have it yourself, to see deeply into the core of your being as to what needs changing. If you want to be a counselor yourself, this might be a place to consider—although, as with the Neptune lines, the negative energies of Pluto can also affect your personal relations. For instance, Pluto conjunct MC (PL MC) or IC (PL IC) can bring some element of power struggle into your home or career. You may find that you are constantly rebuilding or remodeling at this location, which you may try to do instead of inner-level reconstruction and transformation (though the two could be done alongside each other). It can also bring some criminal element too close for comfort to the home base, especially with Pluto conjunct IC (PL IC). In addition, Pluto can be so compelling that the attraction-repulsion principle tends to have sway in relationships. You absolutely must have him or her, but if you cannot, then you'd just as soon be alone while you plan your next moves. This applies to Pluto conjunct ASC (PL ASC) or DSC (PL DSC).

Given that generally the Mars, Saturn, Uranus, Neptune, and Pluto lines are lines to avoid, how can you avoid them if you were born along one or more of those lines? You can't, really, because the natal chart affects you for life no matter where you move. But you can soften the extent to which those issues affect you for life by moving to another location, though to some degree you will always be dealing with the possibility of both their positive and negative manifestations. The wisest approach is to know all the potential negative manifestations in advance so that you can spot them when they arise and change the probable outcome.

Below are planetary combinations or clusters whose midpoints conjunct ASC, MC, DSC, or IC will add to your store of information regarding which lines to seek out or avoid. (Remember how important it is to check not only the actual point of crossing of planetary lines, but also all along the same line of latitude anywhere in the world up to 2° away. One degree to exact is strongest.)[49] Note that unless the combinations involve Sun/Jupiter/Uranus/Pluto or Moon/Jupiter/Uranus/Pluto, generally it is not a good idea to

---

49. One can see this visually, and now also very quickly, by numerical order on the Astro-Carto-Graphy latitude crossings sheet, which is included with each A-C-G map.

move to a place that has more than three planetary lines passing through it. Another exception would be if you needed an intense infusion of planetary energy temporarily to encourage rapid growth and self-awareness. For this purpose, areas close to the North and South Poles would be a good bet for a short, intense stay. All of us have a series of planetary line groupings there, which is one reason why they are not well-populated places and definitely not comfortable for most people. Here, then, are some planetary combinations that are useful to know, and their meanings apply as much to questions of geographical location as to timing.

Good luck, success: Sun/Jupiter, Moon/Jupiter, Jupiter/ Uranus, Jupiter/Pluto, Sun/Jupiter/Uranus/Pluto, Moon/ Jupiter/Uranus/Pluto.[50]

Good health: Sun/Jupiter, Moon/Jupiter.

Parties, good times (and potential for overindulgence): Venus/Jupiter.

Violence: Mars/Pluto, Mars/Neptune/Pluto, Sun/Mars.

Dangers, accidents: Mars/Uranus, Saturn/Uranus, Uranus/ Neptune, Mars/Uranus/Neptune.

Very hard work or hard times: Mars/Saturn, Saturn/Pluto, Mars/Saturn/Neptune.

Divorce: Saturn/Pluto, Saturn/Uranus/Pluto.

Illness, alcohol or drug addiction: Sun/Neptune, Mars/ Neptune, Sun/Mars/Neptune.

Illness or physical weakness only: Sun/Saturn/Uranus, Sun/Saturn/Uranus/Pluto, Sun/Saturn/Neptune, Sun/Saturn/ Neptune/Pluto.[51]

In one case, a man won a house through a lottery when T. (transiting) Uranus came into close hard contact with N. (natal)

---

50. Either natally, or by timing or relocation, lottery winners, for example, whose birth charts have been researched and verified, have usually shown Jupiter/ Pluto, or Jupiter/Uranus/Pluto planetary lines at MC or ASC and/or the same planets crossing at birth or relocation latitude.

51. In certain cases Pluto ASC lines can also be very hard on the health, especially if the person is not used to living on this line. Example: A man moved to his Pluto ASC line and suddenly underwent several near-death operations for pancreatic cancer. The Pluto energy is very demanding of deep-rooted change, starting bodily in this case.

Jupiter and N. Moon. This Moon/Jupiter/Uranus combination was even more ripe to happen because the natal chart showed N. Moon and Jupiter square N. Venus and Uranus (2° orb), i.e. Moon/Jupiter/Venus/Uranus, a propensity for good fortune (Jupiter/Uranus) emotionally (Moon) or through houses (also Moon).

Geographical Clues: Career and/or Financial Success[52]

Considering the raft of top-grossing American entertainers in recent years whose incomes far exceed those of America's top-grossing executives, it seems fitting to include some of the entertainers for whom we have accurate birth data. Bruce Springsteen and Arnold Schwarzenegger, for example, were among the highest-paid entertainers during 1987 and 1988, and others included in this category happen to be either entertainers or well-known public figures. (All birth data is listed in Appendix B.)

Arnold Schwarzenegger
Body builder turned movie actor/producer and real estate investor

Born in Graz, Austria (15E26, 47N05), Schwarzenegger has Mercury and Venus ASC lines going through his birthplace. These are favorable for business, but not as spectacularly favorable as the lines going through or close to Los Angeles, where he moved to begin his movie career in the 1970s: Jupiter MH and Mercury and Venus DSC.[53] (His two-year income for 1987-88 was reported to be $43 million.) This combination might be a party signal for a less disciplined person, but Schwarzenegger's natal chart shows a very disciplined combination of Sun conjunct Saturn and Pluto (within 5° and 7° orbs, respectively), as well as natal Moon in the Saturn-ruled sign of Capricorn. Notice how the West Coast United States is generally more favorable for him than the East Coast, where his wife since 1986, television journalist Maria Shriver, lives and works in between visits in this bi-coastal marriage. The midpoint for the Moon MH and Uranus IC lines runs right through New York City,

---

52. All the maps appearing in this chapter are copyrighted by Astro·Carto·Graphy and are reproduced with their permission.

53. Though most astrologers refer to the Midheaven as the MC (from the Latin "medium coeli" meaning "middle of the sky"), A·C·G uses MH as their symbol for Midheaven for ease of use by non-astrologers. For the remainder of this chapter, the MH symbol will be used alongside the A·C·G maps.

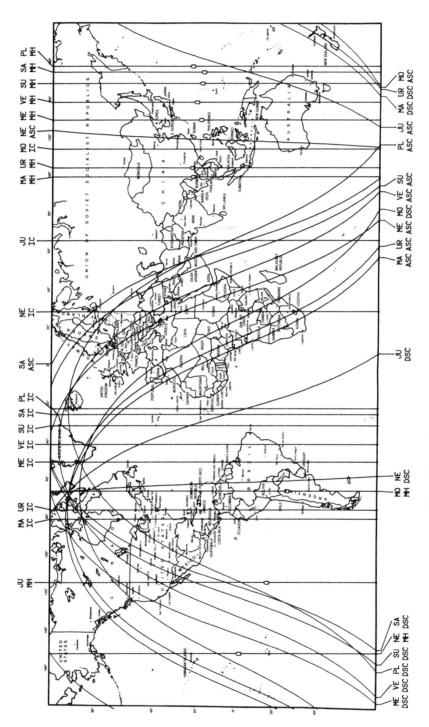

Astro-Carto-Graphy Map for Arnold Schwarzenegger

Maria's home town. (Moon = woman, involved in exciting [Uranus] work, related to the electronic [Uranus] media; she is perhaps full of surprises [Uranus], and Arnold's sense of a home base [Moon] there is subject to last-minute changes [Uranus]. No wonder Arnold stays based in Los Angeles!)

Bruce Springsteen
Rock star, musician and songwriter

Born in Freehold, New Jersey (74W17, 40N16), where the fortunate Jupiter/ Uranus midpoint comes into hard contact by 3' orb to natal MH, affecting career, Springsteen also was born with natal Sun close to the Cardinal axis, at 0° Libra 43', and natal Pluto nearby on the same axis, at 17° Leo 29'. These combined signatures contribute to his being known for his national and international scale of success, though most of his musical style and content comes from his working-class New Jersey roots.

It is interesting to note that he remains based in New Jersey, at the same latitude where Venus/Jupiter, Venus/Pluto, and Saturn/ Uranus crossings occur elsewhere in the world. These planetary combinations do not contribute to making life easy for Springsteen, who, although his income for the two-year period 1987-88 was reported at $61 million, apparently gives so much away to charity that he was doing at least one benefit concert for himself in 1988 to help defray his expenses for his self-initiated divorce from his first wife, actress/model Julianne Phillips. In terms of the planetary crossings, when Saturn and Uranus (push-pull) are vying for influence with Venus (love and money), even the fortunate Jupiter/ Pluto crossing has trouble winning out. The Saturn/Uranus influence is scrappy and potentially divorce-prone, and no doubt contributes toward making his natal Sun square Uranus even more wildly and recklessly energetic. Rather simple in his actual living style and clothing, he has shown this mainly in his performance style, in which he often gives his many loyal fans four to five hours' worth of sweating, hard-driving music per performance. I should add that the underlying Saturn/Uranus influence at the birthplace (New Jersey), which thus affects his whole life's destiny, is not as obvious at first as the more even-handed and diplomatic Venus-ruled Libra natal Sun. But we are scratching beneath the surface here.

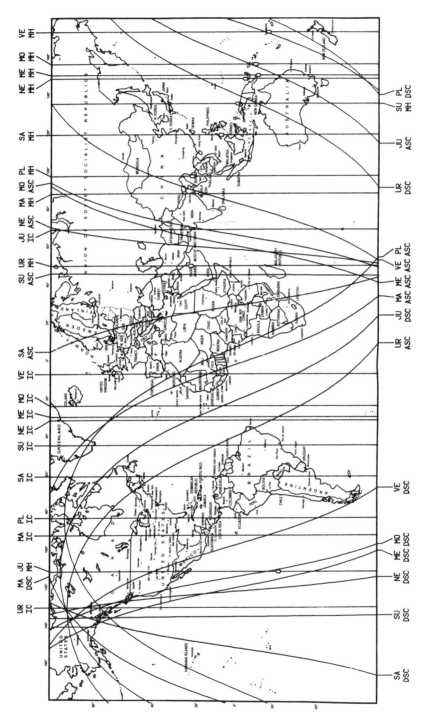

Astro-Carto-Graphy Map for Bruce Springsteen

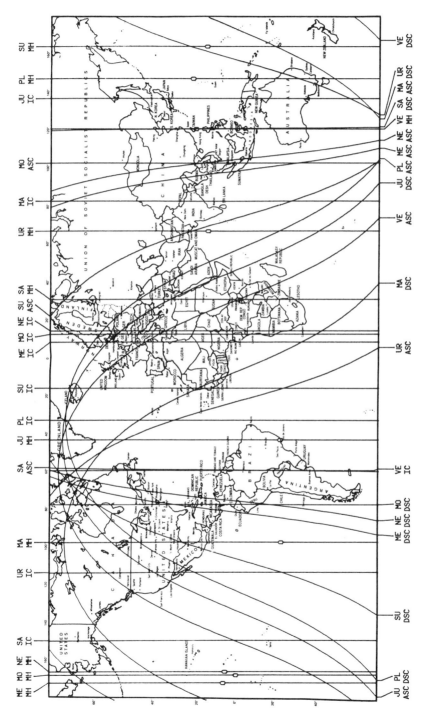

Astro-Carto-Graphy Map for Dustin Hoffman

Dustin Hoffman
Movie and stage actor

Born in Los Angeles (118W15, 34N04), Hoffman has Jupiter ASC at his birthplace, which is also the American movie capital, and the Uranus IC line is nearby. This combination, called a Jupiter/Uranus paran, is a fortunate one, and we will run into it frequently with these individual examples of career and/or financial success. Also, like Springsteen, Hoffman's natal Sun is 1° from the Cardinal, world-connecting axis, at 16° Leo 02'.

Hoffman has carved out a remarkable niche for himself as an actor who is not afraid to take big chances, to play unusual roles, and to stand by his own uncompromising aesthetic convictions— something quite uncommon in Hollywood. The seriousness and integrity of his artistic motives is reflected in Venus/Saturn crossing at the equator. This is not necessarily an easy combination, but, linked with the lucky Jupiter/Uranus paran at his birthplace, he has managed over the long haul (Saturn) to use his art (Venus) and earn his money (Venus) in a highly lucrative way (Jupiter/Uranus) without sacrificing his serious views (Saturn) about what kind of roles he is willing to play. Currently earning somewhere upwards of $5 million per picture, Hoffman has distinguished himself in numerous lead roles in movies as diverse as *Rainman* (1988), *Tootsie* (1982), *Midnight Cowboy* (1969), and one of his first pictures, *The Graduate* (1967). He also produced and brilliantly acted the part of Willy Loman in Arthur Miller's *Death of a Salesman*, a Broadway revival that was also made into a movie in 1985.

Shirley MacLaine
Movie actress/producer, dancer, author

Born in Richmond, Virginia (77W27, 37N33), MacLaine was never one to stay close to her birthplace. Her many travels are well documented in her various books, and the likelihood that everyone would know about her travels (and her career and relationships) is reflected astrologically in her having ASC, MH, and Moon's Node all on the Cardinal axis. Her enduring good fortune with the public as an actress and author is highlighted by her natal Jupiter/Uranus midpoint coming into hard contact with both natal Moon and Pluto. This planetary combination also describes how her various personal metamorphoses (Moon/Pluto) would not only go well but be lucky for her (Jupiter/Uranus).

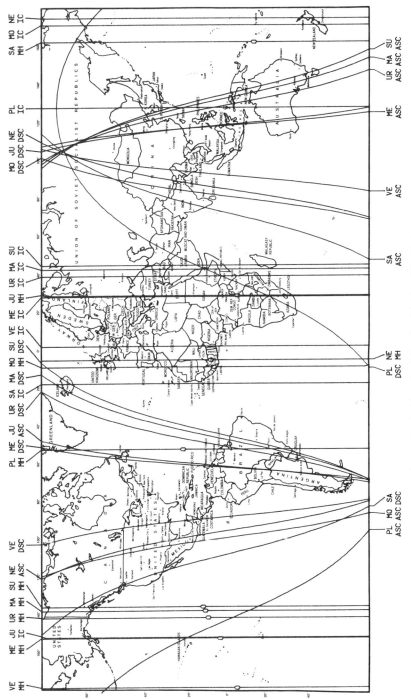

Astro-Carto-Graphy Map for Shirley MacLaine

When the lines on the A·C·G map run very close together, you know you have a close hard contact, either by conjunction (0°) or opposition (180°). Her Mercury/Jupiter lines run close together, as do Moon/Neptune. Note that the Mercury/Jupiter ASC lines run down through the western coast of South America, where MacLaine experienced many unusual happenings and wrote (Mercury) about them with exuberance (Jupiter) and philosophical zeal (Jupiter).[54] The same lines run through eastern Africa and central Egypt, near Cairo, whose ancient pyramids also had a strong influence on her. Her natal Moon/Neptune conjunction reflects the dreamer (and dancer and movie artist) who eventually became a spiritual seeker. Many of the locations where MacLaine has done much of that seeking, to date, are shown by where those lines run. Moon/ Neptune ASC lines run down through the southwestern United States, near Santa Fe, New Mexico, where she did extensive past-life work with Chris Griscom at the Light Institute of Galisteo. (This is documented in MacLaine's book, *Dancing in the Light*, 1986.) These lines continue south through central Mexico, where she was inspired by the ancient Mayan culture. Similarly, in western China, Nepal, Tibet, and northeastern India near Calcutta pass the Moon/ Neptune DSC lines. Her spiritual experiences in Nepal and Tibet were documented in her books *Don't Fall Off the Mountain* (1970) and *You Can Get There From Here* (1975).

Notice the confluence of lines in eastern China. MacLaine was the first to lead a women's delegation to China in the 1970s. Notice also how the Saturn DSC line runs down through the Pacific Northwest, where she has a home, and near Los Angeles, where she has another home. MacLaine, the peripatetic traveler, actress, dancer, author, and producer, usually goes to one of these two homes to focus in (Saturn) on her next project and to do serious and concentrated (Saturn) studying, reading, and writing. These are places that discipline her to bring all the far-flung pieces together. She has used this Saturn line well.

---

54. Many of these experiences were documented in her book *Out on a Limb* (1983), which was subsequently made into a television mini-series that she starred in, playing herself and co-writing the screenplay. In addition, she wrote a book about the making of the mini-series called *It's All in the Playing* (1987). Mercury/Jupiter can keep the story rolling as long as it is expanding and expansive.

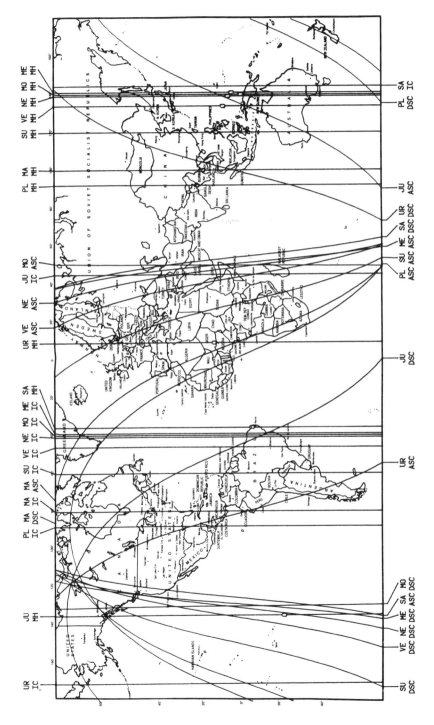

Astro-Carto-Graphy Map for Robert Redford

SHIRLEY MacLAINE
April 24, 1934
3:57 p.m. EST
Richmond, Virginia
  77W27
  37N33
ST 5:55:59
Meridian houses

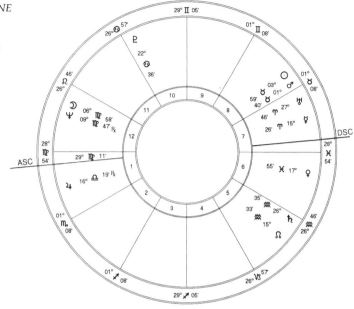

Natal Horoscope for Shirley MacLaine

ROBERT REDFORD
August 18, 1936
8:02 p.m. PST
Santa Monica, California
  118W29
  34N01
ST 17:57:23
Meridian houses

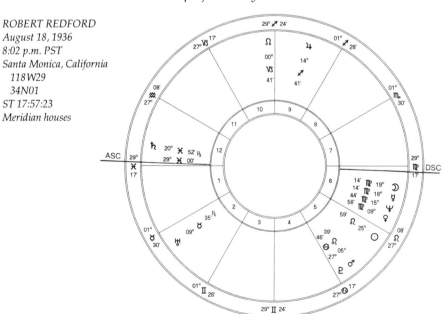

Natal Horoscope for Robert Redford

Robert Redford
Movie actor/director/producer

Born in Santa Monica, California (118W29, 34N01), Redford shares with MacLaine the natal ASC, MH, and Moon's Node on the Cardinal axis, furthering the likelihood of a great deal of travel in the life, and the likelihood that no matter where he lives, moves, or travels, the whole world tends to know about it. (Redford has managed to keep his private life much more private than MacLaine, and this is reflected astrologically by his having most planets well below the horizon except for his elevated 9th-house Jupiter. He also hasn't written any autobiographical accounts!) Notice that Redford has a Saturn ASC line passing just west of Hollywood, but, unlike MacLaine, he spends as little time there as possible, even though this is the movie capital of the United States. His personal philosophy and ethics have tended to put him more and more at a remove from the Hollywood "hot topic" movie, although he has done well by Hollywood and has the fortunate Sun/Jupiter and Moon/Venus crossings at the same latitude. Instead, Redford has tended to establish his bases in the American Southwest (New Mexico) and in Provo, Utah (111W39, 40N14), where he is off the potential goldfish bowl Cardinal axis (though to some extent this is always with him as his natal coordinates, even if somewhat softened and modified when he is in Utah).[55] In Provo, Utah, the fortunate Jupiter/Pluto midpoint comes into hard contact with the relocation MH, as does the natal Sun with relocation ASC there —which is where he has established his Sundance Institute to encourage and develop actors, writers, directors, and composers working in the film arts.

With Saturn rising natally, there is the potential for much self-discipline and hard focus, especially in relation to his work, with natal Mars (work) and Saturn (focus) in hard contact. In recent years he has concentrated his attention cinematically on the issues of ethnic and minority groups, including Hispanics and American Indians, and politically on environmental issues.

Mark Spitz
Swimming champion

Born in Modesto, California (121W00, 37N39), Spitz has

---

55. Oftentimes astro-mapping is as useful in telling you what locations to get away from as where to go.

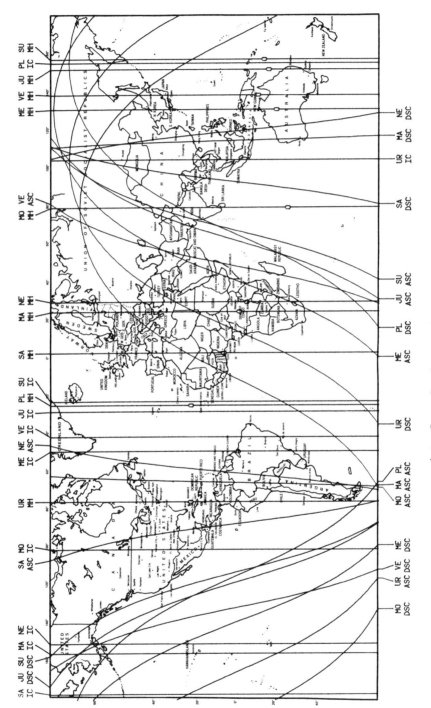

Astro-Carto-Graphy Map for Mark Spitz

Sun/Jupiter DSC lines at his birthplace as well as Pluto ASC (within 7°). This is a strong planetary combination for success, and one would expect to see either a strong Sun/Jupiter or Mars/Jupiter for a sports champion. He won a record seven gold medals at the 1972 Summer Olympics, which were held in Munich, Germany (11E34, 48N08) August 26-September 10, 1972. His Mars/Saturn midpoint runs just east of Munich, indicating a lot of hard work there, and a tremendous amount of discipline (Saturn) applied to a sport (Mars). Fortunately, he also has Venus/Pluto and Moon/Mars crossings at the same latitude elsewhere in the world, contributing passion for the sport (Moon/Mars) and an intense desire (Venus/Pluto) to win. (Count in also the natal Sun/Jupiter/Pluto.)

Spitz has also announced his intention to make a comeback as a swimmer in the 1992 Summer Olympics scheduled for Barcelona, Spain. His Saturn MH line right through Barcelona augurs well for career staying power.

Christina Onassis
Heiress

Born in New York City (73W59, 40N46), Onassis was on the one hand blessed with a colossal inheritance (Jupiter/Pluto midpoint on her natal ASC, Jupiter/Uranus midpoint on her natal Sun), and on the other hand somewhat cursed with an inability to feel deep contentment and joy in her life. There were always hopeful signs that she was moving in that direction, as she married each of her four successive husbands, and gave birth to her much beloved daughter Athina in January 1985. She was seriously considering husband number five when she visited Buenos Aires, Argentina, and died there suddenly on November 19, 1988 (at age 37) of an apparent heart attack. Though a suicide was ruled out, no doubt her intensive dieting, followed by compulsive binges and combined with abundant use of amphetamines and tranquilizers was more than her physical body could handle.

Her birth latitude holds a telling combination of planetary crossings: Venus/ Jupiter (an excess of the sensual pleasures, not knowing when to stop them); Moon/Saturn (sadness, and feelings of depression); and Venus/Neptune (unrealistic expectations in love matters, false loves, over-obligation in friendship, unclear about the value of money and confusing it with love). She also had Saturn close to the Cardinal axis, which, rather than giving her the

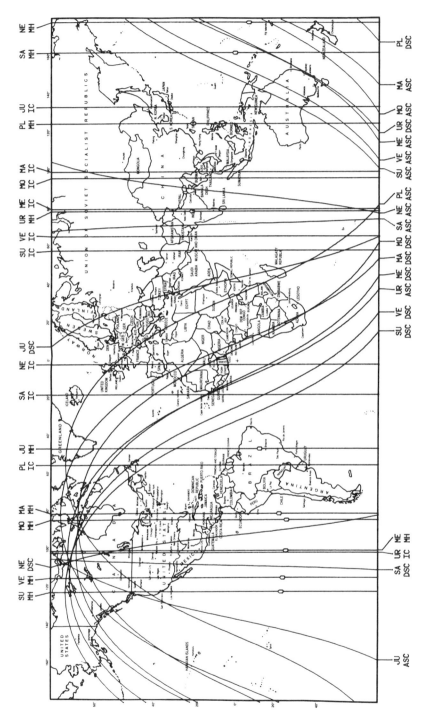

Astro-Carto-GraphyMap for Christina Onassis

necessary discipline in life, tended to darken her outlook, so that often it was depressed and depressive. (When Saturn's influence is not used constructively, one feels only that part of its energy which constrains, and thus feels emotionally depressing.)

On the Onassis A∗C∗G map (see opposite page), Greece lies between the generally fortunate Jupiter DSC and Pluto ASC lines, but she chose instead to buy homes and settle in Paris and Switzerland, where her Pluto ASC line runs strong. As we have noted earlier, Pluto lines are not easy ones to live on for long unless your life's work is Plutonian, such as unearthing people's subconscious layers, as Carl Jung's was (see footnote 68, p. 117). In her case it contributed to the constant upheavals and obsessions (Pluto) in her relationships (ASC), forcing her to constantly reevaluate her character and her life. Pluto ASC lines can also be very hard on the physical body, because they force a relentless and deep level transformation which can sometimes only be begun on the physical level.

At the time of her death, Onassis was spending time on her Pluto IC line in Buenos Aires. The IC is related to one's roots, one's origins, and one's endings. As it happens, her father Aristotle Onassis started out in Buenos Aires in 1923 with a few hundred dollars in his pocket. In short order he revived a family tobacco business, gained dual Argentinean/Greek citizenship in 1925, and moved into the import-export business before buying his first ships in the early 1930s. This was the beginning of the great Onassis fortune which his daughter Christina inherited at age 23 and then passed on to her daughter Athina, the sole Onassis heir.[56] Athina's inheritance is estimated to reach upwards of $1 billion by 2003, the year she turns 18 and has legal access to her own money. (Another level of meaning for Pluto on the collective level is large amounts of money, especially as in other people's money, money gained through the public, partners, or the deceased; and the general concept of the recycling of financial or other resources.)

Merv Griffin
Entertainer, TV host, real estate investor

Born in San Mateo, California (122W19, 37N34), Griffin made his first big success as a television personality and as the TV host of

---

56. Athina was three years old at the time of her mother's death in November 1988.

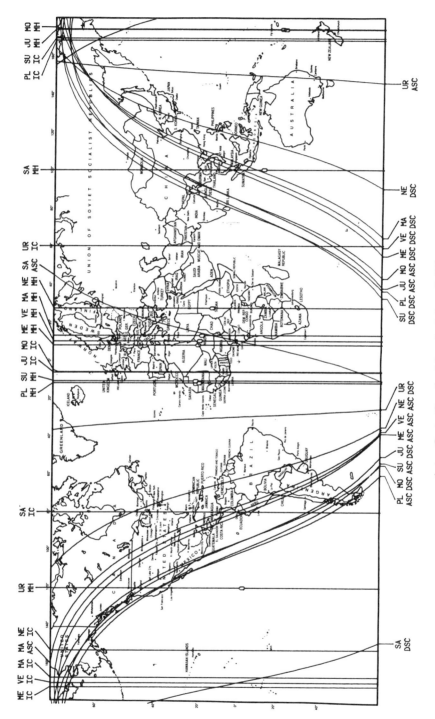

Astro-Carto-Graphy Map for Merv Griffin

The Merv Griffin Show (1961-1986), coming up the ranks initially as a singer and pianist. He also inspired the TV show, *Wheel of Fortune* (1973), the most lucrative game show in American television history, which he later sold to Coca-Cola in 1986 for $250 million.

Once again we have the tell-tale success signature, in this case Sun/Pluto ASC, Moon/Jupiter DSC (7° orb), and Uranus MH, all of this natally, which is close to Los Angeles (118W15, 34N04) where he established himself not only in television and radio but also in real estate. Jupiter/Saturn crossings occur at the same latitude as Los Angeles, and this combination concerns buildings, among other things. Over the years Merv Griffin has had substantial successes in his real estate investments.

Griffin has four sets of Venus/Saturn crossings at the equator, affecting his whole life at any location. Dustin Hoffman has two sets of the same crossings, but unlike Hoffman, Griffin doesn't have so much seriousness (Saturn) about art (Venus) as seriousness about money and games of chance (both Venus). After the $250 million sale of *Wheel of Fortune,* Griffin advanced himself into "the Forbes 400."[57] As of late 1988 his holdings were reported in Forbes magazine as exceeding $300 million.[58]

Geographical Clues: Relationship Choices

Grace Kelly
Movie actress turned royalty

Born in Philadelphia, Pennsylvania (75W10, 39N57), Grace Kelly was a highly successful movie actress in Hollywood for five short years (1951-1955) before capturing the heart of Prince Rainier of Monaco and marrying him April 18, 1956. (She was 26 years old.) This marked her total retirement from films. Although she thought she would be returning to the medium, it became increasingly difficult for her to reconcile being a movie star with her new royal position and duties. (But as Grace Kelly or as Princess Grace, her natal Moon's Node [intimate relationships], located in the 7th house of partnerships, hints that a relationship might eventually take precedence over other matters, including a career.)

---

57. "The Forbes 400" consist of the 400 richest people in the United States, as reported annually in late October in a special issue of *Forbes* magazine.

58. Merv Griffin is a longtime advocate of astrology, and often invited various well-known astrologers to be guests on his TV talk show. He introduced Nancy Reagan to Joan Quigley, the San Francisco astrologer suddenly much in the news during the astrology-and-the-White House publicity fracas in May 1988.

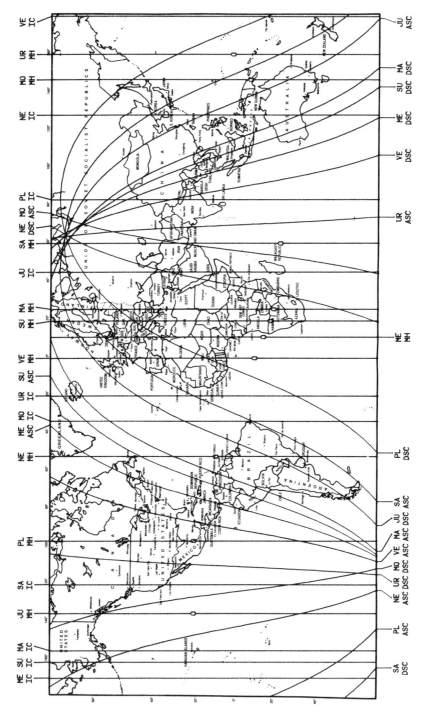

Astro-Carto-Graphy Map for Grace Kelly (Princess Grace)

At her birthplace, the fortunate Jupiter/Uranus midpoint makes a hard contact to her natal Midheaven and the Moon's Node, benefiting her career and social aspirations. It is a combination which tends to promote being "at the right place at the right time."

Relocation to Hollywood puts the angles of her chart 1/2° from the Cardinal axis, and thus puts the world in touch with her as a movie actress. However, the Saturn IC line runs just west of Hollywood, making it a difficult place for her to live long-term due to the demands on her time and on her private life. Jupiter/Neptune crossings at the same latitude made it somewhat easier for her to succeed there, but the actual experience of living and working in Hollywood would not have been enthralling for her due to the Saturn IC line *and* Saturn 2° from the Cardinal axis.

Her ease in making such an international move to Monaco is reflected in a natal chart with planets spread out over eight signs and eight different houses. This is a typically big traveler, at home in many places around the world.

Monaco (7E23, 43N42) presents a brighter picture for her than Hollywood, putting her natal Sun/Venus midpoint close to conjunct the relocation Monaco Midheaven, signaling the love and mostly peaceful life she found there as Princess Grace, wife, and mother of three children. Also, the Mercury MH line runs close through Monaco, which enabled her to communicate more directly with more people on an everyday basis and to connect more with children. Because of her royal (and ex-movie star) status, she stayed in the news (another Mercury function) right up to the time of her death in a car accident in September 1982. Natal Mars does make hard contact to the relocation Monaco ASC, which (along with her natal Sun conjunct Mars) shows the need for a great deal of physical activity and the potential for violence at this location, especially if the physical (and sexual) energy is not used and released.

Elizabeth Taylor
Movie, television, and stage actress

Born in London, England (0W06, 51N31), Taylor started getting married on May 6, 1950 (at age 18), and with little interruption had seven husbands by the time she divorced Senator John Warner in 1982. (Actually, there were six husbands, but she married Richard Burton twice.) One of the closest hard contacts in her natal chart is a Venus/Uranus conjunction. Love (Venus) can be erratic and full of

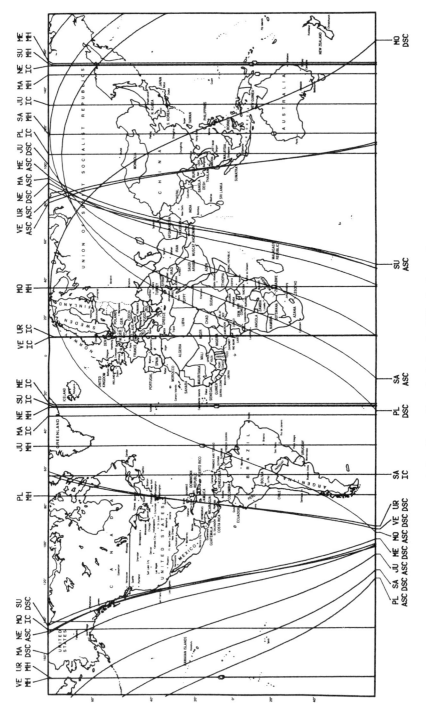

Astro•Carto•Graphy Map for Elizabeth Taylor

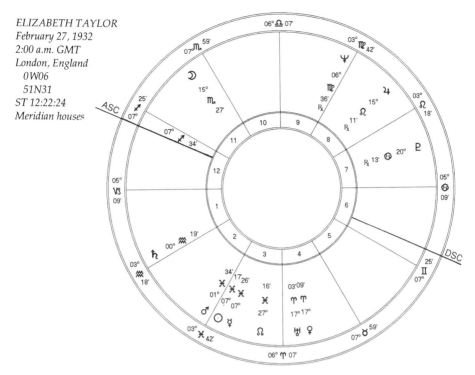

ELIZABETH TAYLOR
February 27, 1932
2:00 a.m. GMT
London, England
  0W06
  51N31
ST 12:22:24
Meridian houses

Natal Horoscope for Elizabeth Taylor

many surprises (Uranus) in such a case, but that is because the individual yearns for and enjoys the unexpected element in love matters, and so attracts them!

The Venus/Uranus IC lines run down right through Switzerland (where she has a home in Gstaad, and where Richard Burton settled in his final years, near Geneva), and through northwestern Italy near Rome (where her celebrated and much reported romance with Richard Burton began on the set of the movie *Cleopatra* in 1963).

Rome shows Venus/Pluto crossing at the same latitude: intensity and obsession (Pluto) over love matters (Venus). In addition, due to her natal Moon and Jupiter on the Cardinal axis, Taylor is prone to being in the public eye (Moon), both known for and enjoyed for her many indulgences (Jupiter).

Venus/Uranus DSC lines also pass through or near New York City, Philadelphia, and Washington, D.C., and in fact they are intensified by Pluto MH line crossing the Venus/Uranus DSC line just a few degrees north of New York City. Unfortunately, Moon/Pluto and Venus/Saturn lines are also crossing at Washington, D.C., indicating that Taylor would try to change her image as a woman there (Moon/Pluto), but that it might constrain (Saturn) either her art or her love life (both Venus) to do so. She became a political wife there (from 1976-82) and started eating and drinking heavily to offset her loneliness and boredom.

Speaking of drinking (Neptune), notice how Sun/Mercury/ Mars/Neptune lines pass just to the west of Los Angeles. Taylor has had a tendency to attract actor/dreamer/big drinker husbands, and Richard Burton was the most famous of them all, on all counts. Of course a woman's Sun and Mars lines are not just about her husband(s), they are about her, and Taylor has fought a lifetime battle with some form or other of chemical dependency. The fact that those lines run close to Hollywood means that it is a fact which becomes dramatized there both in film and in real life for Ms. Taylor, especially when she resides in Los Angeles, as she has in the near decade since her divorce from Senator John Warner in 1982.

Neptune is also concerned with idealism, and with her close Sun/Mercury/Mars/Neptune combination, Taylor would tend to put her loves on a pedestal. As she herself says "... I always chose to think I was in love and that love was synonymous with marriage. I couldn't just have a romance; it had to be marriage."[59]

Richard Burton
Movie and stage actor

Born in Pontrhydyfendigar, South Wales (3W51, 52N17), Burton's success with the public was second only to his success with women. Astrologically, the Moon symbolizes both women and the public, and his natal chart shows Pluto/ Jupiter/Uranus/Moon all angular, confirming the strong likelihood of this success. Unfortunately, his tumultuous private life tended to overwhelm whatever self-discipline Burton could ultimately muster, which, with Sun closely conjunct Saturn, should have been ample. However, in the natal chart, Sun/Saturn is also in soft aspect (either 60° or 120°) to most of the other planets in his chart. This tends to make a person slip into the assumption that they can do anything, in this case discipline oneself, without too much effort. (Yet another example of how hard aspects, or contacts, are truly the key to the manifestation of events.) Burton's career as a dramatic actor, which

59. *Current Biography Yearbook* 1985, p. 411, excerpted from a *Life* magazine interview (Dec. 18, 1964) by Richard Meryman.

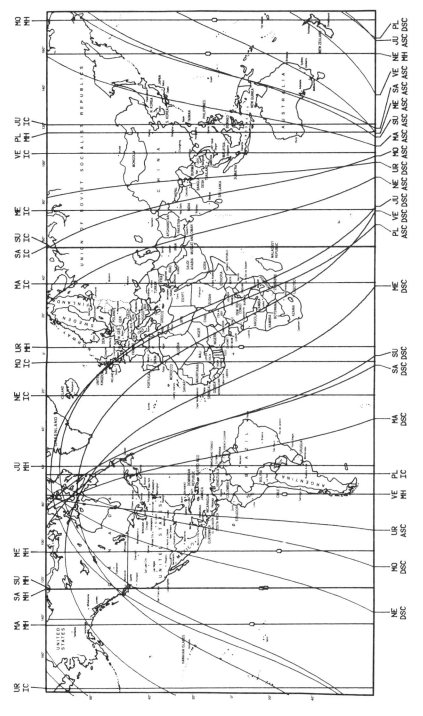

Astro·Carto·Graphy Map for Richard Burton

started off so brilliantly in London in the late 1940s, took a nose dive somewhere in the late '60s and '70s, with intermittent splashes of greatness, as he took on many Grade B movie roles without thought to their quality but probably with an eye to maintaining his increasingly higher standards of living.

As it turned out, Burton was known for his womanizing long before Elizabeth Taylor came into his life, but she is considered, by his public, of course, to be his greatest love of all—and probably she was, judging from his posthumously published diaries (1988).[60] She was wife numbers two and three, out of five. They were married for a total of 11 years (1964-74 and 1975-76) and continued to do television and stage work together after the second divorce in 1976.

For Burton, the fateful meeting place, Rome, shows Jupiter DSC line just to the west of it and Pluto ASC line nearby. Jupiter is generally fortunate, especially with Pluto, but it can also be excessive. Crossing near the same latitude as Rome elsewhere in the world are Moon/ Mercury lines (a lot of discussion and newspaper coverage [Mercury] about one's woman/women and one's emotional life [both Moon]), Saturn/ Neptune lines (making one's dreams [Neptune] come true [Saturn]—for better or worse); and Sun/Neptune lines (the idealized male or artist, the big dreamer and potential drinker, as was also the case).

In London, Burton started out in life with the fortunate Jupiter/Pluto lines there and Moon/Uranus midpoint close by to the London relocation Midheaven. Moon/Uranus can be a changing situation (Uranus) with women (Moon), leading to domestic (Moon) instability (Uranus). His first marriage to a Welsh actress, based in London, had to operate unconventionally and was eventually torn apart by it.

In Hollywood, like so many of the actors discussed here, Burton also has the Saturn line nearby, but in his case it is Sun/Saturn and they are at the Midheaven. It should or could have been a place where he pulled himself together careerwise, but instead, what it stood for (i.e. self-discipline) seemed to elude him; and the relative lack of it, at times perversely apparent in Burton's life, contributed greatly towards his untimely decline and towards his turbulent,

---

60. Richard Burton died of a brain hemorrhage in Geneva, Switzerland, on August 5, 1984. He was 58 years old. In recent years he had been in increasingly frail health, which resulted at least in part from his lifetime of heavy drinking. And, as in his life, the major media coverage of Burton's funeral focused predictably on Elizabeth Taylor, whether she would or would not appear, and how Burton's widow felt about it all.

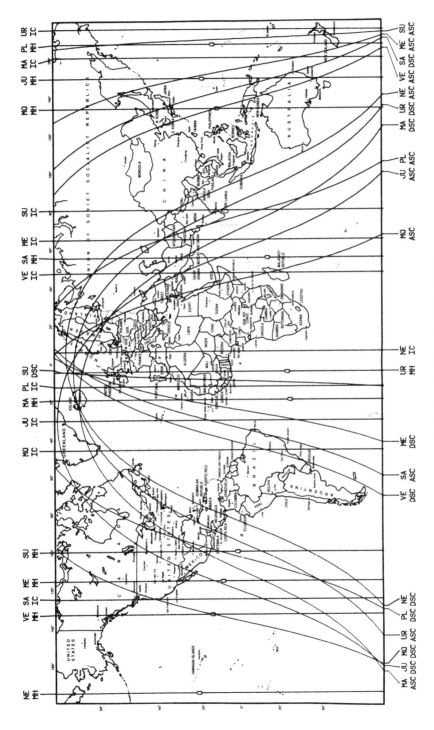

Astro-Carto-Graphy Map for Greta Garbo

though admittedly colorful private life. (For further material on Burton see Chapter 4, under Second Saturn Return, pp. 161-162.)

Greta Garbo
Movie and stage actress

Born in Stockholm, Sweden (18E03, 59N20), Garbo was unusual for something not unheard of in other professions, such as tennis or the ballet—retiring from one's career while young and beautiful and at your peak. (Grace Kelly didn't realize that was what she was actually doing at age 26 when she married Prince Rainier.)

Garbo made movies from 1924, when she was 19, up until 1941, when she was 36, and then suddenly, mysteriously stopped. She was and is still regarded as a screen legend, and the sense of mystery she exuded on screen in the '20s and '30s followed her the rest of her life. In the movie *Grand Hotel* (1932), she had a line which also followed her: "I want to be alone."

Garbo was known to prefer her solitude and privacy ultimately over any marriage or partnership, though she did have a love affair with fellow actor Gilbert Roland in the late '20s, and a friendship of some sort with conductor Leopold Stokowski in 1938.

Astrologically, her natal Saturn in hard contact to natal Moon's Node denotes a tendency for intimate relationships (Moon's Node) to either be conservative (Saturn), to cool off quickly (Saturn), or to cause her to feel constricted (also Saturn). I suspect a combination of all three was operating, which may have prompted this remark by fellow actress Lillian Gish: "Garbo's temperament reflected the rain and gloom of the long, dark Swedish winters."[61] The Saturn line (hooked up with the Moon's Node, which is not shown on the A·C·G maps) runs just west of Hollywood as an IC line, as did Grace Kelly's. For both of them, Hollywood was not a comfortable place to live long-term. In addition, Garbo has Mercury/Saturn midpoint angular there, meaning that she probably felt constrained (Saturn) by what she did and did not say (Mercury) in public, and by how it was reported in the press (also Mercury). That probably also increased her resolve to travel incognito, as she did many times with a female companion, with a slouch hat and a pseudonym for disguise. (Mercury/Saturn is a combination also symbolizing

---

61. Leslie Halliwell, *Halliwell's Filmgoer's Companion*, 8th ed., 1985, p. 425.

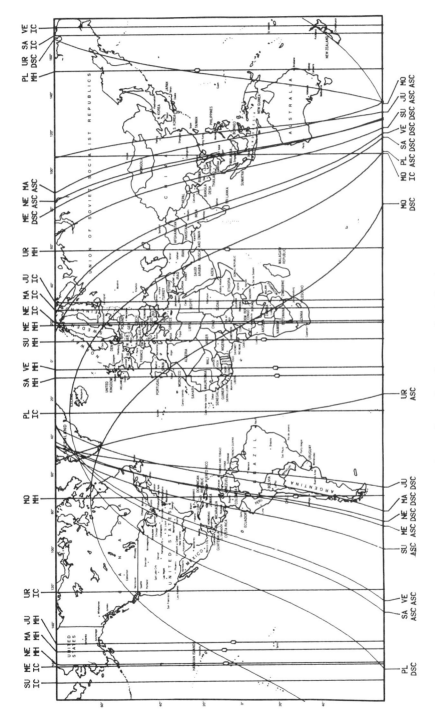

Astro•Carto•Graphy Map for Yoko Ono

travel—thoughts [Mercury] of separation [Saturn], and thus parting and travel.)[62]

Eventually, Garbo had homes in at least three countries. One home was in New York City, where her Uranus ASC line runs straight through. The Uranus ASC line at any location tends to make one steer clear of committed relationships and to yearn for the freedom to explore one's personal identity unimpeded by constraints of any sort, especially social constraints. You can see how Garbo might prefer New York City.

Yoko Ono
Artist and musician

Born in Tokyo, Japan (139E45, 35N40), Ono met her life's most fateful match to date in John Lennon in London in 1968.

One factor not mentioned so far is checking out which lines on the A·C·G map run through the mate's birthplace on one's own map.[63] Yoko Ono has the more traditional Venus line through Liverpool, Lennon's place of birth, and he has a Venus line running on his map just west of Tokyo, Japan. This is the classical love match combination, although Ono has some other messages coming from planetary crossings at the same latitude as Liverpool, England, elsewhere in the world. First is Moon/Uranus and Venus/Uranus, definitely an unconventional relationship, with emotions and domesticity (Moon) expressed in unusual ways (Uranus), and a very original, if not idiosyncratic and nonconformist (Uranus) way of revealing both their art (Venus) and messages about global peace (Venus). At their "Bed-In for Peace" (1969), Yoko and John stayed in bed in their Canadian hotel room for a number of days, and invited media journalists to come by, photograph them, and talk with them, urging the world to "Give peace a chance."

Another crossing Ono has at Liverpool is Mars/Pluto, which can symbolize not only the aggressive (Mars) crowds (Pluto) which tended to follow them everywhere they went, but also physical

---

62. See Mercury + Saturn definition in Witte-Lefeldt, *Rules for Planetary Pictures: The Astrology of Tomorrow*, 5th ed., 1959, p. 156.

63. Richard Burton has Jupiter/Pluto and Moon/Uranus midpoint through London, Elizabeth Taylor's birthplace, identifying the "magnificent obsession" of it all (Jupiter/Pluto), and yet the emotional unreliability (Moon/Uranus). Through Burton's birthplace in South Wales, Taylor has Moon/Mercury (a lot of emotional discussion), Sun/Moon (the husband and wife, the love match, the ultimate alter-ego), and Moon/Neptune (emotions based on idealistic and perhaps unrealistic and shifty grounds).

violence, which was how John died, by an assassin's bullet, December 8, 1980. Mars/Pluto is also the development and transformation (Pluto) of one's work (Mars). John and Yoko influenced each other a great deal artistically, and while they were together it was chiefly through John Lennon that Yoko Ono moved more into the arena of music and away from that of the visual arts.

John and Yoko lived together in New York City from 1971 to 1980, and after his death in 1980 she stayed on there through 1988. In New York City, Ono has Sun ASC and Moon MH lines close by, echoing *her* dominance of their public life and career aims (Moon MH), and *his* dominance of their private life (Sun ASC). Crossing at the same latitude elsewhere in the world is Moon/Saturn and Moon/Mars. Moon/Saturn echoes the sadness that would come to represent New York City, the place where she was widowed and where she grieved over the untimely loss of her husband. It also symbolizes her becoming a mother for the second time at age 42: older (Saturn) mother (Moon). (She lost custody of her daughter by Arthur Cox in the mid-1960s, partly due to her bohemian lifestyle before and after meeting John Lennon.) She was also 7-1/2 years older than Lennon, and in that sense the older or more mature (Saturn) woman (Moon).

Moon/Mars is related to being a wife and a hard-working woman, and Ono did look after their business affairs, especially while Lennon went into retirement for five years. Notice that New York City does not represent a violent place for her personally, but a place where she could experience some deep sadness (Moon/Saturn).

John Lennon
Musician and songwriter

Born in Liverpool, England (2W58, 53N25), John Lennon's romance with and marriage to Yoko Ono on March 20, 1969, was not always so popular with the public, especially since many accused Ono of being the main cause of the Beatles' breakup. He and Ono claimed the Beatles were heading in that direction anyway, regardless of her influence. Nevertheless, her influence over all aspects of his life was unmistakable, and it could be said from the various written accounts, even from her own authorized cinematic account (*Imagine: John Lennon*, 1988) that he depended upon her too

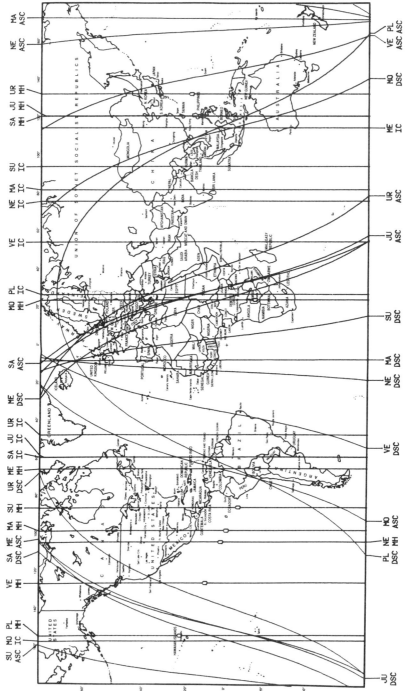

*Astro*Carto*Graphy Map for John Lennon*

much and gave up much of his creative and personal autonomy because of her. There is some hint of this from several astrological factors.

First, the Sun DSC line runs through his birthplace, and thus applies to his entire life's destiny. The DSC position is considered to be that of the mate, the other, though it is difficult to separate what is projected, traditionally the ASC, from what one attracts, traditionally the DSC. In any case the natal chart shows natal Sun and Moon's Node in the 7th house of partnerships, along with six planets in the western hemisphere (the receiving side of relationships and actions). This would confirm not only Lennon's ability to succeed in business partnerships, as he did to monumental artistic and financial heights with the Beatles, but his tendency to place the major thrust of his artistic and personal energy in working closely with others, as he later did with Yoko Ono after the Beatles disbanded.

Also, at his birthplace, the Sun/Moon crossing is near the same latitude elsewhere in the world, as is the violence-portending Mars/Pluto. Masses of people (Pluto) had strong to violent feelings about John Lennon and his music. This is further echoed by natal Mars (one's work, and also potential arguments or violence), not only angular in the birth chart, but its zenith located on the equator, affecting the entire life. The Sun/Moon crossing on the birth latitude places great emphasis on partnerships and marriage as a be-all and end-all in life.

In London, where he and Ono met in 1968, he is still close to the birth chart Sun/Moon crossing and also to the Moon/Uranus crossing: the woman (Moon) who is unconventional and iconoclastic (Uranus), and the breaking up (Uranus) of the domestic establishment (Moon).[64] Lennon was married with a son when he met Yoko Ono, who also happens to have three natal planets in Uranus-ruled Aquarius, including the Sun at 29° Aquarius 23'. (The 29th degree tends to promote the extremes of wherever it is located.) In any event, this is definitely an Aquarian (Uranus) woman (Moon).

In New York City, Lennon has no planetary lines per se, but a Sun IC/Pluto ASC crossing at a nearby latitude further identifies

---

64. Richard Burton also had a Moon/Uranus crossing at the latitude of London. Burton's previous London-based marriage was broken up by Elizabeth Taylor, just as Lennon's was by Yoko Ono.

how Lennon felt he could pull in and enjoy retirement at this location (Sun IC), even though there was always some pressure (Pluto) from his public, his fans, and his intimates (Pluto ASC) to develop and transform himself. One form of pressure came early on in his American residency, when he fought a legal battle with the U.S. Department of Immigration to stay in the U.S. After U.S. officials caught him with a small amount of marijuana at the airport, Immigration sent him deportation orders. Documents produced later showed that these orders originated with the Nixon administration, which was politically motivated to deport Lennon. (Pluto is also related to underhanded maneuvers by a hidden or unidentified source.) Finally he was allowed to stay, and several years later one of his obsessed fans (Pluto) staked out the entryway to Lennon's building (ASC) and, through a violent act (Mars/Pluto), caused the maximum personal transformation (Sun/Pluto) through death (Pluto).

Wallis Simpson
Duchess of Windsor, royalty by marriage

Born in Blue Ridge Summit, Pennsylvania (77W28, 39N43), Wallis (then Spencer) made her first short trip to Europe with her aunt in the summer of 1927, at age 31. At that time, she was freshly divorced from her first husband, Win Spencer, and was soon to marry her second husband, Earnest A. Simpson, a prosperous American-born British subject whom she met in New York, and settle with him in London in the summer of 1928. By November 1930, her expanding social schedule was such that she met Prince Edward (heir apparent to the throne of England) for the first time, and immediately seemed so interesting to him that he urged her presentation at court, which occurred in June, 1931.[65] Together, Wallis and Earnest Simpson had an increasing amount of social interaction with the Prince, from June 1931 up until around October 1934, when the love affair between Prince Edward and Wallis Simpson first became obvious to others. By 1934, Wallis was 38 years old. She was once divorced, currently married, an American, a commoner, and totally unacceptable to be Queen of England.

---

65. These dates are documented in *The Heart Has Its Reasons: The Memoirs of the Duchess of Windsor* (1956) and are later confirmed in the Stephen Birmingham biography, *Duchess: The Story of Wallis Warfield Simpson*, 1981, p. 41. Both of them show that the Duke in his memoirs had erroneously recounted their first meeting as being in the winter of 1931, one year later.

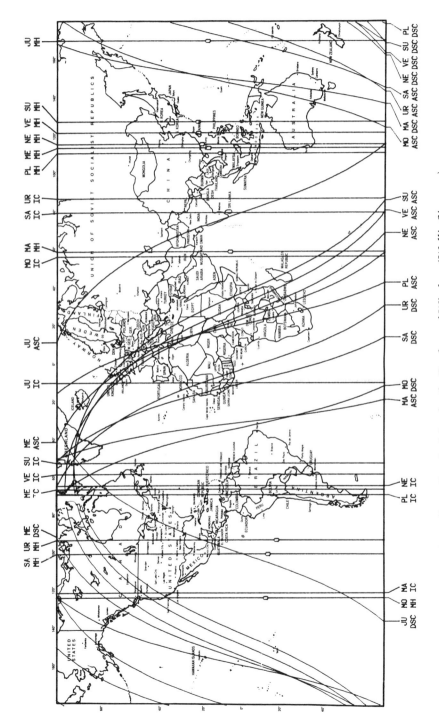

Astro-Carto-Graphy Map for the Duchess of Windsor (Wallis Simpson)

Nevertheless, she and Prince Edward were in love.

Notice the bountiful number of planetary lines (five) she has running through England, and all of them ASC (relationship-oriented) lines. Not that life was entirely boring for her in America, but this many planetary lines brings on a high level of intensity and eventfulness! The fact of her natal Sun 45' from the Cardinal axis also gives at least one clue that the world might eventually know something about her identity and her actions. But first, let us look at this exceptionally close and abundant combination of planetary lines: Sun/Venus/Neptune/Mercury/ Pluto, and make a coherent sentence out of it. She fell in love (Sun/Venus) with an unobtainable man (Venus/Neptune), and because of it masses of people (Pluto) had much to say (Mercury) and were extremely affected by the radical turn of events (Pluto) she brought about due to their obsessive and intense love affair (Sun/Venus/Pluto). In the end, their love (Venus) brought about a major sacrifice (Neptune) in relinquishing the throne, although she did attain part of her idealized goal (Venus/Neptune) in marrying Prince Edward, later the Duke of Windsor. Unfortunately, her total rejection by the English royal court was the saddest part of the large-scale destruction (Pluto) of her dream (Neptune) to be Edward's queen. Edward actually was king for a short 11 months before abdicating the throne in 1936 to marry "the woman I love." They married in France on June 3, 1937, two months after she obtained a divorce from Earnest Simpson. From then on, Wallis Simpson carried the title of Duchess of Windsor, though she was legally denied a share in his royal rank of duke.

In London, the Duke's birthplace, she also has several planetary crossings at nearby latitudes elsewhere in the world: Moon/ Neptune, Sun/Pluto, and Mercury/Venus. In this case Moon/ Neptune concerns a woman (Moon) with a dream and unrealistic intentions (Neptune), who wants to see her man (Sun) make some radical changes (Pluto) so that she can continue to enjoy the social life (Mercury/Venus) she's become accustomed to living. Unhappily for both of them, Edward as king tried unsuccessfully to make those changes when he announced he would marry Wallis Simpson. What he precipitated instead was a major English constitutional crisis, and the government forced his abdication in 1936. Wallis Simpson had singlehandedly changed the course of the British royal succession.

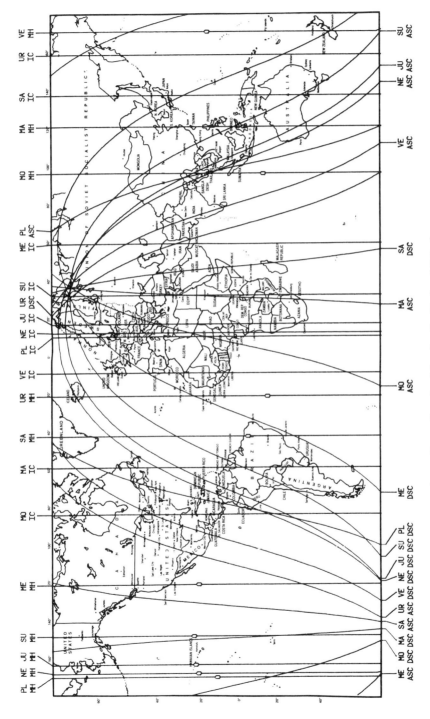

Astro·Carto·Graphy Map for the Duke of Windsor

Duke of Windsor
Formerly King Edward VIII, member of English royal family

Born in Richmond, England (0W18, 51N27), the facts of the Duke's story with the Duchess have largely been told above, except to add that they lived peacefully together for 35 years of marriage until his death in 1972.[66] That time was spent mainly in France, with much jet-setting around the world, and six years in the Bahamas (1940-45) after the Duke was appointed Governor of the Bahamas. He had been extremely popular with the English public up until the time he announced he would marry Wallis Simpson in 1936. (He was then age 42, and she was age 40, apropos of which see Chapter 4, "Mid-life Crisis, Ages 39-45.") Thereafter he was surrounded by controversy for several years (natal Mars on the Cardinal axis), and largely lost any real personal power or stature in the world as a member of royalty. Nevertheless, he and his Duchess continued to enjoy their social cachet in a round of activities with fashionable people throughout the world.

In London, the Duke has Venus/Pluto midpoint right at the IC, which is an indicator of a passionate, intense, and in some ways obsessive (Pluto) love relationship (Venus). In London also, the Duke has Mercury DSC line sweeping through, indicating his ease in talking (Mercury) with the public, and then after his demise, the extent of media coverage (also Mercury) that would follow him. Mercury is not considered a particularly royal planet, and it is definitely not duty-oriented, which is further confirmed by his elevated natal Uranus in the 9th house showing us that the Duke was not one to bow to conformity, and in the matter of choice of wife, felt he had the freedom to choose (Uranus) no matter how unconventional (also Uranus) her background and how seemingly improper by conventional standards.[67]

The Duke's planetary crossings at the same latitude as London include Mercury/Venus, Mercury/Mars and Jupiter/Saturn. The

---

66. He was interred at the royal burial ground at Frogmore, England, and in accordance with his wishes, after her death in 1986, her body also was flown from France to England to be buried next to him. The Duke and Duchess of Windsor were not accepted together in England in their lifetime, but they were allowed to be joined together there at death.

67. Grace Kelly, later Princess Grace, had her Mercury MH line near Monaco, and though she appeared to tend to her royal position and duties happily enough, there was some talk of her discontent at not being able to continue to make films. Nevertheless, her sense of duty (Saturn) was evident in life, at 2° from the Cardinal axis. For the Duke, his Saturn was mainly in hard contact to his natal Moon, showing that duty (Saturn) might weigh heavily on his emotional equilibrium (Moon), and cause him undue strain.

Mercury/Venus combination is related to the enjoyment of a social life, to a certain ease in playful party mode, and to expressing himself verbally. Venus ASC also hints at a love relationship which could evolve from that social life, and out of which much aggressive publicity (Mercury/Mars) might arise. In his case also, the Jupiter/Saturn crossing has a clear definition. The Saturn MH line concerns the kingly duty expected of him; Jupiter DSC is related to a more expansive way of life that he came to prefer, and that did not hamper his style or his mobility, especially in relationships.

At the Duchess' birthplace in Pennsylvania, he has his Pluto DSC line sweeping through just to the east—not a typical love line, but then this was not a typical situation. Her presence in his life (DSC) changed his position irrevocably (Pluto). Other planetary crossings on *his* map at *her* birth latitude include Mars/Neptune and Moon/Jupiter. She required a major sacrifice (Neptune) of his royal role, his inherited job (Mars), although apparently she made him very happy (Moon/Jupiter) and was presumably worth the heavy sacrifice.

Geographical Clues: World Leaders' Lives in Jeopardy

John F. Kennedy
Politician, U.S. President, 1961-63

It is of paramount importance to ensure the physical safety of our world and national leaders, and if Astro•Carto•Graphy and Cyclo•Carto•Graphy maps could have been used in 1963, these tools would have proved invaluable. (Unfortunately, they weren't developed for more widespread use until 1976.)

We know that JFK was assassinated while in a motorcade in Dallas on November 22, 1963, but even 27 years later we still don't know who did it. The intense and sudden violence that we all witnessed on television, and that terrible sense of collective loss is very Plutonian. So is the ongoing mystery of it, and the repressed secrets that have probably been withheld from the public since 1963. These are all symptomatic of Pluto, as is the Mafia, whom many people suspect of setting up assassin Lee Harvey Oswald and others (even if the government-appointed Warren Commission was determined to say that Oswald acted alone, and to squelch the numerous and divergent eyewitness reports that still persist).

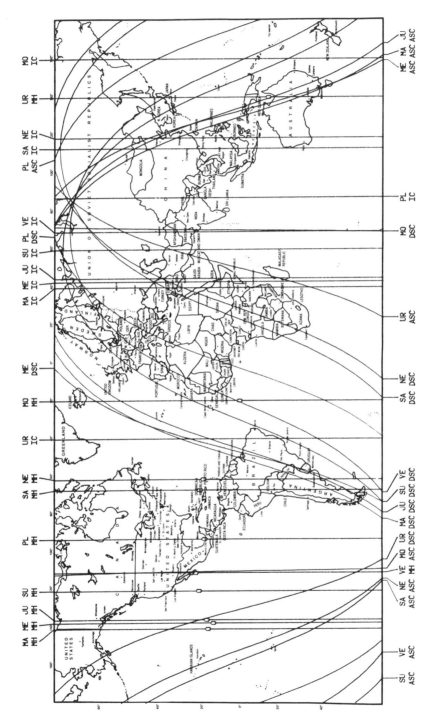

Astro•Carto•Graphy Map for John F. Kennedy

As it happens, JFK's Pluto MH line runs just east of Dallas, definitely close enough to count, and potentially dangerous for any public figure because it can attract such passionate and violent feelings about the individual at that location.[68] Also Dallas and Fort Worth, more than any other American cities on or near his Pluto MH line, happen to have a combination of three planetary crossings at the same latitude elsewhere in the world that spell out danger and sudden, surprising turns of events (Sun/Uranus and Mars/Uranus), and self-sacrifice (Mars/ Neptune). In each case, either Mars (aggression) or Uranus (surprising acts) are on the ASC or DSC, the relationship axis where one is projecting, attracting, acting, and acted upon. (John Lennon had Pluto ASC crossing Sun IC at the same latitude as New York City, where he was shot.)

In addition, a C·C·G map for JFK for November 1963 (or for a period of at least 18 months either side of it) would have shown Pluto/Pluto crossing at the Dallas latitude, a Sun/Moon/Pluto crossing at same, and Mars/Pluto crossing at the equator. The latter highlights a particularly dangerous, violent-prone year for JFK, and the planetary crossings of both the C·C·G and the A·C·G maps pinpoint Dallas. Therefore, any violence planned with JFK as the target was "ripe" to succeed in Dallas, especially in 1963.

Gerald Ford
Politician, U.S. President, 1974-76

When we consider the potential violence and strong feelings around Plutonian energy, especially for a world or national leader, it would seem prudent for the Secret Service to pay particular attention to a President's Pluto lines. Better still, that President should avoid those locations altogether, at least while in office—as it is the power that the President represents that attracts the violence, and the desire by some fanatic(s) to remove his or her presence from the face of the Earth.

Gerald Ford's Pluto IC line runs right through San Francisco, California; Portland, Oregon; and Seattle, Washington. There were two attempts on Ford's life by would-be assassins, both of them in

---

68. Pluto lines do not always symbolize violence, especially when the energy being used there is some other kind of "unearthing" activity, such as research into the subconscious layers. Carl Jung, for example, lived peacefully to the age of 86 on his Pluto IC line and Sun DSC line. His work involved the uncovering and transformation (both Pluto) of the content of those subconscious layers of the mind.

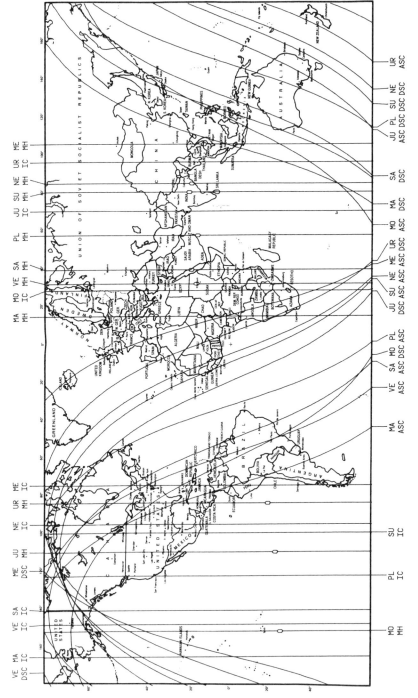

Astro•Carto•Graphy Map for Gerald Ford

September 1975 within 17 days of each other, and both of them in San Francisco. Not only is it remarkable that they were so condensed in time and space, but also that both would-be assassins were women! Ford's Moon/Uranus crossing lines are within 1° of the San Francisco latitude. As seen before, Moon/Uranus can represent an unusual, highly unconventional woman (as Yoko Ono is described), but in this case the Pluto line adds the possibility of either radical changes or developments through or by a woman, or violence perpetrated by a woman, as was nearly true in this case. The first one was Lynnette Alice "Squeaky" Fromme, age 27, an avowed follower of Charles Manson, the cult leader and mass murderer; the second one was Sara Jane Moore, age 45, a social misfit whose bullet missed Ford by five feet and hit a taxi driver, who was not injured seriously. Both women are serving life sentences.

Ford's C•C•G map for 1975 is also instructive in pinpointing that year as a time to avoid the Pluto IC line locations, especially San Francisco. Crossing at the latitude of San Francisco on his 1975 C•C•G map were Pluto/Pluto, Sun/Pluto, and Saturn/Pluto. Also conjunct the Pluto IC line was a secondary progressed Mars, making it a Mars/Pluto coupling, and the fourth warning signal that this was a dangerous place for him to visit in 1975. Luckily, he escaped unhurt.

Mohammed Reza Pahlavi
Shah of Iran

Though he was absolute monarch of Iran from age 21 in 1941, Pahlavi was not formally crowned Shah of Iran until 1967. By 1978, the boiling ferment of Moslem fundamentalist fever was overflowing in Iran and, after unsuccessfully trying to deal with the strife and insurrection, the Shah and his family were driven from the country in early 1979. The Shah was now increasingly a broken and sick man, requesting and being denied asylum in the United States, though he was allowed in briefly for an operation at a New York City hospital. Finally, Egypt granted him permanent asylum. He died at a military hospital near Cairo July 27, 1980.

The planetary lines near Teheran (his birthplace and residence for many years) are Mars/Saturn MH and Moon ASC. These are not particularly fortuitous for a monarch, even though he was actually

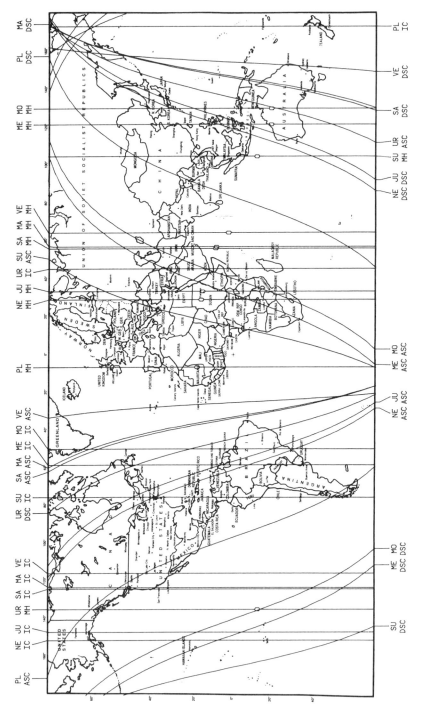

Astro·Carto·Graphy Map for Mohammed Reza Pahlavi, Shah of Iran

ruler of Iran for 38 years. Mars/Saturn not only represents exceptionally hard work, but it can be a death symbol, and at the top of a ruler's chart could definitely be read as "death to this ruler and his heirs."[69]

The Moon represents the public, and in itself is not bad for a ruler to have angular; but in this case Moon/Mars/Saturn together signify that his public is aware, on some level, of his ultimate demise and contributes to bringing it about. Mercury ASC/Uranus IC crossing at the same latitude as Teheran tells us that communications move very fast for him there and, in combination with Mars/Saturn at the Midheaven, means that he may not be able to keep up with the sheer surprising pace (Uranus) of communications and latest news (Mercury), and in fact would try to stamp it out (Mars/Saturn), increasingly resorting to police terrorism and torture to do so. In January 1979, the Shah was overthrown by followers of the Ayatollah Khomeini, a Shi'ite Muslim leader. The Shah and his family fled to Cairo, where Jupiter and Neptune lines straddle the Midheaven. Jupiter/Neptune is a combination denoting the speculator, with all its potential for the big risk, the big gain, and the big loss. In his case, Cairo saw his last hour of the big (Jupiter) sacrifice and loss (Neptune). He had lost everything that mattered to him, although his family was safe.

Mahatma Gandhi
Spiritual and political leader of India, lawyer, champion of civil rights

As we've been learning, Pluto is a major planetary energy for death, violence, terrorism, and radical transformations of all sorts. So it is not unexpected to see Pluto at its zenith on the equator of Mahatma Gandhi's chart, symbolizing a lifetime in which he was surrounded by all of the above. There were any number of places where violence was a possibility for him. Even though he could not bring ultimate peace between the many religious factions in India, chiefly the Moslems and the Hindus, he contributed enormously to Indian independence from Britain in 1947. His method for doing so, and his own supreme message, was *satyagraha*, passive resistance.

---

69. In ancient times, and in fact up until several centuries ago, astrologers did not look at just anybody's natal chart. Other than a few members of the nobility, it was mainly the king or queen's chart, or that of whomever was ruler. Depending on the amount of power accorded that ruler, the ruler's chart was and still is regarded as reflecting not only the destiny of the individual but of that regime or presidency. That is why, when a ruler dies or is killed in office, such as President John Kennedy, a whole nation dies with him for a time.

Gandhi's awareness of civil rights issues began in South Africa, where, with the Saturn IC line running nearby Capetown and Sun/Saturn midpoint on the northeast coast, he would naturally experience repression of some sort. In this case, it was his first encounter with racism.

In India itself, he has the Mercury ASC line sweeping down through the center of the country and near New Delhi, where he was based and where he was shot January 30, 1948 by a Hindu fanatic who objected to 's tolerance for the Moslems.[70] Gandhi was 78 years old and attending a prayer vigil at the time to help abate recent Hindu-Moslem hostilities in New Delhi.

Mercury by itself does not bring violence. (The Duke of Windsor's Mercury ASC line goes through London.) However, it does keep one in the news and somehow in constant communication with the people, especially when one is at that location. At New Delhi, the Mahatma also has Moon/Uranus midpoint almost exactly at the Midheaven, echoing the close bond he shared with the Indian people (Moon) in the chaos and the ongoing campaign for independence (Uranus), which he led by unusual means (Uranus)—passive resistance. This was his lifelong aim, and India finally won its independence in 1947, symbolized for him personally by his triumphant planetary lines through London (Venus/Mars/Jupiter/Pluto), where he was sent for various negotiations between India and the British government.

Gandhi's greatest sadness was that, at its independence, India was divided into a Moslem state (Pakistan) and a mainly Hindu one. Through Pakistan, Gandhi has the Uranus MH line, with the Uranus zenith (equalling in some ways the native's epitome of chaos or rebellion) just south of Karachi, the largest city and former capital of Pakistan. Remember also that, as India's most potent spiritual and political leader at that time, the positions of his Uranus MH line through Karachi and his Uranus zenith near there are powerful

---

70. Prime Minister Indira Gandhi was also killed by assassins (two Sikhs) outside her home in New Delhi on October 31, 1984. (She was almost 67.) The reason she was working at home was because her astrologers had warned her of impending danger, and she had sought to avoid it. Unfortunately, the ongoing strife with Pakistan was her legacy as well as Mahatma Gandhi's. Her Saturn ASC/Uranus DSC lines run up through northwestern India near New Delhi and through Pakistan, symbolizing her lifelong difficulty dealing with the Moslems and the Sikhs, who settled in northern India and opposed the Moslems. In many ways Saturn/Uranus is about reconciling the old with the new, the conservative with the liberal. The outcome can be death in such a struggle, and death is among the layers of meanings in the Saturn/Uranus symbol.

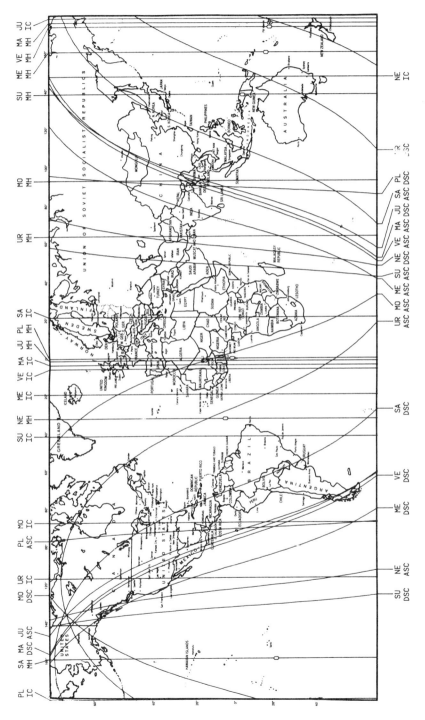

Astro•Carto•Graphy Map for Mahatma Gandhi

symbols of *India's* troubles.

There is a similarity here to Lord Mountbatten (see pp. 128-132), in that both of them, in their late 70s, were killed not so much because they were at a dangerous location as because they represented an extremely strong political symbol for the assassin(s) to strike at. The same could be argued for any potent political leader, such as an American President, except that astrology does pinpoint some highly dangerous geographical locations and time periods more clearly (such as JFK's and Gerald Ford's), indicating that with proper care, they might have been avoided.

Leon Trotsky
Russian revolutionary, journalist, leader in the founding of the U.S.S.R.

A Russian leader who advocated a worldwide socialist revolution of the working classes, Trotsky spent his life fighting for his cause with either the sword or the pen. He was exiled to Siberia twice, was clever enough to escape twice, and proceeded to change his country of residence often, moving back and forth to Russia depending on his deftness and on how much he was in favor with the Russian powers-that-be. He returned to Russia again in 1917 to organize and lead the Bolshevik seizure of power, though he fell out of favor with Lenin's successor, Joseph Stalin, and was expelled from the party in 1927 and deported in 1929. His was truly a strife-torn life, which was not over even with his deportation. Trotsky continued to oppose Stalin in his writings, and was accused of an anti-Soviet plot in the Moscow treason trials of 1936-38.

Geographically speaking, he moved around a great deal, from his birthplace at Ivanovka in the Ukraine (30E28, 46N58) to Leningrad, Siberia, London, Turkey, France, Vienna, New York City, Norway, and finally Mexico City, after the Soviets pressured Norway to expel him. Clearly this was not just a man with wanderlust, but a man whose very nature and character allowed him no rest at any location.

We will examine his last location only, as there are too many to consider all of them here. Trotsky settled in Mexico City in 1936 and lived there until his murder on August 20, 1940 (at age 61), by a man whose identity and motives are still not understood. Notice that on the same latitude as Mexico City (19N24) is his Mars zenith, the epitome of what Mars can represent, from work to aggression to

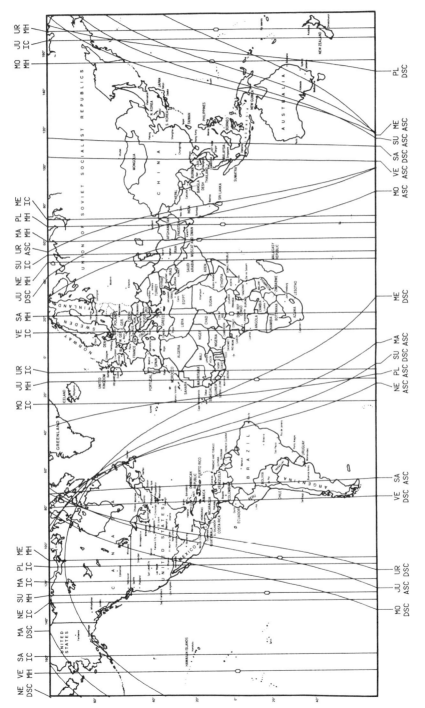

Astro-Carto-Graphy Map for Leon Trotsky

violence. Not only is that a forceful symbol for the ideological civilian and military battles Trotsky waged all his life, but so are the other A*C*G markers for Mexico City. His Jupiter ASC line runs through there, which should have been luckier for him, but remember that Jupiter can be involved in excesses of anything, including ideas. Also crossing at that latitude are Moon/Mars (strong to violent emotions), Moon/Pluto (obsessive to transforming emotions), Moon/Mercury (emotional about ideas and thoughts), Mercury/Jupiter (writing or communicating a lot and enthusiastically, like Shirley MacLaine, with her close hard contacts of Mercury and Jupiter), and Mercury/Uranus (a lively, unconventional mind that desires freedom of thought). For a revolutionary leader, writer and thinker, this location would not be conducive to a serene retirement, let alone keeping him out of trouble.

Czar Nicholas II
Last of the Romanovs, ruling dynasty of Russia, 1613-1917

Trotsky's ideas and actions contributed significantly to paving the way for the Russian revolution in 1917 and to the downfall of a 304-year reign. Just to make sure the Romanovs would not attempt to regain power, Czar Nicholas II, the Czarina Alexandra, and their entire family were shot in Ekaterinburg (now Sverdlovsk) on July 16, 1918. (The Czar was then 50 years old.) Any other surviving Romanovs fled abroad.

Czar Nicholas II had ruled Russia from 1894 (age 26) to 1917, when he was forced to abdicate. His reign continued much along the lines of his father, Alexander III, who scarcely educated him in the affairs of state and whose policies were to suppress any political opposition and persecute the minorities. With such an unenlightened rulership, and his distraction with military affairs, not only were revolutionary groups proliferating, but also Czarina Alexandra and her close adviser Rasputin were often left to control the government. The Czar's devotion to his wife and family appeared to surpass his devotion to anything, and they kept themselves largely insulated from the Russian social and political scene.

Born and based in St. Petersburg, Russia[71] (30E15, 59N55), Czar

---

71. St. Petersburg was renamed Petrograd in 1914, and again renamed Leningrad at Lenin's death in 1924. It was the Russian capital from 1712 to 1918, replacing Moscow.

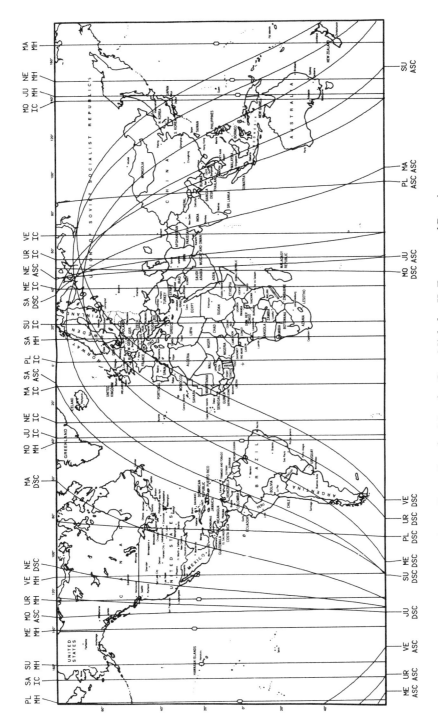

Astro·Carto·Graphy Map for Czar Nicholas II, Emperor of Russia

Nicholas is a fascinating example of an historical figure born at a high latitude, whose life plays out all the many features symbolized on the A·C·G map.[72] First of all, no fewer than ten of his planetary crossings are right on or near 59N55 latitude elsewhere in the world, and five of them are within a fraction of a degree of crossing that exact latitude. Those five are as follows: Sun/Venus (attention to the pleasures and luxuries of life, being in love, attention to the female); Saturn/Uranus (clash of the old and the new, the conservative and the liberal views and actions, such as Indira Gandhi's Saturn/ Uranus line through Pakistan and New Delhi, where she was killed); Venus/Neptune (idealized love, love sacrifice, potential to give way to or be over-obligated to the female); Moon/Saturn (emotionally repressed or depressed and/or, as head of state, repressing the people, or being repressed by the people as the Duke of Windsor experienced in another way in England); and Venus/Saturn (tendency to be very serious, cautious and conservative about money and love). The remaining crossings include Moon/Neptune (a confusion about what is going on with the people, also emotionally idealistic, especially about his wife and the public) and Pluto and Mars/Uranus, with the potential danger and violence inherent in their meanings. Remarkable also are the number of planets whose zeniths are at the equator: Pluto, Moon, Jupiter, and Neptune nearby. This means that, for his entire life (1868-1918), there was a strong possibility of a sweeping (Jupiter) revolution or drastic transformation (Pluto) of his people (Moon), which might have gone more in his favor if he had not been so relatively blind and unconscious (Neptune) in his social and political perceptions. Remember that when assessing the horoscope or A·C·G map of a national or world leader, the implications of all the natal planetary energies move to a much larger scale and scope.

Lord Louis Mountbatten
British royalty and military man

Lord Mountbatten was the great grandson of Queen Victoria and a cousin of Queen Elizabeth II (who married Phillip Mountbatten, later Duke of Edinburgh). He was also a British admiral who was considered a World War II hero after leading commando raids in Europe and commanding Allied operations in

---

72. On any A·C·G map, it is typical to have more crossings at the higher latitudes, at approximately 60° N or above. Thus anyone born or living there must deal with the stress of many planetary influences simultaneously.

Burma from 1943. After the war, he became Viceroy and then Governor-General of India until 1947, when he was in charge of winding up the negotiations for the independence of India and Pakistan in the same year. (Notice his Neptune and Pluto MH lines straddling New Delhi and central India. Neptune/Pluto can definitely be the destruction [Pluto] of a dream or an ideal [Neptune], as India's independence was for England.) Other posts he held were those of First Sea Lord of Great Britain (1955), Admiral of the Fleet (1956), and Chief of the Defense staff (1959-65). Clearly this was a man who tended to attract and move into confrontational circumstances in life, either as military man or as negotiator. For this reason we are seeing as much if not more information from his natal horoscope chart as from his A✦C✦G map, which is why it is shown on p. 131. You will notice an unusual arrangement of the planets, which astrologers call a "see-saw" type of chart. See-saw arrangements can show five planets opposite another five planets, or sometimes up to seven planets opposite three, as is the case with Mountbatten's chart. This connotes much attraction to polarized situations which can be fought or negotiated, and need some type of conflict resolution.[73] Mountbatten's chart, even by comparison to Richard Nixon's and Ralph Nader's (see footnote 73, below), is extremely polarized, with one wedge of planets within a 59° range and the opposite wedge within a 29° range. Note the close opposition involving two Personal Points: Moon opposite Uranus—the country (Moon) is in a highly changeable state (Uranus); and Sun opposite Saturn—the man and statesman (Sun) is under pressure to do his patriarchal duty (Saturn). So, even with the easygoing Mercury/Venus ASC lines running through Ireland, southwestern England, and France, the whole story is more evident in this case in the patterns in the natal chart and to some extent in the planetary crossings for Sligo, Ireland.

Mountbatten was on a pleasant outing (Mercury/Venus), a fishing trip August 27, 1979, with members of his family one mile off the coast of county Sligo in northwest Ireland when his fishing boat

---

73. Other strong examples of this type of chart are the natal charts of Richard Nixon (U.S. President, 1969-1974, whose polarized and mostly antagonistic relationship with the American press climaxed in 1972-74, when two *Washington Post* investigator-journalists uncovered the Watergate scandal, forcing Nixon to be the first President ever to resign, on August 9, 1974); and Ralph Nader (American lawyer and safety and consumer advocate, whose relentless efforts have affected the actions and policies of the automobile and nuclear industries as well as those of the government and various other industries in the United States).

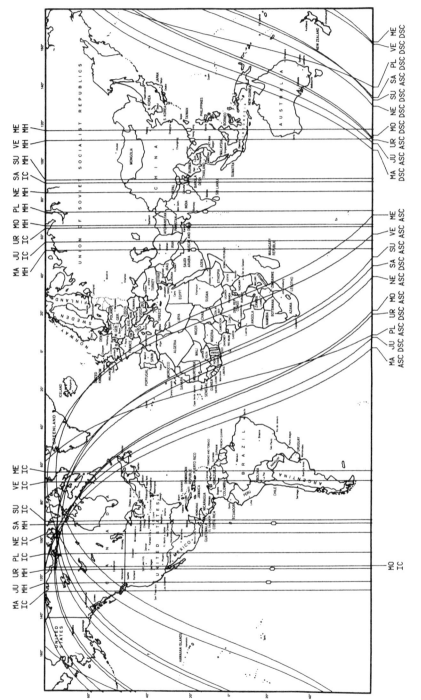

Astro·Carto·Graphy Map for Lord Louis Mountbatten

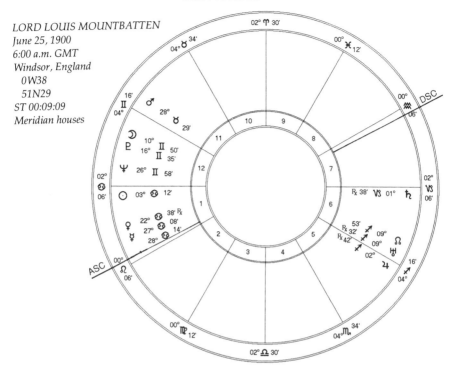

Natal Horoscope for Lord Louis Mountbatten

was blown up by a bomb planted by members of the Irish Republican Army. He was killed instantly, as were his daughter, his 14-year old grandson, and the boatboy. Several other family members were seriously injured. Mountbatten (age 79) was reported as having "...no particular connection with sectarian conflict in Northern Ireland."[74]

Planetary crossings within 1° of Sligo's latitude (54N17) are Sun/Pluto (the man [Sun] is transformed [Pluto], moves into another stage of development)[75], Saturn/Pluto (it is difficult to make changes [Pluto] when one is blocked by conservative ideas [Saturn]), Venus/Mars (a pleasant time, especially socially or romantically), and Mercury/Jupiter (a lot [Jupiter] can be said [Mercury] with great enthusiasm [Jupiter]).

These are not all foreboding combinations, especially the last two, but Mountbatten just happened to be enjoying himself that day

74. *Facts on File*, Aug. 31, 1979, p. 641.
75. John Lennon had Sun/Pluto planetary crossings at the latitude of New York City, where he was shot December 8, 1980, and JFK had Sun/Moon/ Pluto crossings at Dallas, Texas in his 1963 C·C·G map.

in August of 1979 in Sligo, Ireland, and he just happened to be at the center of some controversy, as usual.[76]

Geographical Clues: Astronauts' Lives in Jeopardy

To date, there have been two major disasters involving American astronauts, both at Cape Canaveral, Florida. The first was a fire on board the command module of Apollo 204, January 27, 1967, which killed all three astronauts inside. The second was the explosion of the *Challenger* shuttle January 28, 1986, killing all seven astronauts on board, including schoolteacher/astronaut Christa McAuliffe. Accurate birth data is available on all ten astronauts, for whom I checked out geographical clues to the tragedies via astro-mapping. What I expected to find, especially for the astronauts killed at ground level in 1967, were strong and unmitigated planetary combinations for sudden violence at the same location or latitude as Cape Canaveral. What I found instead was that no one geographical location, not even Cape Canaveral, was unusually dangerous for any of them.

There is probably an inherent logic in this finding in that astro-mapping is based on the horizon, and when one is off the surface of the Earth, this type of map no longer applies. (It is geared for specific longitudinal and latitudinal coordinates on the Earth.) The fate of the astronaut victims in the 1967 ground-level fire is less easy to explain as to the lack of violence signals from the astro-mapping, except to say that astrology works strongly not only by astronomical factors, but also by purely symbolic, metaphorical factors. In that sense, we would have to admit that all astronauts are aiming and training to go into outer space, which is off the horizon, as noted. Nonetheless, the C∗C∗G maps do show interesting action at the equator in most cases, applying geographically to the whole Earth in general. Most of the factors are either progressed Pluto or Uranus zenith at the equator, or crossings such as Saturn/Uranus/Pluto, Sun/Saturn/Pluto, and Sun/Pluto at the equator. These are all combinations we have seen many times now indicating violence and social turmoil in the charts of world leaders whose lives were in jeopardy.

Also, on examining each of the natal horoscopes of the

---

76. See material on Mountbatten under Mahatma Gandhi, p. 124.

astronauts, it seems that their entire approach to life was one of pioneering, with the potential for physical danger always present. Timingwise, there were significant clues that each was headed into circumstances that had potential for maximum danger. This is especially loud and clear in the NASA corporate chart and in the mundane charts set for Cape Canaveral leading up to and including the moment of each space-program disaster. (See Chapter 4, pp. 211-220.)

Geographical Clues: Criminal Types and Criminal Acts

Charles Manson
Cult leader, mass murderer

The leader of the infamous Manson family, a communal band of hippies slavishly devoted to Manson, he led them in the ritual killing of Sharon Tate (then eight months pregnant by director husband Roman Polanski) and a group of her friends. It was the night of August 9, 1969 in southern California.

Notice the Mars/Neptune DSC lines running nearby southern California. In a more highly evolved person, Mars/Neptune could indicate a talented filmmaker, musician, photographer, dancer, or even spiritual leader. But with the least amount of slippage and deviation, Mars/Neptune can be highly dangerous, because it has to do with giving up the will to act (Mars) and giving it to someone else (Neptune). One's own ego and ability to take action (Mars) melt into the communal will (Neptune) for any purpose—often, if negatively oriented, drug or alcohol-induced. (The Manson family was known to be big drug-users.) There was also some evidence in this case that murder victim Sharon Tate, her unborn baby, and her friends were part of a ritual sacrifice (also Neptune).

At the same latitude as his Cincinnati, Ohio birthplace (84W31, 39N06), Manson has Sun/Pluto crossing, which is a recurring planetary combination for murder *victims* at the location of their death (including John F. Kennedy, John Lennon, and Lord Mountbatten). Sun/Pluto can be a radical or violent transformation which is acted upon you or which you enact upon others in some fashion. It would appear that Manson, who is currently serving a life sentence, has moved deeper into the most negative and violent levels of personal and collective power and control evocative of Pluto's symbolic meaning. Manson has never shown a sense of

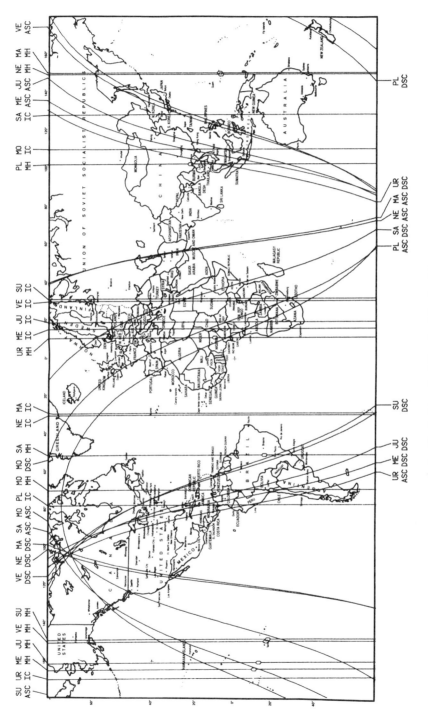

Astro-Carto-Graphy Map for Charles Manson

remorse for the Tate murders, and while in prison has unfortunately continued to inspire some of his followers to violent acts, including Alice "Squeaky" Fromme, who pulled a gun on President Gerald Ford in San Francisco on September 5, 1975. The gun turned out to be unloaded, but for the intention of her act she also is currently serving a life sentence in prison.

Jim Jones
Cult leader

Jim Jones has the dubious distinction of having powers of persuasion so phenomenal that he successfully prevailed upon nearly a thousand of his followers to join together in mass suicide in November 1978. (He was 47 years old.) He had led this group, called The People's Temple, from San Francisco to Guyana in 1977. (Guyana is on the northern coast of South America.) On the A·C·G map, Jones's Sun IC/Mars DSC lines come together in Guyana. On the positive side, Sun/Mars is physically or sexually active and probably athletic, but where there is the slightest divergence from normal behavior, this can become a potentially violent and dangerous combination. The ego and sense of personal identity (Sun) becomes too aggressive (Mars) about expressing its power. In Jones's case, he was regarded by outsiders to his group as a manic-depressive with paranoia and delusions.

This sense of egomaniacal power would not have been so obvious in San Francisco, where he started out with his followers. At San Francisco's latitude (elsewhere in the world) is the planetary crossing Sun/Neptune, which can be full of self-delusions (Neptune) but may appear (Neptune) to be highly spiritual, pure, and selfless in its desire to benefit only the communal good (also Neptune). Once in Guyana, the Sun/Mars energy took over for Jim Jones, aided and abetted by the energy of his planetary crossings at the Guyana latitude. They include Jupiter/Uranus (which is normally fortunate, and, buoyed by the expansion of Jupiter, extends the new opportunities and horizons of Uranus) and Venus/Jupiter (the sensual-indulgence combination that says "Let's have a party!"). He did call a very excessive (Jupiter) party (Venus), and everyone came and did what he doubtless assured them would amount to the party of a lifetime.

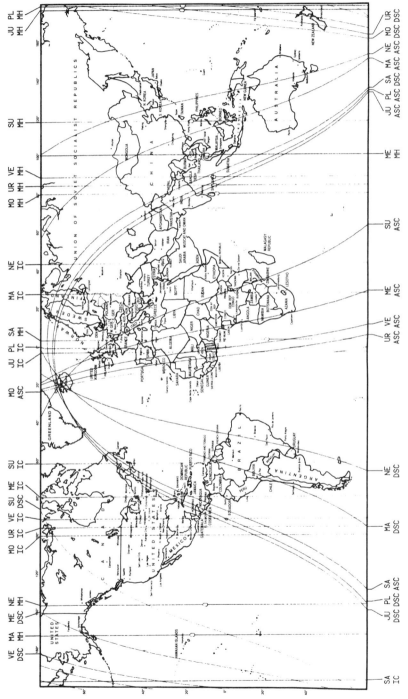

Astro-Carto-Graphy Map for Jim Jones

John Wayne Gacey
Serial murderer

Known up to that time as "an outstanding citizen" by most accounts, it came as quite a shock to the family, friends, neighbors, and acquaintances of John Wayne Gacey that he had murdered 32 young men and boys, all of whom he had sexually assaulted in a sadistic fashion and buried in his cellar. He was indicted for the murders January 13, 1979, at the age of 36.

The location for these horrendous deeds was Chicago (also his birthplace), near where Gacey's Sun/Moon/Neptune lines share the MH/IC axis and Mars DSC line is 5° from being exact. Also the natal Mars/Saturn midpoint (denoting hard work, possible repression, and at times death) is on the DSC, within 1/2°. As we have seen, Mars signifies abundant physical and sexual energy and/or aggressive behavior. It is not easy to have Mars on the DSC axis, as it can promote or attract potentially aggressive behavior, i.e. fights or quarrels in yourself or in others.[77] In Gacey's case, it was unusual that he also had a potentially ego-denying and self-effacing planetary combination at the other angular axis of the chart. His natal Sun conjunct Moon opposite Neptune (close to the MH/IC axis) indicates that his sense of himself (Sun) in relation to the opposite sex (Moon), especially his wife, would be dissolved (Neptune) or diminished in some way.[78] As it happens, his second wife divorced him because of sexual impotency.

Once again we see where combinations of Sun/Mars/Neptune are deceptively dangerous, because in an unbalanced individual the ensuing actions become justifications for having *lost* power in some

---

77. Examples of Mars on the DSC axis of noncriminals include Robert F. Kennedy, who as a lawyer, Attorney General (1961-64), U.S. Senator (1965-68), and later presidential candidate (1968) was never afraid of a confrontation and did attract his share of troubles with Jimmy Hoffa and the Teamster's Union, civil rights, and finally an assassin, who shot and killed him June 5, 1968, shortly after he had claimed victory in the California Democratic presidential primary. Another example is the American stage and film actor Sean Penn, who, although widely respected for his talents as an actor, has been in the news repeatedly on account of his verbal or physical fights, usually with photographers or film crew who have not noticed that this is a very private celebrity with a very explosive temperament. (More on Sean Penn in Chapter 4.)

78. Even with the most positive manifestation of Sun/Moon/Neptune, there is a denial of the physical, sexual connection in the process of spiritualizing the relationship, otherwise known as a platonic relationship.

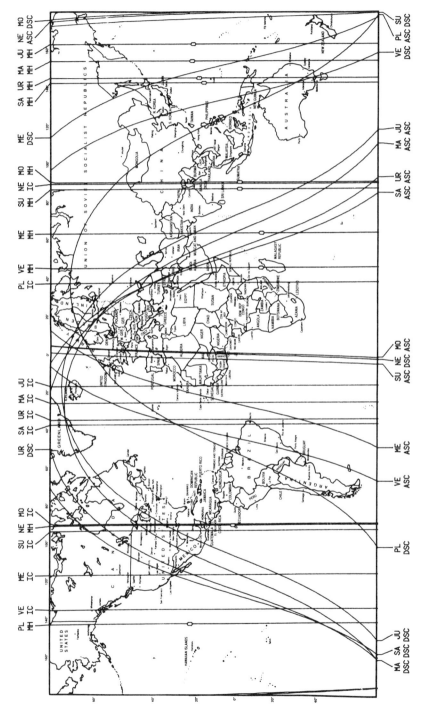

Astro·Carto·Graphy Map for John Wayne Gacey

other major arena of life.[79]

As if the planetary lines through or near Chicago do not tell enough about Gacey, here are the planetary crossings close to Chicago latitude (41N53): Uranus/Pluto (a desire for changes [Uranus] that are total and drastic [Pluto]); Sun/Mars (a desire to be physically, sexually active [Mars], and, if a man [Sun], to show your prowess [Mars] in some way, to be aggressive [Mars] about presenting your identity as a person [Sun], as Jim Jones was in Guyana in 1978); and Saturn/Uranus (the conflict that can arise from pitting the old [Saturn] against the brand new and perhaps unconventional [Uranus], the conservative and proper way of doing things [Saturn] versus the totally anarchical and rebellious [Uranus]). As we have already seen in the cases of various world leaders, including Indira Gandhi and Czar Nicholas II, Saturn/Uranus lines or crossings can indicate so much polarization of opposing views or energies that murder or death can result.

Richard Speck
Murderer

On the night of June 13, 1966 there were nine student nurses from the South Chicago Community Hospital in their dormitory rooms. By the time the night was over, a man named Richard Speck had gained entry to the dormitory, knifed and strangled eight of the nurses, and raped one of them. One lone nurse out of the nine hid under her bed, watching and listening in horror until it was all over and she knew she had survived.

The perpetrator of these hideous crimes was Richard Speck (age 25), who had recently moved to Chicago from Dallas, where he lived from 1947 to 1966 and where he was still wanted for burglary, with a previous criminal record of 37 arrests, including those for burglary and disorderly conduct connected with excessive drinking.[80]

On June 13, 1966 Speck had also been drinking (Neptune) and

---

79. Sun/Neptune and Mars/Neptune are also strong potential combinations for drug or alcohol abusers (or chemical dependency of any sort), because of the personal power (Sun, Mars) that has been willingly relinquished or sacrificed elsewhere (Neptune), supposedly at times for the common good (also Neptune), as in the case of Charles Manson.

80. At Dallas, Speck has the Sun/Neptune midpoint 2° from the Midheaven axis, which for him was problematic enough, but the drug and alcohol (Neptune) problem instantly became even worse when he moved back to his NE ASC line in Chicago, where he had not lived since he was six years old.

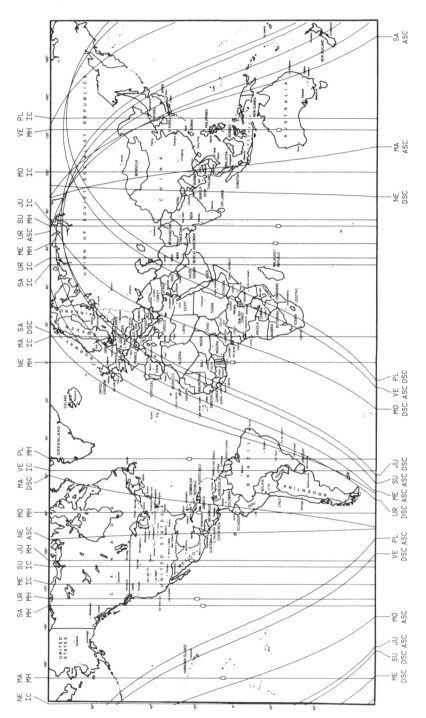

Astro-Carto-Graphy Map for Richard Speck

taking drugs (Neptune), so it is not surprising to see the Neptune influence so strong in his birth chart. He was born in Monmouth, Illinois (90W39, 40N55), which is very near the Chicago crime location (87W39, 41N52), especially by latitude.

The birth chart shows Neptune on the Cardinal axis (his lens on the world) conjunct ASC and square MC, both of which are also on the Cardinal axis, and indicate his career and relationships could be well known. In this case, his career as a criminal and his relations with his victims became big news in 1966.

Other than the facts of his alcohol and drug habit and his criminal record, we also know that Speck had been previously married and divorced and that he claimed to hate his ex-wife. Given that fact, we note that the planetary crossings at the latitude of Chicago are Moon/Neptune and Venus/Uranus. Moon/Neptune has to do with idealizing (Neptune) women (Moon), possibly feeling (Moon) overly obligated to them (Neptune). With a criminal mind and the influence of drugs and alcohol (Neptune), one could resolve to make a sacrifice (Neptune) of the women (Moon)—any women (Moon). Nurses, by the nature of their occupation can also be described as Moon/Neptune.

Venus/Uranus, as we noted earlier in the chart of Elizabeth Taylor, is related to extreme changeability in the love life. In the chart of a criminal type, we have the possibility of the sexual thrill-seeker who is not easily satisfied with one traditional or stable relationship, especially if he tends to view most relationships unrealistically (Neptune ASC) and, as in this case, through a drug- and alcohol-induced haze (Neptune).

Bruno Hauptman
Convicted kidnapper, murderer

Kidnappings, especially by terrorists or fanatics, have unfortunately become all too common throughout the world in the 1970s, '80s, and early '90s. But in 1932, before television and media hype, the kidnapping and murder of the Lindbergh baby stood apart as *the* kidnapping of the century. The baby was the son of Charles and Anne Morrow Lindbergh. Charles Lindbergh was considered a national hero after he had astonished the world by making the first solo, non-stop transatlantic flight, landing in Paris on May 31, 1927. For this he received unprecedented acclaim, and later, unfortunately, a tragic blow, when his son disappeared March 1, 1932,

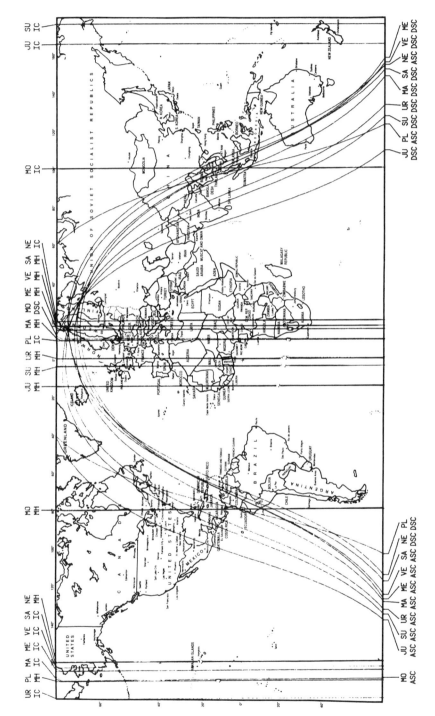

Astro-Carto-Graphy Map for Bruno Hauptman

from their Hopewell, New Jersey home.

The convicted criminal, Bruno Hauptman, a carpenter by trade, had a history of criminal activities in Germany beginning in 1919 (at age 20), when he was sentenced to five years in prison. Soon after, he moved to the United States. He was caught and arrested for the Lindbergh kidnapping and murder in September 1934, and was tried January 1935. He received the death sentence February 13, 1935, at age 35.

We have spoken earlier about the extreme stress associated with being born at or going to a location where more than three planetary lines are angular simultaneously. It is like tuning into several radio stations simultaneously. You can't distinguish one from another, and the confusion and the static grate on one's nerves. If left on indefinitely, it would probably cause permanent nerve damage and who knows what else. Such a situation is present in the natal chart of Bruno Hauptman (p. 60). He has a case of "mutable mode overload." Every single planet and Personal Point in the chart is closely connected in a mutable sign except one, Jupiter. This is a person with an extremely highly charged character and destiny, which is only amplified by the natal Sun conjunct Uranus (4° orb), symbolizing the body, ego, and identity (Sun) electrified, shocked, and yearning for the unusual experience (Uranus). It is unusual in my experience to see all of these components in one chart.

When his Sun/Uranus conjunction is projected as planetary lines onto the A·C·G map, the natal Sun and Uranus are seen to be actually rising near Hopewell, New Jersey (74W46, 40N23). This would further overexcite and catalyze someone at this location if his character were already potentially out of balance.

Without supremely enlightened parents and teachers to direct such a high-voltage person, it would be difficult for him to get a solid grip on life with a destiny like this, in addition to which there is a Mars/Pluto crossing right on the equator. This gives the individual a lifelong acquaintance with, if not taste for, violence.

IV
When on Earth?

Everybody's Big Picture: 29-1/2 Year Saturn Cycles

I feel good and I don't feel age. I've never
felt age. I felt "how do I feel," and it's not
chronological age anyway. You see, dear,
if you are doing your creative work, you
don't have age or time as such. And
consequently you're not caught in it, so
you go on.

—Louise Nevelson, in a CBS
Sunday Morning television
interview, 1979.

The indefatigable sculptor Louise Nevelson was 80 years old
when she made the remarks above. She died in April, 1988 at the age
of 89, and she never slowed down much up to the time of her death.
Although her particular character freed her from the conventional
limits of chronological age, it would be fascinating to know what
she said about age and the passage of time at around age 21, or
25-26. My guess is that she was more impatient about the subject at
those earlier ages. Frequently I have heard and overheard young
people at those ages bemoan the fact of their most recent birthday.
They are often disappointed with the idea of growing older,
bewildered and uncomfortable that they have not achieved more.

The average human life—as opposed to the average dog's life,
for example—has certain definite advantages in terms of
understanding the passage of time, over which astrologers consider
Saturn to rule. And since Saturn does rule over *time*, at least
measurable time, astrologers put a great deal of stock in the cyclical
patterns of Saturn—which just happen to coincide with the time
length assigned to the very important secondary progressed lunar
cycle equaling 29.531 years. Saturn, for its part, takes 29.458 years to

orbit the Sun, and so, in the life of a human being, it is said that, when an individual has experienced at least one "Saturn return" (i.e. Saturn returning to the point where it is located in the natal chart), then there is something about life that they can finally fathom. Before that, there is a good possibility that a person does not understand how time really operates, gets impatient, and makes the wrong decisions about career, relationships, domestic arrange-ments, etc. It is easy to get panicky before the first Saturn return and think that time is running out, that this is the last chance for—you name it—or to do—you name it.

As odd as it may seem at first, there really is an interesting parallel to the behavior of a dog—which of course never experiences a Saturn return and, maybe even more importantly, also never gets to observe other dogs who do. Therefore, the eager-beaver, super-excited dog is crazy with delight when you come home or take him on a hike, and just as upset at times when you are not going on a hike, and, God forbid, leaving the house for the day. It is hard for them to get used to the idea that you will be back, that there will be other hikes, other days. Human beings are supposed to know better because they have the advantage of experiencing a Saturn return.

Everybody's Big Picture: The 7-Year Saturn Quarters

So is there nothing before age 29-1/2? Yes, Saturn makes a square (90° angular relationship) to its natal position about every 7 years and every 21 years, and an opposition (180°) about every 14 years. Saturn makes one complete revolution in its orbit around the Sun in 29.4575 years (29 years, 167 days), which, if you divide by 4, does not equal 7 exactly. It comes out to be 7.364383, and even then we have to understand celestial mechanics to see that the strongest likelihood of Saturn being within 1° to exactly square or opposite its natal position will be in the time period between the 7th and 8th birthdays, or between the 14th and 15th birthdays, for example, with some effects at various times within 3° to 5° of exactness up to 1 year preceding and up to 1-1/2 years after the 7th, 14th, 21st, 28th, 35th, etc. birthdays. For the strongest contacts, one can get the calendar dates in the ephemeris.[81]

---

81. See Appendix A, Section 5: "The Ephemeris: What It Is and How to Use It."

If you think of the parallel to the lunar cycle, which is 29.531 days (even though we cannot easily observe Saturn in the heavens at the second, third, and fourth quarters), the symbology of the quarter phases is much the same—except that it is oriented towards Saturn-ruled things, especially those denoting societal boundaries. (See pp. 24-25 for a reminder of the meanings assigned the four quarters of the lunar cycle.)

Imagine the four points of the compass as the four cardinal points of the zodiac, and wherever the natal Saturn is becomes the starting point at 0° Aries. Every 90° (which for Saturn is also approximately every 7 years) is a distinct phase change and pivotal turning point, when we check in with Father Time, so to speak. There are also noticeable phase changes in between, at the 45° angular points, but here we will concern ourselves only with the fourth harmonic phase changes that occur every 90° from the starting point. Below is a brief summary of how this applies to Saturn's quarter cycles.

1) First Quarter (Conjunction, 0°)—New start, fresh beginnings
    Age 0 to 7 years
    Age 28-29 to 35 years
    Age 58-59 to 65 years

2) Second Quarter (Waxing square, 90°)—Spreading your wings, crisis in action
    Age 7 to 14 years
    Age 35 to 43-44 years
    Age 65 to 72 years

3) Third Quarter (Opposition, 180°)—Crystallization and clarification of what society wants from you.
    Age 14 to 21 years
    Age 43-44 to 49 years
    Age 72 to 79 years

4) Fourth Quarter (Waning square, 90°)—Release of the old ways, of traditions learned that do not suit you as an individual adult; reorientation to the new.
    Age 21 to 28-29 years
    Age 49 to 58-59 years
    Age 79 to 87-88 years

The most graphic example I have ever seen of how this works, at least up to age 28, is in the British film entitled *28 Up*.[82] It is a sociological documentary which follows the same group of young people at ages 7, 14, 21, and 28. Right in front of your eyes, you see how this diverse group of individuals grows older, develops, and reacts to Saturn's nudging pressure to grow up and to be responsible, which most of the group interprets as a pressure to conform rather than a pressure to seek out their own uniqueness. It is easy to understand how this can happen, because the very nature of Saturn as an astrological symbol is about the many boundaries that we set up in our society, our educational system and our government. The sad paradox is that, while we teach individuals to be "civilized" human beings in the first 28-29 years of life, at the same time we often strip them of any hope of finding their uniqueness and their special talents. It is not a settled question, however. Parents, educators, and media policymakers, especially advertisers, are not solely responsible for making children conform. Kids pressure themselves to conform, perhaps because they see it as a necessity in order to survive and succeed.

There are a few exceptions to this when a young person chooses to move ahead faster in life earlier and is naturally impatient with the standards of conformity set by his or her peers. Astrologically, this is symbolized by a combination of 1) no planets retrograde in the natal chart, or possibly just one planet retrograde (usually an outer planet, beyond Mars), and 2) a fast Moon, a natal Moon whose orbital speed immediately prior to birth exceeds 13°10' in a 24-hour period. Although there is no guarantee that this will be a lifetime advantage, these astrological factors tend to make young people focus sooner on their special abilities and their unique approaches to life, making them less susceptible to peer pressure or societal pressure, especially in regard to choice of career or vocation.

First Waxing Saturn Quarter: Age 7

The first waxing Saturn square at age 7 marks the first dawning of our intellectual forces and the first formal structuring (Saturn) of our mental, emotional, and intuitive processes when we go to school. It is an extremely sensitive time, because while the inner

---

82. Directed by Michael Apted, *28 Up* was originally made for British television and was released as a full-length documentary film in 1985.

creative powers are still amazingly active and receptive, they are also in real danger of being jolted too soon by a world which threatens to be bigger and more important than the inner world known up until then. If not nurtured with great care at this juncture, it is easy to separate too quickly from our creative sources and to join the "big, real world" too soon.

The fascinating thing is that, because of various factors, especially the slower frequency of our brain waves from infancy to 7 years old, we operate very much then on the inner conscious levels, where we experience little of the physical dimensions of time and space. This is the best place to develop high levels of intuitive awareness, because they are still connected with the waking consciousness while also connected to the deepest subconscious or superconscious layers. It is the level of brain activity most sought after in meditation and states of deep relaxation, including hypnosis. Many adults working in intensely creative areas, as well as meditation training, consciously try to remain in a relaxed state during the work day (resulting in slower brain-wave frequencies) until a lot of outer activity, such as telephones and loud talking, automatically speeds them into the range of higher brain-wave frequency, called beta frequency—where work can be done and life can be lived but not on such a calm, relaxed, and potentially inspired level. Excessive beta-level activity can lead to hypertension, high blood pressure, and many other related diseases of the "civilized" world (Saturn).

Since the waking consciousness of a child from birth to around 7 years old is at the slower brain-wave frequencies most of the time (infants in the delta and theta range), a tremendous amount of information is being absorbed at a highly intuitive level. Some educators even feel that if you intellectually force-feed a child at this stage, you are stripping away some of the most creative input that might otherwise nourish that person for an entire lifetime. Rudolf Steiner (1861-1925) was one such educator and philosopher, and his schools, known internationally by the name of Waldorf schools, have an extremely enlightened way of emphasizing and encouraging the child's imaginative and creative forces. The process is such that, in the first grades (ages 6-7), when the child is introduced to the *idea* of reading (a very complex and advanced intellectual skill, after all), it is not in an impersonal, didactic, and socially pressured way (a typically negative manifestation of

Saturn's potentially authoritarian energy). Instead the child develops a love of speech, of oral verse work, of the aliveness and the sound of each letter of the alphabet, and how consonants and vowels work together in a very coherent and imaginative way.

By contrast to most first-graders, Waldorf students are writing and learning their own pictorial vocabulary before they are reading books written by anyone else. In fact, the first book they read is their own little book that they have written. By the end of second or third grade, they are reading other people's books, but even if some children are not doing this yet, there is no fear or chastisement. They have been given the basic pictorial vocabulary and the love of language and storytelling. With that instilled in them, it eventually does bring out the sheer excitement of reading rather than the apathy that is unfortunately all too evident in many of our public schools. The reputation of Waldorf graduates indicates that this type of education most often leads to rapid intellectual development that rarely constricts the innate creative flow.

The first Saturn square is, unhappily, all too often manifested as a societal and parental stifling of the individual creative imagination. I mention Rudolf Steiner and the Waldorf schools as an example of what seems an illuminating way of dealing with a child up to age 7, and in fact beyond that up to age 14. Anything that is within the realm of Saturn that the child learns too soon or too forcefully will stifle creativity and individuality considerably. For instance, even though surveys measuring the effect of 30 some hours of television watching per week "have not proved conclusively" that these kids are developing less well intellectually, emotionally, and physically, can they really have immediate proof of the creativity that might be stunted by having too much media input and electronic bombardment, especially when we know what a high proportion of it consists of advertising?

Strictly speaking, advertising falls under the realm of Neptune, but it is still the process of creating a desire for real goods (Saturn) that often have peer status (Saturn) connected with owning them or eating or drinking them, whatever the products may be. This situation carried to excess (which is not uncommon) can promote a further deadening of those early and delicate wellsprings of creative ingenuity, separating the child perhaps forever from their maximum use and inspiration.

First Saturn Opposition: Age 14

In many primitive tribal cultures, age 14 is considered a time when young boys undergo rigorous tests, physically and emotionally, that mark the irrevocable passage from boyhood to manhood. From here on they are capable of mating sexually, but with that privilege comes a multitude of responsibilities (Saturn) to support their family and community. Although the modern civilized world delays this process, often for at least another seven years, and usually never formally makes a ritual test out of it as is still done in certain tribes, there are still some ceremonial vestiges of this ancient though now uncommon tradition. The Bar Mitzvah is probably the best known of these, in the Jewish tradition, when a boy at his 13th birthday undertakes new religious duties and responsibilities and makes a rite of passage into manhood. In modern times, girls have been included in this ritual and have the Bat Mitzvah on the 13th birthday.

One of the main uniting themes here is the entry into puberty, which is considered to be reached legally at age 14 for boys and at age 12 for girls. Remember that, just as there may be a discrepancy between what is considered legal and what is actually happening biologically, Saturn does not reach its exact squares and oppositions precisely at the 7th, 14th, 21st, etc. birthdays, but is on its way in and out of that hard contact for up to a year before and up to 1-1/2 years after that 7th-year-cycle birthday. But it is a perfect analogy to the Saturn *opposition* to its natal position that a young person is then *confronted* at age 14 with the reality of his or her sexual coming of age. It may not mean what it once did in terms of societal and family responsibilities, but it causes the person to acknowledge on the one hand a loss of childhood innocence, and on the other hand a gaining of a whole new set of possibilities in life, including sexual relationships and pregnancy. Often this coincides with the first real testing of the parental authority, and in a sense the Saturn opposite Saturn symbolizes confronting the key authority figures outside as well as inside oneself. The outside authority figures are obvious enough, but by inside oneself, I mean the sense of authority to command any situation. Because this demands a point of view, it often coincides with the young person's assuming a rather strong point of view on many subjects which shortly before, he or she would have scarcely cared about at all. That is because the desire to be seen as a real, worthwhile, and memorable person suddenly lurches to the fore. The irony is, of course, that the personality has been conspicuous and evolving steadily since infancy, and does not necessarily need a jolt to push it into a renaissance of self-flowering. So yes, it is good to crystallize (Saturn) one's thoughts on various subjects, but if the crystallization process is motivated too much from a desire to prove one's worth as a human being, then the educational and socialization process during those years from 14 to 21 is once again (as in the previous quarter, from age 7 to 14) in real danger of short-circuiting the natural creative evolution of that human being.

First Waning Saturn Quarter: Age 21

> When you're young, you have all these things to worry about—should you go there, what about your mother. And you worry, and try to decide, but then something else comes up. It's much easier to just plain *decide*. Never mind—*nothing* is going to change your mind. I did that once when I was a student at MIT. I got sick and tired of having to decide what kind of dessert I was going to have at the restaurant, so I decided it would *always* be chocolate ice cream, and never worried about it again—I had the solution to *that* problem.
>
> Richard Feynman, *"Surely You're Joking, Mr. Feynman!": Adventures of a Curious Character*, 1985, p. 235.

Even one of the world's greatest theoretical physicists can attest to it, as Richard Feynman does in the above quote. There are so many decisions to make at around age 21! And it seems as if one will be saddled forever with the weight of the consequences of those decisions. But a person at this age still hasn't experienced the first Saturn return, and so in a literal and symbolic sense, is not as aware that many changes can still be made without great loss or self-sacrifice and, perhaps even more momentously, without losing face.

It is an intriguing turning point at the fourth quarter of Saturn, especially the first one at age 21, because much has been learned and absorbed from family, teachers, and peers about how society works, its rules, regulations, stipulations, and so on. But only now is the time really ripe to try one's own set of values, one's own ideas and philosophy of life, career, relationships, domestic arrangements, etc. That is because the time is now also ripe to throw out some of the ideas that never fit in the first place. (In addition, one's early 20s coincide with the first Uranus square, i.e. transiting [T.] Uranus squares natal [N.] Uranus, a combination also demanding that we tune into our most unique qualities as individuals, and not necessarily those indoctrinated by anyone else.) This is not to say that rampant rebellion is the key, but that some degree of rebellion might even be appropriate at this age.

The very nature of Saturn is conservative, protective, and defensive of the old ways. Its energy is like the elder statesman who has been entrusted to preserve, protect, and defend the old way of life that has worked for his generation and probably many generations before him. When there is a hard contact to Saturn, the symbology tells us that it is only fitting that we will come into some kind of crunch with the old, inherited ways. We will question them and shake them up somehow. We did not get the expression "This does not square with that" out of nothing. It is hard to square it, but it is possible, and then usually we get to the bottom of something. Given that age 21 or thereabouts marks Saturn's waning square, it is clear that the crunch will involve releasing whatever has become too calcified. This can be a good influence on Saturn-ruled institutions, because any structure can definitely get too rigid. So as difficult as relations can be between the generations, the older generations owe a debt of gratitude to the 21-29 age group for perpetually preventing the onset of societal rigor mortis. (The 39-45 age group helps a lot with this too, as we shall see in the upcoming section.)

In some ways it is ironic that age 21 was designated long ago as "the age of majority." One is no longer a minor, one can legally vote, and one can legally drink alcohol, though the age for that has been modified periodically. And, as noted, it is also the age when the greatest questioning of one's elders is likely to begin.

Allowing leeway of a year either side for Saturn's ingoing and outgoing orbits, notice how, with each of the Saturn four quarters up to age 21, there is something new that civilization offers. At age 6-7, you can go to school! At age 14, you are capable of adult sexual relationships! At age 21, you can vote, drink, and enter adult society! Notice also that the privilege in each case carries with it much implied duty and responsibility and how, after 21, the other Saturn quarters become fuzzier and fuzzier as to what we can have and what is expected of us in society's terms. The first Saturn return has a strong personal effect, which will be discussed in a moment, but only after age 29-1/2 are we really dealing with our very own concepts of what we think we want to do.

The catch is that, if from ages 21 to 29 we have not questioned what is expected of us to see if it fits, then we will be due for a crisis at the first Saturn return and, if not then, then at the next Saturn quarter, or the next one. It is not hard to see that the less you examine your life circumstances to make sure they are genuinely yours and not just preset on automatic, then the greater the crisis, especially the longer you wait. There are so many major timing clues in the 39-to-45 age range, including the second Saturn opposition at ages 44-45, that often those who somehow waffle through the previous Saturn quarters do not escape this one. That is why the 39-45 age stretch is so potentially exciting—and so potentially grueling. Often this is when people first seek out an astrologer, if not when they're in their mid-30s.

First Saturn Return: Ages 28-29

If age 21 is society's "coming of age," then 28-1/2 to 29-1/2 is truly astrology's "coming of age" for any person, of any sex, race, nationality or creed. When Saturn, as the ruler of Time, has finally come around once, it is like the clock striking twelve at midnight on New Year's Eve. You *know* it is the new year; and in this case, you know you have experienced one whole round of what life has to offer. You got born, spread your wings in childhood, again in puberty as you examined what civilization had to offer and what it wanted from you, then you reoriented yourself after keeping what you wanted to absorb, and releasing what was no longer useful or suitable to you. Four long seasons of approximately 7 years each, not unlike spring, summer, fall, and winter in their symbolic and literal events.

Often young people set goals for themselves which round off into neat decades. By age 30, they should have achieved thus and so, often including house(s), car(s), marriage, kids, high income level, and educational degrees, though not necessarily in that order. And just as often it is not so neat, because the Saturn return comes along by age 29-1/2 and demands that we have done our homework, so to speak. If we are in a career only to please the family and earn a lot of money, it will often collapse or fizzle at this time. It is the same with marriage, or any serious relationships. We often speak of "the test of time," and surely Saturn, as Time's symbolic planetary ruler, is testing us every time it comes around by hard contact, but especially at the time of the return. It is a moment of reckoning, like counting the returns, literally, and it is also a moment of second chances to start over.

You may be one of the lucky ones who actually did make all the right decisions prior to age 29-1/2. You chose and kept what was good and right for you, educationally, relationship-wise, and career-wise, and you discarded what was wrong for you. In your case, you would be starting to reap the benefits for all that, and for your hard work. People would be starting to reward you with more status, more pay, and, inevitably with Saturn, more responsibility.

An interesting irony about the Saturn return is that it culminates a Saturn quarter (ages 21-29), when it is most appropriate for us to question the values, advice, and inherited wisdom of our elders. Yet it is also the period when we are still strongly influenced by what our society-at-large considers appropriate goals in life. So, not surprisingly, the 21-to-29 age group, before experiencing the first Saturn return, is both often interested in advice and equally disdainful of receiving it, inwardly if not outwardly. It is easy to see how that confusion would arise. Even using astrology, it is hard for them to realize that you are giving them their own messages rather than yours. The astrologer is only the translator of that message. For example, several years ago I had a client in his early 20s who would carefully note how I advised him to deal with certain situations that came up, based on his natal horoscope and the timing to it. Then he would methodically proceed to do the absolute opposite of what I suggested, just to see how it would turn out! I had to admire his spirit of adventure and willingness to experiment, except that I was suspicious when he never wanted to tell me how it worked out.

In any case, up to age 29-1/2, we are still keenly aware of trying to meet society's demands, and our decisions are often made accordingly. The idea here of "pulling one's weight" is such that we are still usually measuring (a Saturn-like concept) by some societal standard that is collectively understood. For this and many other reasons, I hated to see the documentary *28 Up* end at age 28, because these lives we saw unfolding before us were just starting to get interesting.

The 7-Year Saturn Quarters: A Summary

The Saturn squares and oppositions are not something to be dreaded, but their effects are real, and as such they mark turning points that have also been noted by some educators, psychologists, and sociologists—most of whom doubtless have no knowledge whatsoever of Saturn's full, half, and quarter cycles. So what is the advantage of understanding them astrologically? The advantage is understanding more deeply what is going on every 7.364 years, knowing with certainty that Saturn will continue on its cyclical path, and that the depth and breadth of its astrological symbology teaches us something about the practical reality of Saturn, of how it demands that we set limits and manifest something that is important to us, something that can make a contribution to civilization. If we get caught up in the part of Saturn that becomes overly concerned with status, ambition, and pecking order, can we really blame Saturn? I think we cannot, because it is just the negative and exaggerated version of a basically good and useful thing. Without the limits and the discipline that Saturn sets, especially by symbolizing the formality of measuring linear *time* itself, we would find it difficult to accomplish anything on Earth. The 7-year sectors marking the full, half, and quarter Saturn cycles teach us about the formalities of living together in a civilization. The planetary energy of Saturn was never intended to symbolize the retarding of natural growth, but all too often we interpret its cautionary and realistic presence as a withering, draining, and depressive aging process. This usually happens when we have nothing to shape or form. If the outline of your life is vague and scattered, then you can be sure that the basically benefic energy of Saturn will feel most unbenefic as it attempts to recreate some sense of much-needed order. If we do not get the message the first couple of times around, then Saturn can give it to us again in a most heavy-handed manner.

Other Big Turning Points for Everyone

Given that the Saturn cycles show strong lines of demarcation for certain eras in our lives, especially up to age 29-1/2, let us now look at everybody's most dramatic turning points throughout the adult life:

1) Ages 28-29-1/2:   First Saturn return

2) Ages 39-45:   a. Transiting Uranus opposite natal Uranus, ages 39-43, early or later within this range, varying by generation.

b. Transiting Neptune square natal Neptune, ages 41-42.

c. Transiting Pluto square natal Pluto, age can vary from 37 to 91. See chart next page.

d. Transiting Saturn opposite natal Saturn, ages 44-45.

3) Ages 58-59 1/2:   Second Saturn return

4) Age 84:   First Uranus return

The Mid-Life Crisis: Ages 39-45

Since the first item above has been discussed in some detail in the previous sections, let us move on to the second item, very often known as "the mid-life crisis." The etymology of the word "crisis" and its various definitions is a pungent reminder. It comes from the Greek *krisis,* meaning decision, from *krinein*—to decide, or to separate. The medical definition precedes all others in most dictionaries. Here's a typical entry: "the turning point in the course of a disease, when it becomes clear whether the patient will recover or die."[83]

My point is not that life or mid-life is a disease, but that the crisis at this point is probably universally akin to no other. In fact there is often the sense that, if one does not or cannot turn a certain corner at this time in life, then it feels as if some form of death is imminent—or perhaps even longed for. It is remarkable the number of outer planets that make the square or opposition to themselves during a 6-year period. This is intensified for those born between 1940 and 1991 because, due to the strange orbit of Pluto (as shown in the diagram on p. 47), the Pluto square occurs at an earlier and earlier age, early enough to coincide with the other big celestial combinations that everyone experiences from ages 39 to 45.

---

83. *Webster's New World Dictionary,* Second College Edition, 1984.

Transiting Pluto square natal Pluto

Years born	Average age of Pluto square[84]
1800-1810	88-89
1810-1820	89-91
1820-1830	91
1830-1840	89-91
1840-1850	86-89
1850-1860	83-86
1860-1870	80-83
1870-1880	75-80
1880-1890	71-75
1890-1900	65-71
1900-1910	59-65
1910-1920	54-59
1920-1930	49-54
1930-1940	45-49
1940-1950	40-45
1950-1960	38-40
1960-1970	37-38
1970-1980	37-39
1980-1990	40-43
1990-2000	43-48

Although I know of no formal research done on the subject, I would deduce from the above chart that the age group born between 1940 and 1992 would probably experience a more intensified mid-life period than those born earlier or later in the century. However, those doubling their second Saturn return with a Pluto square at age 59 (1910 births) would have the opportunity for a potential crisis delayed until age 59! Needless to say, without some extra compassion and understanding, it would be easy for those born between 1900 and 1940 to assume that later generations are

84. The closer your birth year to the start of the decade, the closer your average age of Pluto square to the upper end of the age spectrum. For example, 1900 births have the Pluto square at age 65. Born July 26, 1875, Carl Jung experienced his Pluto square at age 78, eight years before his death in 1961.

overreacting to or even bungling life in their early 40s. Another parallel is that the years 1940-1992 are speeded up in terms of global developments, symbolized by Pluto (a generational bridge planet) moving more and more rapidly through this part of the zodiac at this time. Unless the sections in Chapter 2 describing the planets are still fresh in your mind, you may now want to review the pages on Uranus, Neptune, and Pluto, because an understanding of the basic symbology of these planets, and in fact all the planets, is crucial to an understanding of how they affect our lives in human terms. As with any transits, major or minor, further detail comes from the house positions being activated as well as from the rest of the chart.

The Mid-Life Crisis Transits

T. = Transiting planet
N. = Natal planet

T. Uranus Opposite N. Uranus
Ages 39-43
(earlier or later in this range, depending on the generation.)

The iconoclastic and potentially rebellious nature of Uranus pushes us to seek the outer limits of our individualities. If we have not taken those big chances before now, Uranus confronts us with that awareness and gives us a big shove towards doing what is necessary. Uranus often provides an opportunity that comes with sudden surprise or shock, which feels pleasant or unpleasant depending on our resistance to it.

T. Neptune Square N. Neptune
Ages 41-42

One's hopes, dreams, ideals—in fact, all goals in idealized terms —are tested by Neptune square to itself. It is as if one's obligation to oneself to be true to the initial dream gets a giant nudge now.

T. Pluto Square N. Pluto
Age varies from 37 to 91 (see chart, p. 158)

Pluto pressures one to new levels of self-discovery here by uncovering hidden aspects of one's past or present, and by forcing, at times ruthlessly, the destruction of something over which you thought you had complete power and control.[85] This often affects one's home and profession, though you also ought to check Pluto's natal and transiting house position for further details.

T. Saturn Opposite N. Saturn
(Ages 44-45)

Careers and relationships which were tested at the last Saturn square 7 years ago now undergo another big test to see if they hold up. If they do not, they will deteriorate and collapse rapidly; if they do, you will receive strong material evidence that you are on the right track in the eyes of the rest of the world. The opposition often symbolizes a confrontation of some kind.

The Second Saturn Return: Ages 58-59-1/2

How you experience the second Saturn return depends a great deal, as with all the Saturn cycles, on how you handled the previous quarter, half, and full cycles of Saturn. So when somebody seems to be getting away with murder, he or she doesn't ever, really. Somehow Saturn, the great disciplinarian, appears and acts in his own way to each of us. If there is a planet of karma, Saturn is it.

It is very odd sometimes how Saturn keeps reminding us of his symbolic as well as literal presence. Today, for instance, I open the newspaper to read the following lead paragraph on the front page:

> Aerospace executive Ed Greer has resurfaced seven years after abandoning his wife, two sons and the corporate life to become the vagabond beach bum his yuppie colleagues fantasized about.
>
> Associated Press, Los Angeles, *The New Mexican*, Feb. 4, 1989. p. 1.

---

85. A recent example of a 42-year old experiencing not only the Pluto square Pluto but Neptune square Neptune is Theodore Bundy. In July 1979 (at age 32), Bundy was tried and found guilty of the murder of two women he had strangled and beaten, and of the attempted murder of three other women. Over a period of ten years, the well-educated Bundy successfully delayed his execution, even though it was becoming clearer and clearer that he was probably responsible for many more murders of women, mainly in the Pacific Northwest area. Finally, he ran out of appeals and elaborate legal strategies and decided to confess to numerous rape murders (out of the 32 or more of which he was suspected). He was executed in a Florida State Prison on January 24, 1989, at age 42.

This is an exaggerated situation, to be sure, but the timing shows a dramatic example of a mid-life crisis in which, as in the dictionary definition of a crisis, Bundy reached "the turning point . . . where it becomes clear whether the patient will recover or die."

Ed Greer left without a word on September 10, 1981, and FBI agents finally located him in October 1988. Birth data was not available here, but, judging from the circumstances and from his photograph, I strongly suspect he either left at around age 28 and came back at age 35, or he left at around age 35 and came back at age 42. In any case, Greer's solution to his life situation was hardly a model one, but it is somewhat typical of the extremes that may arise if a person feels totally locked into his or her circumstances.

You begin to see how, even though there are many chances to begin again, somehow there is a cumulative effect, so that by the second Saturn return, if you are not doing what you like (and preferably love), if you are not in relationships that you like (and preferably love), and if you are not living where you like (and preferably love), then you will get a multitude of signals letting you know that your previous goals, wishes, and plans were faulty, wrongly-based, and backfiring all over the place. But what is faulty, you might ask? It is certainly not wrong to want to make a lot of money, for instance, but it *is* wrong to do it by compromising your basic honesty and integrity. In the newspaper story above, the subject Ed Greer is quoted as telling a coworker before he disappeared in 1981, "Never become too good at something you hate. They'll make you do it the rest of your life."

The stage and screen actor Richard Burton openly courted both the high life and a kind of contempt for his craft, which, given the high level of his talent, prevented him from truly fulfilling his promise as one of the great actors of the 20th century. One might have foreseen this somewhat years earlier from his response to veteran actor Laurence Olivier, who, during the Elizabeth Taylor/ *Cleopatra* scandal in 1963 in Rome cabled Burton: "Make up your mind, dear heart. Do you want to be a great actor or a household word?" Burton's reply was "Both." On other occasions he had made remarks such as "An actor is something less than a man, while an actress is something more than a woman" and "I've done the most awful rubbish in order to have somewhere to go in the morning."[86]

In February and March 1984, Burton experienced his second Saturn return and was due to have another go of it in October 1984.

---

86. All Burton quotations are from Leslie Halliwell, *Halliwell's Filmgoer's Companion*, 8th ed., 1985, p. 168.

As was mentioned in Chapter 3, self-discipline (Saturn) was never a comfortable issue for Burton, and most of the time he acted as if he could do well enough without it. But when Saturn makes its return (in this case in combination with T. Pluto conjunct N. Mars, and T. Uranus square N. Moon), you cannot avoid looking at what you've done with your life and whether you have manifested what you planned. When its effects are also on the N. Sun, as in this case (with Burton's N. Sun conjunct N. Saturn), then Saturn seems almost to be pressing on the body (and mind and willpower) to make good the promise. It is a very real pressure. Burton was not only physically weak from his many cumulative years of high living, but he had not fulfilled his promise. He died in Switzerland of a brain hemorrhage on August 5, 1984, at age 58 years 9 months. The media coverage was noticeably muted and mixed, almost as if the public felt cheated of their opportunity to witness a truly great theatrical talent.

It may seem that 59 is too late to start again, but it is not if you want to enjoy the rest of your life. You may think you are enjoying it, but if the terms of enjoyment are false or hollow, with no peace of mind and no sense of benefiting humanity in any way, then Saturn's message is that the structure you have created for your life needs to be torn down and rebuilt once again. In some ways, it may feel like a larger risk at this age, especially financially, if you are planning on retirement at age 65. But not even these national or legal guidelines can fool the wisdom of the Saturn cycle. Saturn's message again and again is to let there be structure to your life, but not so much so that you feel trapped or imprisoned, and not so comfortably that you support a tendency to smugness or complacency.

The Uranus Return: Age 84

As noted earlier, Uranus is about your uniqueness as an individual. Its planetary influence cares little what the rules and regulations say, so if you have not loosened up and let yourself be more liberated from Saturn's structures at the Uranus opposition (ages 39-43), or at the Uranus squares (early 20s and early 60s), then you get another big chance at age 84 to be your own person. There is an interesting new aspect to this era of the personal life, in that you're less susceptible to the pressures and anxieties of your previous way (if not philosophy) of life.

One example is that of an 84-year-old woman who abruptly divorced her second husband, to whom she had been married some 15 years. The marriage had not been an especially happy one, but she had borne with it out of the basic conservatism of her generation towards the general idea of divorce. (Her first husband had died.) Finally, an incident arose that was just too much. She could suffer it no more. However, along with this unusually late-in-life divorce came a tome that she wrote for her family, called *Anatomy of a Marriage*. In it she sought to explain to her younger relatives what she had been through, what she had done, and why she had to do it! It is not always easy to take in that strong Uranian breath of fresh air, even at age 84.

It may also be that by age 84 your personal destiny indicates that you have done all you wanted to in the physical dimension of Earth life, and your greatest desire for liberation (Uranus) is that of the soul from the physical body, or physical death.

Joseph Campbell, the legendary mythologist, writer, and lecturer, died in Honolulu on October 30, 1987, five months before his 84th birthday. At that time, the Uranus opposition was 5°, or 3-1/2 months approaching its exactness (along with some exact low-energy cycles, including T. Neptune in hard contact to N. Sun/ Mercury/Jupiter, T. Saturn in hard contact to N.Moon/Pluto, and the highly changeable T. Uranus opposing secondary progressed Sun). The newspapers reported that Campbell died "after a brief illness."[87]

He had just completed a set of six highly stimulating and popular one-hour documentaries for PBS television with journalist Bill Moyers, entitled *The Power of Myth* (later made available in book form under the same title, published 1988). In several of the episodes, he spoke inspirationally and almost glowingly about the death process and the spiritual preparation necessary to meet one's death with no fear—in fact, with joy. It seems certain that many people absorbed this message who may not have done so otherwise. And what a perfect metaphor for a famous mythologist to die within a day of Halloween, the time of the ancient ritual when the souls of the dead are both honored and cajoled. But then Campbell always believed in the inherent aliveness of symbols, and their messages.

---

87. Quotation and date of death reported in *Facts on File,* November 6, 1987, p. 832.

Personal Big Turning Points

Now that we have looked at what planetary cycles will come for everyone at certain ages, let us move on to an area that necessarily becomes more complex and intricate—that of the cyclical turning points that can be measured, but that vary from person to person depending on what is in the natal chart and where everything is located in the cosmological scheme of things.

There are a number of factors to take into account. First of all, astrologers use a wide variety of timing techniques in order to cover all the ground. Some astrologers prefer solar and lunar returns, for example, although I do not find those particular techniques as useful and accurate except for solar returns that are also the New Moon or Full Moon. (See under "Relationship Fulfillment: Cycles and Patterns," p. 170.) Within Western astrology, the following are a list of recommended techniques:

1) Secondary progressions, especially the secondary progressed lunar cycle (29-1/2 years) and the charts marking each quarter of the cycle.

2) Transits.

3) Solar arc directions, full, double, and half.[88]

4) Eclipses, solar and lunar.

5) Solstice and Equinox charts (especially the Winter Solstice chart, for yearly trends).

6) Transiting lunation cycles (especially for short-range timing).

7) Natal Astro•Carto•Graphy maps (for individuals, corporations, or nations), with Cyclo•Carto•Graphy overlays to unite timing with geographical location, if that is an issue.

8) Mundane Astro•Carto•Graphy maps of Solstices, Equinoxes, lunations, and eclipses (mainly for exact timing).[89]

---

88. Solar arc directions (full only) are available in astrological computer software, and are included in the multitude of Astro Communications Services timing options. Also, a solar arc table is available from publisher Ludwig Rudolph (Witte Verlag), Hamburg, Germany. (See Appendix G, p. 276.)
89. Available in the *Source Book of Mundane Maps*, published annually since 1979 by Astro•Carto•Graphy, c/o Astro Numeric Service, P.O. Box 425, San Pablo, CA 94806. (Phone: 1-800-MAPPING).

9) Monthly kinetic mundascope graphs (for exact timing within a 24-hour range).[90]

I will not go into detail here about how all of these techniques work or how they are woven together, other than to say I put all the various timing symbols on one large sheet of paper which covers 12 months, month by month. In any case, there are a few basics, and Chapter 2 already describes how the secondary progressed lunar cycle operates. That is crucial to understand for one's personal big turning points, especially as it deals in 29-1/2 year time spans that begin at different times for everyone.

First, here are a few pointers. Since the language of astrology can become extremely complex, one of the ways that I have found (and that I learned from the Uranian system of astrology) to keep things as simple and clear as possible is to make equations. Normally the astrologer would use the glyph for the planet; ♀ for example, for Venus, and ♀ t for transiting Venus. But here I will spell out all the names of the planets. When I use the = mark, it means that there is a hard contact between planets and/or Personal Points. (Remember, a hard contact is any division of the circle by 4, 8, or 16, but especially by 4 and 8, for the big pictures.) It means that one planetary factor or one set of planetary factors equals another, and so it becomes a sentence. (We have seen a lot of this in Chapter 3, although as yet without the = marks.) The sentences mean the same whether the planets or Personal Points are natal, transiting, or progressed, but we note whether they are N., T., or P. to give a sense of the timing, i.e. how long the planetary picture will be in operation. The essence of the effect on human lives comes from the symbols of the planets and Personal Points themselves, in whatever combination that may be.

You may wonder how it works if the low cycles coincide with the high cycles. My experience and observation has taught me that low cycles with enough preponderance (i.e. strength and volume) will always outweigh a high cycle. However, it is extremely unusual for a high cycle to be very strong and coincide with a low cycle.

---

90. Described further (and with sample graphs) in Appendix A, Section 4, the kinetic mundascope is a valuable technique developed in the late 1970s by Vermont astrologer and researcher James Valliere. At the present time, these graphs can only be found in his *Valliere's Natural Cycles Almanac,* published annually since 1981. You can order this from specialized bookstores or from the publisher: Astrolabe, Inc., Box 28, Orleans, MA 02653. (Phone: 1-508-896-5081, FAX 1-508-896-5289.)

What I have seen are examples of what are normally low cycles, greatly modified and softened by some other factors. Those exceptions will be noted later. Another key thing to remember is that when you have transiting or progressed contacts that last from several weeks to several months (and transiting Pluto can be in the same vicinity for about two years), you obviously have a much more pronounced effect than those which last a day or so. The exceptions are the solar and lunar eclipses, which, when exactly conjunct a Personal Point, are considered to have an effect up to six weeks before and six weeks after the date of the eclipse.

In other cases, at very low physical points, especially where there is a congruence of several low cycles, there is the possibility of physical death by illness or accident. An ethical astrologer in the Western world never predicts death. (It used to be a common practice among Eastern astrologers, especially in India, to predict the time of death, and it may still be.) The client should be made aware of the low cycles, when they begin and when they are over, which is often a great relief to know—but it is not up to the astrologer to predict death as a probable outcome of the cycle or cycles. The wisest advice is one of calm warning, so that if the client is not resigned to death and longing for its onset, then you can help him or her to take extra care in maintaining health on all levels, physical, mental, emotional, and spiritual, until such time as the cycle begins to turn upward again.

The best way to deal with any of these major cyclical combinations is to know what they are aiming at, look for the signals, question what needs to be done differently (if anything), and do not offer heavy resistance to the process. Another hint is to be aware, month by month, year by year, of the integrity that not only builds your structures in life but motivates your adventures.

Below is a brief summary of some abbreviations used in the upcoming sections on cycles and patterns. You may also want to quickly review the list of planetary combinations on p. 78 that occur frequently in geographical location work and which apply equally to timing work.

=   = **Hard contact:** Angular relationship by 4th, 8th, or 16th harmonic.

T.   = **Transiting:** Example: T. Saturn. Orbs for transiting and progressed planets or Personal Points are strongest 1°

applying and are still in effect up to 1° separating. Sometimes consider 1-1/2° applying and separating for slow-moving outer planets (especially Pluto) to Personal Points.

P.   = **Progressed:** As in the secondary progressed system of timing.

N.   = **Natal:** Located in the natal chart.

SR°   = **Stationary Retrograde degree:** The degree at which a planet moves Stationary Retrograde, as seen from the Earth.

SD°   = **Stationary Direct degree:** The degree at which a planet moves Stationary Direct, as seen from the Earth.

☉ E   = **Solar eclipse:** Notable in timing mainly if it conjuncts or opposes a Personal Point. The effects can last from 6 weeks before to 6 weeks after the eclipse.

☽ E   = **Lunar eclipse:** Same as above.

Physical Energy/Health: Cycles and Patterns

In this section, please note the cycles marked as follows:

*Also applies to cyclical patterns for career.

Change-producing, and impossible to say whether **High or **Low** cycle. It depends on how the opportunity is met, but these are usually stress indicators.

*High: 2nd and 3rd quarters of the secondary progressed lunation cycle. Exception: if the 2nd and/or 3rd-quarter charts consist of unfavorable patterns. But if there are favorable patterns, it bodes well for the duration of the chart (from 7 to 9 years).[91]

*High: ☉ E or ☽ E conjunct N. Sun, MC, or ASC: In effect for 6 weeks before to 6 weeks after an eclipse.

*High: P. or T. Jupiter = P. or N. Sun, Moon or MC: Especially

---

91. To obtain the angles of the secondary progressed lunar quarter chart, first calculate the true solar arc, i.e. the elapsed distance between N. Sun and P. Sun using the day-for-a-year portion. Then add the true solar arc to N. MC to obtain P. MC. This is the MC of the secondary progressed lunar quarter chart. Look in your choice of tables of houses under *birth* (not current location) latitude to obtain ASC and house cusps. Meridian House Table 1st house cusp = East Point, so another house table must be used to obtain the ASC.

strong if Jupiter SR° or SD° conjunct N. or P. Sun, Moon, or MC.

*High: P. Sun conjunct N. MC.

High: P. Sun = P. Venus: Stronger if in combination with other **High** cycle patterns.

*High: T. Saturn conjunct N. MC and transiting N. 10th house: Strongest within 1° of N. MC and when T. Saturn is in direct motion, but still in effect in **High** cycle during Saturn's 2-1/2 year transit of N. 10th house. Exception: if you have prepared for this transit in a negative way. President Richard Nixon resigned from office during this transit.

*High: T. Saturn = N. Saturn: Also denotes very hard work.

*High: T. Mars = N. Mars: Especially strong when T. Mars conjuncts N. Mars once every two years. This includes the time T. Mars spends in same zodiacal sign as N. Mars, which averages 5-1/2 weeks, unless T. Mars is retrograde, which brings it up to about 9 weeks.

*Median: T. Saturn conjunct N. ASC or DSC: Exception: **Low** cycle and hard on health if Saturn SR° or SD° conjuncts N. ASC.

*Changeable: T. or P. Uranus = P. or N. Sun: Especially dangerous for men prone to heart attacks or with weak heart conditions. A time for them to cautiously build health maintenance and not overdo or overly stress themselves.

**Changeable: T. or P. Saturn/Uranus = N. or P. Sun: Same as above, although extends further to include danger for known cases of hypertension.

**Changeable: T. or P. Pluto = N. or P. Sun or Moon: Never moving quickly, Pluto is slower and more drastic in its final effects. If the physical body is weak beforehand, this combination may bring a complete breakdown before building it back up. Even if in good health, there is potential for some radical changes in diet and nutrition and in the orientation of the psyche. Moon/Pluto can also indicate a glandular change.

*Low: Last year of the 4th quarter of the 29-1/2 year secondary progressed lunation cycle: Exceptions: if E or E conjuncts N. Sun, MC or ASC, or T. Jupiter SR° or SD° conjuncts N.

Sun, or, especially for a woman, conjuncts N. Moon. Also, if P. Jupiter = P. Sun, as in the example of Meryl Streep. (See Chapter 4, "Time Clues.")

*Low: T. Saturn conjuncts N. IC and transiting N. 4th house: T. Saturn still in effect in **Low** cycle during Saturn's 2-1/2 year transit of N. 4th house. Exception: if your N. Sun is in the 3rd or 4th house. Gerald Ford has a 3rd house N. Sun and became U.S. President (from August 9, 1974, following Nixon's resignation, to January 20, 1977), during which time T. Saturn conjuncted Ford's N. IC and transited the N. 4th house.

*Low: T. or P. Saturn = N. or P. Sun or Mars.

Low: T. or P. Saturn = P. or N. Moon: Especially strong in effect if it occurs in a quarti-lunar secondary progressed chart.

*Low: T. Saturn conjunct N. ASC: Especially strong if T. Saturn SR° or SD° conjuncts N. ASC, and stronger still if it coincides with other **Low** cycles.

*Low: T. or N. Saturn = T. or N. Pluto: Very hard work, sometimes including a sense of being blocked in your efforts.

*Low: T. or N. Jupiter = T. or N. Saturn.

Low: T. or N. Saturn = T. or N. Neptune: Can bring chronic illnesses or infections.

Low: T. Saturn/Neptune = N. Sun or Moon: Same as above.

Low: T. Saturn/Uranus/Pluto = N. Sun or Moon: Intensifies a physically weak condition.

*Low: T. or P. Neptune = N. or P. Sun or Mars: Especially pronounced effect when T. Neptune = N. Sun or Mars.

Career: Cycles and Patterns

Please note: All of the above marked with an asterisk under "Physical Energy/Health: Cycles and Patterns" also apply to "Career: Cycles and Patterns."

High: T. Uranus = N. Venus: Especially fine for artistic creative output, but calls for caution on speculative ventures. Financial circumstances (Venus) can move so swiftly and surprisingly (Uranus) that you lose.

High: T. Jupiter = N. 2-8 house axes: In effect 1° applying and 1° separating. Works extremely well with Meridian houses. (I cannot vouch for any other house system on this one.) The same applies to any combination of planets or Personal Points to the house axes. The 2-8 axis affects the financial status, for better **(High** cycle contacts) or worse **(Low** cycle contacts).

High: T. Jupiter/Uranus or T. Jupiter/Uranus/Pluto or T. Jupiter/Pluto = N. 2-8 house axis: Same as above.

Low: T. Saturn or T. Uranus or T. Saturn/Uranus = N. 2-8 house axis: Same as above.

Low: T. or P. Neptune = N. or P. Sun or Mars: Special caution for speculators (Neptune), who may leap too far too fast here.

Low: T. Saturn = N. Venus: Causes the feeling of constriction and/or loss in the financial position, if not actual constriction or loss, especially with Saturn SR° or SD° = N. Venus. Best approach here is very conservative. [92]

Relationship Fulfillment: Cycles and Patterns

In this section, please note the **Low** cycles marked as follows:

*Critical to the survival of the relationship, especially if more than one of these combinations exist simultaneously. You may want to wait until this critical period passes before making any irrevocable decision on a relationship, although these patterns denote that it can be rough going while you wait.

High: T. ☉ E or ☽ E conjunct N. Moon's Node: Occurs usually only once or twice in a lifetime and often marks the beginning of an important relationship, if other planetary patterns concur.

---

92. I have observed cases where the client had both T. Neptune = N. Sun *and* T. Saturn = N. Venus simultaneously, including Saturn SR° = N. Venus. Over a 10-month period, this caused the person to want to take big speculative chances (Sun/Neptune) to compensate for the sense of financial constraint (Saturn/Venus). The result was big losses in the stock market.

High: Solar return T. Sun conjunct or opposition T. Moon (i.e. either New Moon or Full Moon): The solar return occurs within 24 hours either side of the actual birthday. Calculated from the exact return by degree of T. Sun conjunct N. Sun. Solar return New Moon or Full Moon usually denotes the start of a major relationship or a marriage within a year after the solar return. Princess Diana's solar return July 1, 1981, before her marriage July 29, 1981, to Prince Charles shows a New Moon (within 2°, or approximately two hours approaching it).

High: P. Sun conjunct P. Moon = P. Venus or Jupiter or P. Venus/Jupiter or P. Jupiter/Pluto: Unless unfavorable patterns intervene, such as P. Saturn conjunct P. ASC, this can apply for the entire secondary progressed lunar quarter, from 7 to 9 years. Favorable period for meeting a mate or for a marriage.

High: P. Venus conjunct N. or P. ASC: Similar to above, although not as decisive.

High: T. or P. Jupiter = N. Sun or Moon: Does not by itself guarantee relationship success or a big match, but does guarantee a sense of optimism and expansive well-being that promotes attraction.

High: P. Sun conjunct N. MC: Applies for a woman.

High: P. Moon conjunct N. MC: Applies for a man.

Changeable: T. or P. Uranus = N. or P. Venus: Could cause an unexpected and surprising new romantic relationship to appear, but more likely to be whirlwind than stable. Commitments already established could now experience an influx of some new elements, either potentially creative or potentially disruptive.

Low: P. Sun conjunct P. Moon = P. Saturn, Uranus, or Neptune, or P. Saturn/Uranus, or P. Saturn/Neptune: Can apply for the entire secondary progressed lunar quarter, from 7 to 9 years.

*Low: T. or P. Saturn = N. or P. Venus, ASC, or Moon's Node: The critical state is potentially worsened if the T. or P. planet has SR° or SD° = N. planet or Personal Point.

*Low: T. or P. Saturn = N. Uranus or Pluto: Same as above.

*Low: T. or P. Jupiter/Saturn = N. Moon's Node or ASC: Same as above.

*Low: T. or P. Saturn/Uranus = N. or P. Moon's Node or ASC: Same as above.

*Low: T. or P. Saturn/Pluto = N. Moon's Node or ASC: Same as above.

*Low: T. or P. Saturn/Uranus/ Pluto = N. Moon's Node or ASC: Same as above.

*Low: T. or P. Uranus = N. or P. Moon's Node, MC, or ASC: Same as above.

*Low: T. or P. Uranus in the N. 7th house: Especially the first several years out of a total of 7 that T. Uranus spends in any one house, in this case the 7th (assuming the house divisions used are somewhat equal, such as in the Meridian house system).

*Low: T. or P. Saturn SR° or SD° = N. Sun/Moon midpoint.

Low: T. or P. Saturn = N. or P. Sun or Moon: Can make one feel constrained emotionally, especially with Saturn/Moon, though may not affect relationships adversely if problems are shared with the mate.

Domestic Arrangements: Cycles and Patterns

This section could be entitled "Real Estate: Cycles and Patterns," since it includes that, but it is much more than that, because it is about where we feel at home, where we put our home base. Very often the state of our house or apartment inside and out reflects our emotional state, especially as regards our intimate relationships with those who share our domestic arrangements. This applies also to whatever legal status our home has and the particular advantages we have by either owning or renting our house or apartment. The immediate environment is of great importance too, especially considering the symbology of the home as our womb, so to speak, and also in many ways the direct reflection of our physical, emotional, mental, financial, and spiritual health! So, not surprisingly, when there is a move, a renovation, purchase, or building of a new house, this is always a direct reflection of the state of our health on all levels and of the health of our key relationships, usually marriage.

How many people do you know who bought, built, or renovated a house or apartment only to divorce or die soon thereafter? I know of a great number of such cases, which is not to say they are inevitable, but that there is a basic renewal or renovation (with guaranteed temporary chaos) which occurs here on external levels and must be carried out simultaneously on internal levels. Otherwise, when the house is built or the apartment completely renovated, and nothing has changed on an emotional/spiritual level, especially as regards the intimate relationships, then the physical or emotional well-being suddenly collapses, as probably does the marriage or the relationship in question.

High cycles for purchasing or finding real estate are definable, but they are considerably amplified by having concurrently several of the **High** cycle planetary patterns that are listed under "Physical Health/Energy" and to some extent those listed under "Career." Please bear this in mind. Also in this section, please note the cycles marked as follows:

> *Change-producing, and impossible to say whether **High** or **Low** cycle. It depends on how the opportunity is met, but these are usually stress indicators.

High: T. or P. Jupiter conjunct N. IC and transiting the N. 4th house: Every 12 years Jupiter transits the 4th house for one year, which may not be a consecutive 12 months. (Check the ephemeris for dates.) It is strongest during direct motion, and especially effective if T. Jupiter SR° or SD° = N. IC.

*Changeable: T. or P. Pluto = N. or P. Moon: Pluto in these combinations often symbolizes renovation of some kind, or a move of the domestic base. Note the turnaround point with T. Pluto and all slower-moving outer planets, as the T. planet moves SR, then SD, and passes for the last (usually third) time over the same critical point in the chart. This is when some action may finally occur, the groundwork having been laid during its passage back and forth over the natal planet or Personal Point, and it may not necessarily happen as you expected, especially if it is also during Mercury Retrograde and/or Mars Retrograde.

*Changeable: T. or P. Uranus = N. or P. Moon, MC, or ASC: Same pointers as above regarding planetary movement. Uranus tends to create sudden, surprising situations or opportunities. They are a call to big changes, whether they feel pleasant or unpleasant.

*Changeable: T. or P. Saturn = N. or P. Moon or MC: Exception: T. Saturn conjunct N. MC is less prone to moves. Otherwise, Saturn contacts to the Moon can reflect the sadness around saying good-bye to a people, a place, and an era of your life.

*Changeable: T. Jupiter/Saturn = N. ASC: Usually a change of residence, if not a separation from a person.

*Changeable: T. Neptune = N. Moon: The nature of the changeability here calls for caution and no drastic moves or decisions. The reason for refraining from any major action regarding domestic arrangements during this transit is because it is too clouded and confusing. Often ownership of a property, legally and/or emotionally, is now in question. After N. Neptune has moved in direct motion over the N. Moon and past it by at least 1°, the problem should clear up.

Low: T. or P. Saturn conjunct P. or N. IC or square P. or N. MC.

Low: T. or P. Saturn/Pluto = P. or N. MC.

Shortcuts in Timing Techniques:
The 45° Graphic Ephemeris and the 90° Dial

Now you are beginning to see why people hire astrologers to figure out all the timing for them. It is not simple, but there is a system to it, and there are computer programs to help us—though I have yet to find one that puts all the symbols I want for a year on one large sheet.

Out of an array of astrological software for microcomputers, there are currently two astrological tools which help us to see things right away for a time span of a year or more. The first is the 45°

graphic ephemeris.[93] The second is the 90° dial.[94]

Playing Detective with the 45° Graphic Ephemeris

The 45° graphic ephemeris, as shown on the next page, shows graphically all the planetary movements for one year, in this case 1988. The horizontal lines indicate where the client's natal Personal Points and planets are located. The Personal Points can be drawn in red so that you can immediately focus the most attention on them. You want to see the overall sweep and movement for the year, and any bunchings of planetary lines, especially where the client's natal lines cross the transiting lines for the year. I recommend using a transparent ruler and placing it vertically on the printout graph to see what is happening in certain time periods, if not on exact dates. (*Timegraphs* provides the option of a movable vertical line for use on the computer screen.)

As it turns out, 1988 was a trying year for anyone with a Personal Point at either 27-1/2° of the Mutables (the Mutable signs are Gemini, Virgo, Sagittarius, and Pisces) or at 12-1/2° of the Fixed (the Fixed signs are Taurus, Leo, Scorpio, and Aquarius). If you look closely, you will see why. For Client X, there is really no respite all year long from T. Pluto = N. ASC; T. Saturn/Uranus/Pluto = N. ASC; or T. Saturn/Uranus = N. Sun/Venus. These combinations are all very difficult on key relationships, especially marriage. This

---

93. Available in software format only from Astrolabe, Inc. and from Matrix Software, as of spring 1991. (See Appendix G, p. 275 for their addresses and phone numbers.) Astrolabe's *Timegraphs* (©1989) is a software add-on module for Astrolabe's *Nova, Chartwheels,* or *Advanced Natal Report* programs. With *Timegraphs* you can create your own graphic ephemerides using any planets or any dates. An overlay of horizontal lines shows the positions of natal planets from your chart files. Matrix Software has just recently produced its version of the 45° graphic ephemeris in *Quick-Graphs* (©1991).

Astro Communications Services currently offers a range of graphic ephemerides printouts (either in 45° or 30° format), including those that run from one to five years of transits, with or without natal lines, and up to 85 years of secondary progressions only for any year between 4000 BC and 2500 AD.

Another source is a book entitled *A Year-at-a-Glance: The 45 Degree Graphic Ephemeris for 101 Years, 1900-2001,* by Roxana Muise, 1986 (published by South Western Astrology Conference, P.O. Box 1175, Torrance, CA 90505). Though it does have the advantage of including 101 years' worth of charts of transiting planets, it is not as easy to work with in terms of overlaying natal or corporate planetary positions, depending as it does on a system of plastic sheet protectors and non-permanent markers.

94. Astrolabe produces 360° and 90° dials in both software and non-software format, although, as of late 1990, they are in the process of retooling both dials. Samples of each are shown in the Appendix. Their Chartwheels II program (©1989) currently has the most up-to-date software using 360° and 90° dials, plus pointer or midpoint capabilities with either dial.

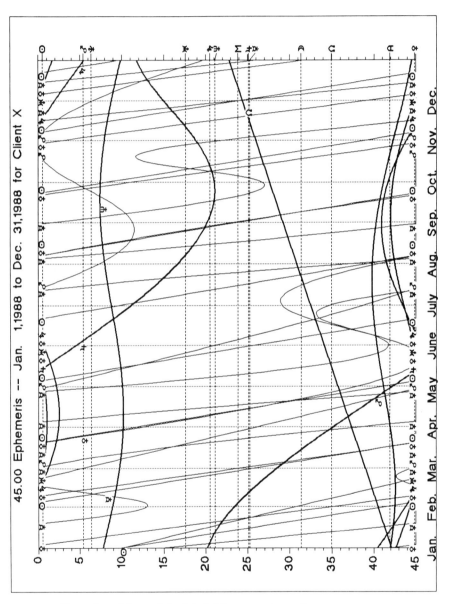

Reproduced from Astrolabe's Timegraphs *software program*

is not to say that everyone experiencing Saturn/Uranus/Pluto in 1988 experienced marriage problems, but those with Moon's Node or ASC at either 27-1/2° of a Mutable sign or 12-1/2° of a Fixed sign would, because those are crucial relationship axes. I have observed other clients who had the bulk of the Saturn/Uranus/Pluto action on the N. Sun, which caused a tremendous number of health problems, especially in one case where T. Neptune was also = N. Mars. It is as if all the energy systems of the body shut down temporarily, especially if the body is weak in some way at the start of the transits, in this case January 1988.

The scenario for Client X in 1988 goes as follows: Much of the first 9-1/2 months was spent planning the building of a new house, which involved a move in late August to an interim house while building was to proceed until spring 1989. (T. Pluto hovering on the ASC axis usually concerns building, moving, and probing relationships.) Problems in the marriage began to worsen as the year wore on, coming to crisis pitch after the move in late August. (By then T. Saturn and Uranus were adding to the confusion of T. Pluto = N. ASC in their intense dynamics of what I call the "Shall I stay or shall I go?" syndrome.)

Finally, on October 13, the couple decided to separate (as T. Pluto was within a fraction of a degree exactly conjunct N. DSC), except several stepchildren were in the picture who were extremely upset about the breakup and caused it to become even more explosive. (Notice even the New Moon on October 10th exactly contacts N. Uranus; and Sun/Moon = Uranus is a very disruptive combination for relationships.) With fireworks and extra aggravation, one would also expect to see Mars in the picture, and indeed it is moving within 1° to an exact square of N. Sun and Venus October 12-November 13. With a Mars SD° = N. Sun/Venus on October 28th, we have even further confirmation of a potentially aggressive situation.

Fortunately, there was no domestic violence, but with all the T. Saturn/Uranus/Pluto/Mars activity moving swiftly onto my client's N. Sun, I became concerned that the ultrahigh stress level would cause her to be accident-prone or susceptible to illness of some kind, even though in late October she appeared to be in excellent health. Noting her close natal Mars/Pluto contacts, I surmised that her usual form of exercise was probably rather strenuous, which she confirmed, and I advised her to change immediately to an alternative type of exercise that was more calming, such as yoga, and to gear herself up to dealing as positively and preventively as possible with the serious potential for accidents or illness.

The story goes on, basically towards my client moving twice (after the October 13th decision to separate)— first, out of the family home in late October, and again in early January 1989 to more permanent quarters. There was a divorce settlement in the works in January 1989, and some confrontations regarding finances, other obligations, and issues of trust and loyalty in December 1988 and January 1989.

Other than advice on the likely course of the relationship and the timetable for all that (which was based on a number of timing methods as well as the proclivity of the natal chart), apparently one of the major contributions I made in this case was towards saving the client's physical health. She decided to follow my advice and give up her strenuous exercise routine from the time she saw me, around October 20th. Even so, and with an attitude of as much calmness and caution as she could muster, the accumulated stress came tumbling out. She had at least one near-accident driving her car, and in November she succumbed to a rare eye disease which caused as much as 40 percent loss of vision in both eyes. It was all very alarming, but finally the outcome showed gradual improvement in the eyes. When she had them examined at a special clinic in January 1989, the doctors noted that if she had not refrained from strenuous exercise during this period, she would have definitely had a stroke! This is surely one of the more dramatic client stories, and yet it is awesome to know that astrological information can be not only useful, but sometimes pivotal.

Playing Detective with the 90° Dial

On the opposite page is an example of a 90° dial, showing the planets, Personal Points, and Meridian house axes of Client X, whose story I have just been discussing and whose planetary particulars we have just seen on the 45° graphic ephemeris. The dial is turned to where the pointer is exactly on the ASC, marked A. When you look at the pointer, all the 4th, 8th and 16th harmonics

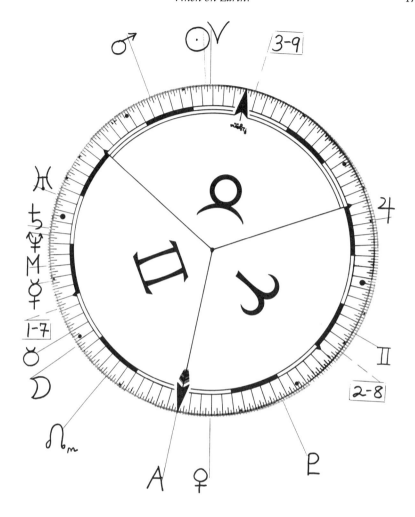

Client X (90° Dial)

are immediately apparent, either at one or the other end of the
pointer or at the dots halfway on either side of the pointer. The three
30° wedges represent the three modes or qualities: ♈ = Aries and all
the Cardinal signs; ♉ = Taurus and all the Fixed signs; ♊ = Gemini
and all the Mutable signs. To start, put the feathery end of the
pointer, or 0° Aries (♈), at 12 o'clock.

For general use, one big tip about the 90° dial is being able to
visualize it when it is not in front of you. Let us say you have your N.
Sun at 7° Libra and you are looking at the ephemeris wondering if

there are any hard contacts to your N. Sun (and later you will check other Personal Points). You imagine the 90° dial in front of you, with the pointer at 0° Aries (♈) at the top of the chart, or at 12 o'clock. (See the unmarked 90° dial shown in Appendix E, p. 271.) First you identify which mode you want, and at what degree. Then you *add* 15° if the planet or Personal Point in question is between 0° and 15° and *subtract* 15° if it is between 16° and 30°. Look across the dial to the mode opposite yours in the circle. In the case of 7° Libra, which is a Cardinal sign, we add 15° and see that 22° of the Fixed is opposite it on the 90° dial. This means that any planet or Personal Point at either 7° Cardinals or at 22° Fixed (and also 22-1/2° from either of these points for finer detail) is going to give descriptive information based on planetary patterns at the 4th, 8th, and 16th harmonics.

With the example on p. 179, we have ASC (A) at 12-1/2° Fixed opposite on the dial, or equal to 27-1/2° of the Mutables. So with T. Saturn conjunct T. Uranus at 27°48' Sagittarius on October 18, 1988, and T. Pluto within 1° orb of hard contact to T. Saturn/Uranus at 11°49' Scorpio that same day, this marks a period of extreme stress for Client X, whose marriage split became formalized on October 13th, just five days before the exact conjunction of Saturn and Uranus, and whose final move from the family home came in late October, close to the T. Mars SD° = N. Sun/Venus October 28th. Meanwhile, as we remember on the 45° graphic ephemeris for Client X, T. Saturn/Uranus/Pluto spent most of 1988 hovering very close to her N. ASC axis, placing long-term disruptive pressure on her relationships. Within 1° is very strong.

Normally I would put several other items around the 90° dial, though I am keeping this one simple for these introductory remarks. Among other things, I pencil in the locations of the secondary progressed planets and Personal Points. (In this case P. Uranus is 22-1/2° from the ASC, for example, and ASC/Uranus usually denotes a move, or a temporary disruption in relationships.) Also, we can see that the 3-9 Meridian house axis is within 1° of the ASC axis. The 3-9 axis is related to our speech, communications, and travel, and, because it is so closely associated with behavior and automatic responses, the 3-9 axis is also concerned with the nervous system, as is Mercury. I was concerned that Client X modify her habits in order to lessen the current assault on her nervous system. Fortunately, she followed my advice, though the trouble she ran into chiefly involved her optic nerves, and, because of the temporary loss in vision, she almost had some automobile accidents and had to stop driving for a while. All of this is well within range of T. Saturn/Uranus/Pluto playing havoc with the basic symbolism of not only the ASC, but the 3-9 axis.

Lastly, note her N. Venus (♀) just 3° from the ASC (A), and N. Sun 3-1/2° away at the other end of the axis, or pointer, equating Sun/Venus by hard contact. Every time T. Saturn and Uranus moved away from the ASC and towards Sun and Venus, as they did February-May and November-December 1988, she experienced the disturbing and chaotic energy of Saturn/Uranus on her physical body (Sun), her finances, and her love life (Venus), and on her basic sense of attractiveness and well-being (Sun/Venus).

The good news is that it is unlikely she will ever again have such a prolonged and difficult planetary combination on her relationship axes. There will be other challenges, of course, but T. Saturn will have moved on, and its tendency to block the changes and cause confusion when in close combination with Uranus and Pluto will be over for some years to come.

Time Clues: Examples of Personal Timetables

Movie stars are always wonderful examples for work like this, not because they necessarily represent the highest caliber of people to emulate, but because, more than anyone else, even politicians and television anchormen and women, their lives are played out before us both on the big screen and in the media. So we develop strong feelings about who they are and what they are about, even if we are all wrong. Neptune rules movie stars, filmmaking, and the making of idols. It also concerns something we all feel we can participate in, if not get lost in.

Accordingly, the next three examples of "Time Clues" come from the silver screen.

Time Clues: A Brief But Meteoric Rise to the Top (James Dean)

James Dean is an extraordinary example of a very rapid ascent to fame, all condensed within the last six months of his life (though he got some taste of it in the last nine months), followed by a sudden and dramatic death in a car crash. Perhaps even more remarkable is the extent to which fame followed him into death, especially in the case of his female fans, who called themselves "widows of James Dean" and came or wrote from all parts of the world after he died. Considering that only one of his three movies had been released by that time, it was an amazing outpouring for a movie star who, at age 24, had barely had time to absorb what this was all about.

Let us turn back the clock to January 1954, just 1-3/4 years before his death. Dean was a desperately poor and struggling actor living in New York City. He had just been cast in a play that was to open on Broadway, *The Immoralist* by André Gide (from Gide's 1902 novel about individuals who are seeking to find themselves in ways that might be at odds with the current ethical standards). The play opened February 8, 1954 (Dean's second-ever Broadway appearance). Though it was considered a flop, running for only 96 performances, Dean's stage presence sparked the interest of Warner Brothers, who were looking for a lead male to play in a film adaptation of John Steinbeck's novel, *East of Eden*. They invited Dean to do a screen test for the part, which he immediately won. He left the cast of *The Immoralist* after only a few weeks, breaking his contract, and went to Hollywood. There, he started work on *East of Eden* with director Elia Kazan and a group of highly talented actors, including Julie Harris, Raymond Massey, and Jo Van Fleet. The play was about two brothers and their rivalry for the love of their father. It was a perfect vehicle for Dean, in that he instinctively knew how to project a smoldering and passionate intensity that did not reflect conventional standards, and a charismatic and high-voltage persona that was simultaneously vulnerable, tortured, and struggling (for parental love, in this case). *East of Eden* was to be his finest movie, though his next movie, *Rebel Without a Cause*, had many similar themes, such as youthful alienation, issues around manhood and what a man should be, and not accepting strictly conventional notions, all played against a backdrop of another father-son relationship.

East of Eden was released on April 9, 1955, and caused a tremendous stir of interest in James Dean—although he was beginning to receive the Hollywood "big star" treatment for several months prior to that.[95] From abject poverty only 14 months earlier, he was now able to buy fancy sports cars, which he loved to drive very fast. He quickly became a serious race-car driver in addition

---

95. Film release dates are from *The International Motion Picture Almanac*, 1985 edition.

to his new role as Hollywood movie star. Many of his fellow actors were unabashedly terrified to ride with him at such high speeds.

In September 1955, Dean had only a few days of shooting left on the set of *Giant*, with Elizabeth Taylor and Rock Hudson, when he made a special request to participate in a road race. At that time, there were some sudden, odd twists and turns in his behavior, such as his going off to spend time in a monastery and saying "good-bye" to many of his friends. His reasoning was that, because he was racing, anything could happen—and indeed it did. But it was *on his way* to the road race that his sports car went careening around a curve and hit another car head on. It was September 30, 1955. James Dean was killed instantly, and a large cult very like necrophilia instantly began.

Not only did the death of James Dean haunt and distress his many fans, but the symbol of what he represented, especially through his roles in his first two films, continued to affect generations of teenagers and young people long after his death. *Rebel Without a Cause* was released 29 days after the tragic accident, on October 29, 1955, and *Giant* followed in 1956. Twenty-three years later, in 1978, the movie *September 30, 1955* was released, once again exploring the James Dean legend, his death, and its drastic effects on many young people. To this day, libraries and bookstores are prone to have all their James Dean material disappear, either through purchase or theft by young people fervently keeping his image and character alive. James Dean would no doubt relish that fact, as he was constantly seeking to make himself more interesting. If he was terrified of anything, it was of being boring. He made an intense study of being interesting, offstage and on, and at that he eminently succeeded.

Now to the astrological sleuthing. When you look at Dean's natal chart (shown on the next page), you will notice that he has all the telltale success signatures we have grown accustomed to seeing in Chapter 3: Jupiter/Pluto (♃ / ♇) at the MC and Uranus (♅) on the 7th house cusp (or equatorial Descendant in this house system), otherwise expressible as Jupiter/Pluto/Uranus angular and Jupiter/Uranus in paran (angular simultaneously), which is an extremely potent combination for good fortune. Notice also, however, that, at the IC, Venus (♀) and Saturn (♄) are also both angular. In fact, the Venus/Saturn midpoint = MC/IC axis, indicating that there is not only great seriousness about his art, but

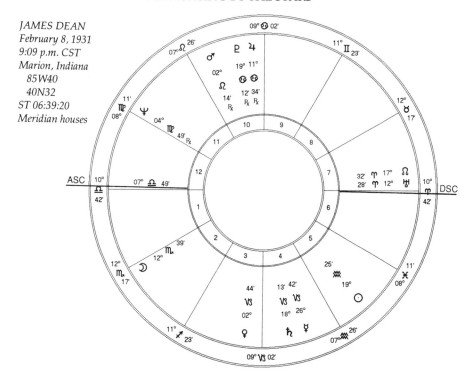

Natal Horoscope for James Dean

also the possibility of great disappointment and delay in love matters. Given the abundant good fortune of having Venus/Jupiter/Pluto/Uranus angular, it is somewhat counteractive to have Saturn also angular. It is as if all systems say "go" except one.

Amplifying the Venus/Saturn combination on the MC axis is also Moon/Neptune (whose midpoint at 8° Libra 44' is within 17' of an exact square to the MC, and thus in hard contact or equal to it.)[96] Moon/Neptune, as we have seen many times, has to do with idealizing (Neptune) women (Moon) or the public (Moon), and sometimes this calls for a great sacrifice (Neptune). In any case, Neptune magnifies the relationship with the public tremendously when on the career or public-image axis (the MC), especially for a movie actor. Add to this the natal Moon and Venus each 2-3° from the Cardinal axis, and you have someone whose perception of the world is almost totally mirrored through his art (Venus) and his emotions (Moon) and, in this case, his public's perception of him

---

96. It is much easier to spot the 45° multiples (or hard contacts) immediately on a 360° or 90° dial, but I present the usual chart format here because more people are used to looking at it.

(Moon) and vice-versa.

Natally, there are several other things to note in passing before we examine what was happening with regard to timing. First, the Moon (☽) is almost exactly on the 2-8 house axis, indicating that his fortunes financially (2nd house) and after death (8th house) would be largely dependent on the public (Moon), especially his female public (both Moon). Another planet exactly on a house axis is Mercury (☿), at 45° from the 3-9 house axis. This will show up in the timing for the critical period in 1955. Mercury relates to communications and travel, and has a natural affinity with matters related to the 3rd house and thus also its polar opposite, the 9th house. Such a combination emphasizes this area of Dean's life, which includes his preoccupation with race-car driving.

Lastly, we notice that Dean has no natal planets in the Mutable mode except Neptune (which is not much help in this instance), and this means that he would lack the basic capacity to adapt, to be flexible, and to adjust to new circumstances in his life, of which he suddenly had plenty in 1955. In combination with this is a chart with a great deal of Cardinality (MC, ASC, Moon's Node, Jupiter, Pluto, Venus, Saturn, Mercury, and Uranus), showing an immense desire for movement and action, but with some confusion and possibly overidealism (N. Mars/Neptune midpoint = N. Sun) about where he is going, and going so fast.

Now let us move to the quarti-lunar secondary progressed Moon chart (i.e. the chart marking this quarter of the 29-1/2 year secondary progressed Moon cycle; see next page). It is a Full Moon chart, a chart designating a time period that is classically concerned with achievement and fulfillment of goals, and it begins for him on June 2, 1954. One can start feeling the effects of the new quarter as much as a few months in advance, and, by the end of February, 1954, Dean was screen-testing for Warner Brothers and moving into a whole new life out in Hollywood. He had virtually leapt out of his former poverty-stricken circumstances and into the mouth of fame and fortune. For such sudden galvanic action in life, one would expect to see a galvanic-looking quarterly chart—and we have it! Every single planet or Personal Point in the chart is in hard contact to another. This is manifestation par excellence, but it is not without its warning signals. The planet Mars, both N. (natal) and P. (progressed) is highlighted at least three times:

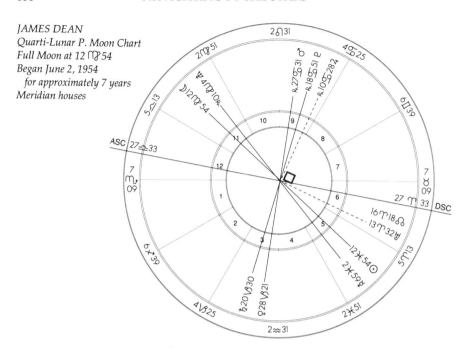

JAMES DEAN
Quarti-Lunar P. Moon Chart
Full Moon at 12 ♍ 54
Began June 2, 1954
  for approximately 7 years
Meridian houses

Quarti-Lunar Secondary Progressed Moon Chart for James Dean

1) P. MC = N. Mars

2) P. Mars = P.Q.L. ASC/Mars/Venus/Sun/Moon[97]

3) P. Mars = P. Mars SD° (due in Nov. 1957)

When you add all this Mars emphasis to an already heavily Cardinal chart (six planets and two Personal Points still in Cardinal signs), and you add in all the 3-9 house activity (including potentially dangerous Mars/Pluto/Jupiter/Saturn there, with Jupiter mostly drowned out), as well as Mercury (denoting communications and travel) on the 5th house cusp opposite Neptune (a desire to magnify [Neptune] one's sense of movement, travel, communications [Mercury] in a dramatic and sensually enjoyable way [5th house]), you have a potentially explosive situation that is ripe to happen any time within the designated 7-year period beginning June 2, 1954. But it is most ripe to happen when the transits and solar arc directions give us the signals. We

---

97. P.Q.L. = Secondary progressed quarti-lunar chart. We watch transits and progressions to this chart for as long as it is in effect, in this case 7 years.

will deal here mainly with the transits.

You can imagine that a person with such a chart who takes up race-car driving had better have razor-sharp nerves and senses. And unfortunately, P. Mercury opposite P. Neptune, though dazzling enough in the movie business, has no place on the race course or even on the highway, where Dean was eventually killed. This is because Neptune not only magnifies one's sense of oneself and one's abilities, but it easily distorts and blurs our ability to see clearly, to act quickly; and Mercury, as luck would have it, rules over the nervous system of the body. We are ready to look now at what was happening with the transiting planets from April through September 1955. *East of Eden* was released April 9, 1955, just as Dean was experiencing the following transits:

1) T. Jupiter = N. Pluto (Feb. 1-April 15)

2) T. Saturn = N. Sun (April 1-May 2)

3) T. Neptune = P.Q.L. ASC/Mars/Venus/Sun/Moon (Nov. 9, 1954-April 30, 1955)

4) T. Pluto = N. MC (March 9-July 3)[98]

Let us make a sentence out of that. Dean would feel the weight of new responsibility and status (Sun/Saturn), which might seem burdensome (Saturn), but he could always escape into drinking, drug experimentation, and fast driving (Mars/Neptune) as well as boozy times romancing women (Neptune/ASC,Venus/Mars/Sun/Moon), though probably not getting too far with them sexually (Venus/Mars/Neptune). He did all of this rather than face the reality that his movie career (Neptune/Mars) was fast transforming itself (MC/Pluto) into something spectacularly fortunate (Jupiter/Pluto) and beyond his wildest dreams (Sun/Mars/Neptune/Jupiter/Pluto).

As the summer approached, he began to experience T. Neptune = N. Mercury/N. 3-9 house axis (June 6-Oct. 15), with a potent T. Neptune SD° = N. Mercury/N. 3-9 house axis on July 7th. Neptune in combination with Mercury can be wonderful for intuitive or spiritual thinking, but, as noted above, it is very dangerous if you habitually drive and move fast (N. Mercury = 3-9, plus stepped-up P. Mars activity and heightened Cardinality). Thus all the drama,

---

98. All the dates given apply to aspects which are within 1° applying and 1° separating.

excitement, and latent danger in his life was reaching a crescendo through natal, progressed, and transiting planets. As of September 1955, here are some transits which either came back into the picture or entered for the first time. The new transits are marked with asterisks:

*1) T. Mercury = P.Q.L. ASC/Mars/Venus/Sun/Moon (Sept. 25-Oct. 7)

*2) T. Mercury SR° = P.Q.L. ASC/Mars/Venus/Sun/Moon (Sept. 30, 6:14 p.m. PST)

*3) T. Jupiter = N. Sun (Sept. 7-17)

4) T. Saturn = N. Sun (Sept. 30-Oct. 19)

*5) T. Uranus = N. Mars (Sept. 19-Dec. 29)

6) T. Neptune = P.Q.L. ASC/Mars/Venus/Sun/Moon (Sept. 11-Nov. 6)

7) T. Neptune = N. Mercury/N. 3-9 (June 6-Oct. 15)

8) T. Pluto = N. Jupiter (July 22-Sept. 25)

Dean's fatal accident took place around dusk on September 30th, within an hour or so of the exact Mercury Stationary Retrograde (which can be precarious for travel, as is described in Appendix A, Section 2).[99] The very fact of the Mercury SR° on *that* day at *that* hour is significant in itself, added to which it is linked up to Dean's secondary progressed quarti-lunar chart by five planetary and Personal Point factors.

Sun/Jupiter gives one a tremendous sense of optimism and expansion, and this is still within a 3° orb on September 30th. It is usually experienced as fortunate, but not always, as we see here. With so many other astrological factors piled up, the expansionary nature of Jupiter is no longer a blessing but rather tends to make one overextend oneself. As for T. Uranus = N. Mars, this is one of the typical accident-prone combinations, as the electrical excitement of Uranus sparks Mars to outdo itself in some form of physical or machine-related activity.

Notice that T. Saturn comes into 1° orb of hard contact (in this

---

99. See also Appendix A, Section 4, regarding Moon Void of Course, its description and specific relevance to James Dean on September 30, 1955.

case, a square) exactly on the day of the accident (Sept. 30). When the outer planets come within 1° of exact hard contact, you start to feel their effects, especially when they are applying (approaching) or on their way into the exact contact.[100] (In this case, T. Saturn is applying, or strongest, up to October 9, but it begins September 30.) The result is such that, with all the latent conditions already in place, T. Saturn imposes a rather depressive effect on all the heady Sun/Jupiter/Mars/Uranus/Neptune/Pluto activity. You could argue that a Saturn transit to his N. Sun might make him more cautious and conservative, and in some cases it might. But here we have overwhelming evidence from his natal, progressed, and transiting planets (and natal and progressed Personal Points) that he is in no mood now to exert caution. In fact, he has made it his life's habit to be uncautious. This is another reason why T. Saturn's strong effects on this 24-year old would be the final trigger setting off all the explosive and dramatic accident-proneness just waiting to happen.

In astrology, it is well understood that a pivotal cultural or political event reverberates into history on many levels. One reverberation is into the lives and destinies of those born within 1 to 1-1/2 years either side of the event. In this case, those born within a stone's throw of September 30, 1955 carry with them some of James Dean's legacy. This is symbolized largely by the outer-planet transits: first the T. Jupiter/Uranus conjunction, occurring twice, on January 6 and May 10, 1955, and secondly the T. Uranus square T. Neptune on June 11, 1955.[101] Jupiter/Uranus is basically a propitious combination, but, like anything fortunate, one can have too much of a good thing. It can get excessive when Neptune enters the picture, as it does when T. Uranus squares T. Neptune. Jupiter expands one's sense of opportunity, the sense that the sky is the limit; Uranus electrifies and excites this concept; and Neptune is capable of magnifying all of the above completely out of proportion.[102]

---

100. This applies also to T. Mercury, Venus, and Mars when they are about to move SR or SD, as in the above case with Mercury.

101. Both Jupiter/Uranus conjunctions occurred in Dean's 10th house of career and social position, adding to the numerous auspicious factors in this arena of his life.

102. Uranus/Neptune can also signify going unconscious, the symbolism stemming from the idea that the sheer excitement of Uranus cancels out the calm oblivion of Neptune, like mixing too many uppers and downers and disappearing into the void. Here is how Witte-Lefeldt describe Uranus + Neptune: "Suddenly incapacitated. Unconsciousness. Checkmated. The transition into the beyond. Crisis. Dead persons. Revolution." *(Rules for Planetary Pictures,* 5th edition, 1959, p. 239.)

This is one of the reasons why James Dean could so ignite and incite the imaginations of young people, even to this day, because of the planetary backdrop against which he briefly flourished and died. It is also one of the reasons why many of those born during this time period developed tremendous difficulty in seeing life optimistically (Jupiter/Uranus) without the use of drugs or alcohol (Neptune). We have many dramatic examples of this, but I will describe just a few. (Obviously this is not the only drug-prone era, but it has a particular ferocity to it.)

Karen Ann Quinlan was born March 29, 1954, with the N. Uranus/Neptune square within 6° orb. She went into a coma on April 15, 1975 (at age 21), after drinking a gin and tonic and taking tranquilizers, and there were also mysterious bruises on her body. Her case is extraordinary in that she was kept alive for years on a mechanical respirator. Even after her parents won a landmark case to get the equipment removed, still she slept on, weighing only 70 pounds by April 1979. She finally died of pneumonia in a nursing home in Morris Plains, New Jersey. It was June 11, 1985. She was 31 years old and had been in a coma for ten years.[103]

Prince Ludwig Rudolph of Hanover, a direct descendant of Kaiser Wilhelm II, was born November 28, 1955, with N. Uranus not only square N. Neptune (3° orb), but also square N. Mars (also 3° orb). N. Mars/Neptune (at an exact conjunction) is already a drug or alcohol-prone combination. When Uranus is added, the excitable factor appears. In this case, the natal chart already shows Sun/ Mercury/Jupiter enhancing an ebullience and sense of jollity that would know no bounds.[104] When Prince Ludwig Rudolph married former fashion model Countess Isabelle von Thurn-Valsassina (age 25) in the fall of 1987, the handsome couple celebrated their wedding with a lavish five-day rock-and-roll fete at

---

103. *Facts on File*, June 14, 1985, p. 456.

104. When Sun/Neptune or Mars/Neptune are in hard contact in the natal chart of a young person who either is known to have drug or alcohol addictions or is known to have parents with a chemical dependency of any sort, it is a clear warning that this individual must steer clear of these forms of Neptune. They should instead pursue other levels of the symbol, such as dance, music, film, photography, and spirituality. Once they are clear of the chemical dependency, the affinity to and talent for one of these other areas will start to become more apparent.

Even if one is not manifesting the drug or alcohol addiction oneself, it is easy to attract it in a mate. This would apply to a man with Moon/Neptune or Venus/Neptune in hard contact and to a woman with Sun/Neptune or Mars/Neptune in hard contact. (We see this in the case of Elizabeth Taylor, although she herself also manifested the addictions as well as attracting mates who manifested them.)

the bride's family castle in southern Austria. (The Prince loved rock music [Neptune] and had plans to be a rock-music producer.) Also lavishly on hand were drugs (Neptune), which each of them had come to depend on for some years but had never yet been caught with, as their aristocratic standing largely shielded them from police investigations.

Then, 13 months later, after the birth of their first child eight months earlier, they celebrated the Prince's 33rd birthday in the usual hedonistic fashion. But this time the fun went too far. The Princess overdosed on cocaine and died of heart and lung edema. (The police found some cocaine, heroine, and syringes on her night table.) Prince Ludwig Rudolph, having tried in vain to revive his young wife, disappeared, totally distraught, and phoned his brother in London telling him of Isabelle's death and of his suicide plans and asking him to look after his baby son. He then drove his sports car to a secluded spot sometime before dawn and shot himself in the mouth.[105]

David Anthony Kennedy is the last example we will discuss of this potentially gruesome planetary heritage. He was the fourth child and third son of Robert and Ethel Kennedy. Like Prince Ludwig Rudolph, he was born into a family of wealth, power, and privilege, and on June 13, 1955, only two days after the exact T. Uranus/ Neptune square, with T. Jupiter within 4°. Also notable is his N. Saturn within 30' of the Cardinal axis, giving him a potential for a conservative, serious, and even depressed outlook on life. (Christina Onassis had her N. Saturn within 1-1/2° of the Cardinal axis, and it manifested very often as depression.)

On June 5, 1968, eight days before his 13th birthday, David Kennedy's father Robert was assassinated in Los Angeles, shortly after declaring his victory in the California presidential primary. Like everyone else, David watched in horror as the story unfolded on the television news, only this time it was his beloved father and he had been the favorite son. By all accounts, he never truly recovered from his father's death and what he represented, which in astrological terms was symbolized by the brilliant dream of Uranus/Neptune/Jupiter. No longer was that shining radiance anywhere to be found in his life, and so he sought to find it in drugs. Whenever he wasn't escaping through drugs, he was faced with the

---

105. *People*, January 9, 1989, pp. 51-52.

hard reality of a bitter blow early in life. Eventually, even with periodic professional help and drug rehabilitation programs, David was unable to overcome his desire to escape. He died of a drug overdose on April 25, 1984 (at age 28), just 30 days after his first Saturn return, a time of reckoning—which can be a cruel one. A hotel employee found him lying dead on the floor of a $250-a-day suite in a Palm Beach hotel.

In a kind of ricochet effect, David Kennedy's life and death, as well as that of Karen Ann Quinlan, Prince Ludwig Rudolph, and many others, all reflect the luminous dreams and the high hopes that were destroyed in an instant, just as with James Dean's sudden and meteoric rise and fall. No one could quite believe how much he captured the imagination of his youthful following. The words of a newspaper journalist musing on the death of David Kennedy really apply to all of them, as he compared the young Kennedy to the character of Quentin Compson in William Faulkner's 1929 novel, *The Sound and the Fury.* Like David Kennedy, Quentin Compson was another "Harvard innocent... [who] wandered about Cambridge under his own burden of fragile and impossible idealism, his own sense of irretrievable loss."[106]

Time Clues: A Consistent, Steady, and Brilliant Rise to the Top (Meryl Streep)

After such dark and brooding themes it is a pleasure to reflect on the life, character, and career of actress Meryl Streep. She is an anomaly in a business which often produces many lives out of balance. Hers would seem to be a life perfectly in balance, her personal and professional reputation crystal clear, and her performances on stage and screen each more demanding and thoughtful than the one before. Even her closest colleagues and associates are impressed or even stunned by the magnitude of her talent, the total professionalism in her conduct, and the incandescent spirit radiating from her character.

How might all this be described astrologically? First, let us look at her natal chart, since one cannot depend on timing alone to bring great results. Greatness has to be already a potential in the natal chart, as well as the propensity to reach a large number of people.

---

106. *Newsweek,* May 7, 1984, p. 52.

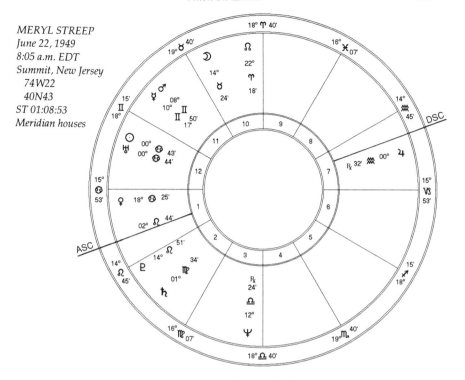

Natal Horoscope for Meryl Streep

At first glance, the natal chart has most of the planets and Personal Points in the eastern hemisphere (the left side of the horoscope), the hemisphere most associated with action and taking the initiative. Jupiter (♃) has prominence in the western hemisphere, the more receptive hemisphere, by being alone there and by being angular, conjunct the Descendant. Venus (♀) is also angular conjunct the equatorial ASC (meridian 1st house cusp), as are the Moon's Node (☊) and Neptune (♆) near the MC/IC axis. This already tells us that there is beauty and charm (Venus), good fortune (Jupiter), prominent career connections (Moon's Node in the 10th house near MC), and some type of Neptunian activity. (In her case, she had classical training for her singing voice [Neptune = music] from ages 12 to 16, and began making television and feature movies in 1977 [Neptune = movies], from age 27-1/2, after theatrical training and experience from 1968, at age 19.) But it is when we start examining the number of her Personal Points to be found on the Cardinal axis (all but the ASC and MC) that we begin to see how extraordinarily forceful Meryl Streep's character and destiny really are. Implied in that is an intimate link-up with the rest of the world, which is what the Cardinal axis is all about symbolically. (As a reminder, its astronomical derivation is described in Chapter 2 under "The Six Personal Points.")

The Cardinal axis here contains Sun/Uranus/Pluto/Moon/ Moon's Node/2-8 axis. (Note also the exact conjunction of Sun/Uranus.) This is an unusually large number of astrological factors, including Personal Points, on the Cardinal axis. It means that the sheer force of her personality and her appearance (Sun), the originality and uniqueness of her presence and her abilities (Uranus), the insistent and at times obsessive drive to transform herself into her many characters (Pluto), heightens her femininity (Moon) and makes all of the above accessible to, and therefore popular with, a large public (Moon), who feel as if they know her personally (Moon's Node). The 2-8 axis on the Cardinals signifies making money and establishing values (2nd house) in a way that ends up being shared by everyone (8th house).[107] Such an active Cardinal axis is like a very active electrical circuit, and it enables her to be highly attuned to a great deal of what goes on in the world in an intimate sort of way. (In her case, it comes alive in the multitude of characters she creates as an actress.) Similarly, the world can tune into *her* with great ease, except for her innermost life, symbolized by the MC, which is not on the Cardinal axis.

Streep also has a rather phenomenal capacity to master accents. Although there are many examples, one of the most awesome to date is her Polish accent in *Sophie's Choice*, which called for her to fracture the English language rather constantly, as her character was just getting a grip on speaking it, or trying to. For such a skill, we would expect to see a well-fortified Mercury and/or 3-9 house axis. Not surprisingly, she has both. The 3-9 axis contains Jupiter, Moon/Venus midpoint, the Ascendant, and 6-12 house axis. Moon and Venus are located in each other's zodiacal areas, called a mutual reception, and it makes this very feminine combination even more beguiling, especially when amplified by the expansionary and

---

107. This is not an easy combination of qualities to have as a child interacting with other children. It evokes an intensity and authority that would seem mostly overbearing to one's peers. And, sure enough, Streep tells of unhappy times in her childhood when she felt unliked and ostracized for being too much of a "mini-adult." She says, "I had the same face I have today and ... the effect wasn't cute or endearing." (*Current Biography*, 1980, p. 388.)

exuberant energy of Jupiter. (For all the variety in her roles, Streep always manages to project an essence of femininity which is unique and never cloying, and also never overbearing, even in her more unsympathetic roles such as in *Cry in the Dark*, 1988.) All of this is then hooked up to the public through the Ascendant axis and through the discipline of the work itself (6-12 house axis), as this is how Streep makes her living. Mercury has great strength through being not only conjunct Mars (forceful speaking) but by being located in Gemini, over which Mercury naturally rules. With Mercury/Mars in an Air sign, she is assured of a fluency in her speech. However, as it is widely square Saturn, she disciplines that fluency so that it does not dissipate into endless talk or heated argument. Mercury is also on the career/vocational ASC/MC midpoint axis (22' orb), assuring that her speaking and communications abilities would be central to her career. With Venus and Saturn both on the career/public-image MC axis, those communications would be through some sort of art form (Venus) and charmingly presented (also Venus), though also finely honed and crafted (Saturn) with seriousness of purpose (also Saturn).

These are the major astrological factors in the natal chart (and there are more corroborating ones) indicating that Streep has the potential, and did have from birth, to become a great artist in some form of verbally communicative art such as film and/or theater. Let us take a look now at four of her quarti-lunar secondary progressed Moon charts. Together they cover a span of 29-1/2 years, from April 1967 to October 1996, and take her from 18 to 47 years of age.

The first one begins April 6, 1967, and, because it is a Full Moon chart, shows the likelihood of Streep's talents coming to the fore at this time (i.e. some time during the 7-year time period of this chart), and getting some serious recognition, probably for the first time. Notice that Ascendant/Pluto/Mercury have progressed to the Cardinal axis—Ascendant/Mercury being new additions. She would now develop and transform (Pluto) her speaking and communicative abilities (Mercury) and convey that to an audience at a grassroots level (ASC), potentially a very large one (Aries/ASC). Uranus is still within 2° of the Cardinal axis, so her uniqueness will be apparent in all of the above.

Another crucial factor in looking at this period is that Sun/Moon = Saturn (within 30' orb), which means that she can be serious now (Saturn), probably work hard (Saturn), and have to pay her dues

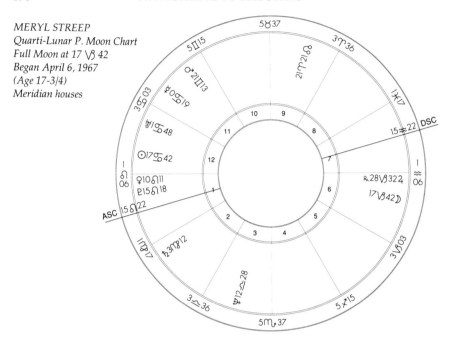

MERYL STREEP
Quarti-Lunar P. Moon Chart
Full Moon at 17 ♑ 42
Began April 6, 1967
(Age 17-3/4)
Meridian houses

Meryl Streep—Quarti-Lunar Secondary Progressed Moon Chart
April 6, 1987 to March 13, 1975

(Saturn), perhaps causing delays (also Saturn). Lastly, with this combination, any truly successful love relationship (Sun/ Moon) is likely to be denied to her (Saturn) during these 7 years. This has nothing to do with her basic attractiveness, or her deservedness; it has to do with Saturn's influence in a cyclical way, causing seriousness of purpose to be more predominant than love relation-ships, and thus largely accounting for delays in this area of her life, among others.

Streep graduated from high school in June 1967, soon after this chart begins, and set off for Vassar College in the fall of 1967. (Pluto/ Ascendant often denotes a geographical move.) During a drama class her sophomore year at Vassar, her acting talent became apparent to her instructor, who immediately cast her in several plays. One of them, *The Playboy of Seville* by Tirso de Molino, was done off-Broadway during a Vassar vacation and was to be her New York City debut. Graduating from Vassar in June 1971, Streep carried on with her theater work in a summer stock company, which continued through the fall and winter of 1971. It was hard work for small pay and small audiences, but she was playing in classics such

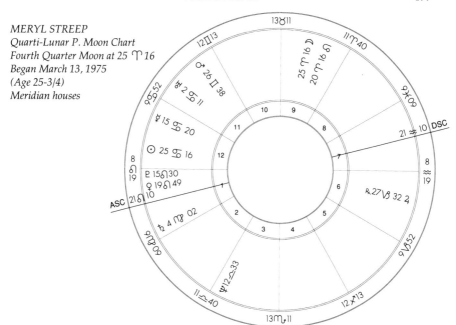

MERYL STREEP
Quarti-Lunar P. Moon Chart
Fourth Quarter Moon at 25 ♈ 16
Began March 13, 1975
(Age 25-3/4)
Meridian houses

*Meryl Streep—Quarti-Lunar Secondary Progressed Moon Chart
March 13, 1975 to October 8, 1982*

as those by Anton Chekhov and George Bernard Shaw and she was learning that, despite its apparent "absurdity" as a way of life, she loved acting and theater more than anything else. She decided to apply to the prestigious Yale Drama School in order to have "an edge" as a successful actress.[108] She was granted a three-year scholarship, and supplemented that with earnings as a waitress and typist. The rest of the time she was in constant demand, and played more than 40 different roles covering immensely different age ranges, cultures, social periods, and acting styles. She worked hard (Saturn), and by all accounts there were no serious romances during this period.

The next chart begins March 13, 1975, just a few months before she graduated from Yale Drama School. This chart is notable for having a Sun/Moon/Jupiter pattern (within 2° and applying, or moving towards the fortunate Jupiter).[109] Saturn has now moved off

---

108. *Current Biography,* 1980, p. 389.
109. This is one of the exceptions to the typical Fourth Quarter Moon chart, which generally shows a reorientation of plans and efforts, and a releasing and waning of energy by the last 1-2 years of the quarter.

the relationship and physical-energy axis, and Jupiter's energy, along with Venus/Ascendant, indicates the strong likelihood of success not only professionally but in personal relationships. Pluto hovers near both ASC and equatorial ASC, but not as close as before, so its obsessiveness and tendency to act alone (Pluto/ASC) move more into the background. In combination with the promise of her natal chart, the astrological picture cyclically is now ripe for some major successes as well as personal happiness in love.

She did some experimental theater in Connecticut the summer after Yale Drama School before moving in August 1975 to New York City (Manhattan). Within days of her arrival, Streep auditioned for Joseph Papp's production of Pinero's *Trelawney of the Wells,* a Victorian period piece due to open October 15th at the Vivian Beaumont Theater in New York City. She got the part and was well received. She continued to be in as much demand in New York theater as she had been at Yale, only now she had the wider public recognition and media attention of New York. By the summer of 1976, she had met John Cazale, another actor, with whom she was to have her first serious romantic connection. Meanwhile, Streep's reputation was gathering momentum, and by early 1977 she was moving into television and feature films. March 1977 marked her television debut in the CBS dramatic special, *The Deadliest Season.*

Now we pause for a moment to zero in on a 12-month period within this 7-year time frame, that of October 1977 through September 1978. It was one of the most intense years in the 7-year period, if not in her life. One could say that it is not quite the Sun/Moon/Jupiter rosy romantic picture that was promised in the 7-year chart, but in an unusual way it was, and this was also the year Streep experienced her first Saturn return, one of life's most critical turning points.

By late October 1977, T. Pluto was crossing her N. 1-7 axis (that of intimate relationships), showing that some new development was changing the relationship picture—in this case, with Cazale. N. Saturn is also within 1° orb of the N. 1-7 axis, and so one might deduce that either a difficult development (Saturn/Pluto), or a difficult separation (also Saturn/Pluto) was in the works. It turned out to be the latter. John Cazale was dying of cancer.

As Streep's first Saturn return was moving into full force (within

1-1/2° orb) November 19-January 3, and stationing there December 11th, she made the decision to put all her professional commitments on hold in order to be with Cazale during his last months. T. and N. Saturn in the 2nd house of values revealed itself to be beyond the sheer business of financial income, which is another 2nd house consideration. Meanwhile, several major outer-planet transits were coming to Personal Points, either by secondary progression or by transit, and stationing there, adding to their power and significance as markers of pivotal life events.

With T. Neptune = N. ASC/6-12 axis January 15-May 27, this added to her sense of obligation and willing self-sacrifice (Neptune) and could have also brought some confusion (Neptune) as to what was happening with her work life (6-12). T. Neptune was applying, or strongest up to March 20, when it made its station. Also T. Uranus came to the Cardinal axis within 1-1/2° orb December 1, 1977-June 3, 1978, applying or strongest to April 27 and making its station February 19. This means that the electrical and potentially shocking effect of T. Uranus was activating almost every part of her life and her being, what with her Sun/Moon/Uranus/Pluto/Moon's Node/2-8 all on the Cardinal axis.

John Cazale died in March 1978, his passing out of Streep's life signalled by this large host of astrological markers, including a solar eclipse on April 7 conjunct her MC. Her first Saturn return came again and for the last time to its point of exactness (within 1° applying and separating) July 27-August 16, and yet another passage of T. Uranus back over the Cardinal axis and her Sun/Moon/Uranus/Pluto/Moon's Node/2-8 axis from September 13-November 6, as well as a last passage of T. Pluto over N. 1-7/Saturn, showing a last separation of sorts. Streep was to share her mourning for John Cazale with a new friend, sculptor Donald Gummer. That friendship soon blossomed into love, and they married in September 1978, shortly after she had closed in New York Shakespeare Festival performances as Katherine in *The Taming of the Shrew*.

In September 1978, Streep also received an Emmy award as the outstanding lead actress in a limited series from the Academy of Television Arts and Sciences. She had played in a 9-1/2-hour miniseries aired in early 1978, *Holocaust*, about Nazi Germany's

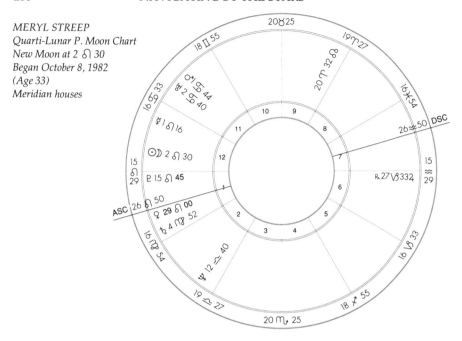

MERYL STREEP
Quarti-Lunar P. Moon Chart
New Moon at 2 ♌ 30
Began October 8, 1982
(Age 33)
Meridian houses

Meryl Streep—Quarti-Lunar Secondary Progressed Moon Chart
October 8, 1982 to June 28, 1989

persecution of the Jews. The long months of production in 1977 had kept her from John Cazale's side, and now he was gone. Even their last work together in the movie *The Deer Hunter* was soon to be released on December 14, 1978.[110] It was the end of a poignant and extremely important period for her, heralded by the beginning of her new life with husband Donald Gummer. (Uranus/Pluto does speak of sudden beginnings and endings, sudden deaths and rebirths.)

Meryl Streep is an example of one of the exceptions to the usual unfolding of events of a fourth quarter Moon chart (hers ending October 8, 1982), except that there was an increasing reorientation from theater to film work, especially as of 1979, four years into the 7-year period. Because of the strong role Jupiter plays, both in that chart and in the New Moon chart beginning October 1982, there is an expansionary quality—although classically a waning Moon tends to cause decreasing energy, especially in the last year or two of the cycle. But in her case, she continued to play more roles in more

110. All movie release dates are from *The International Motion Picture Almanac*, 1985 edition.

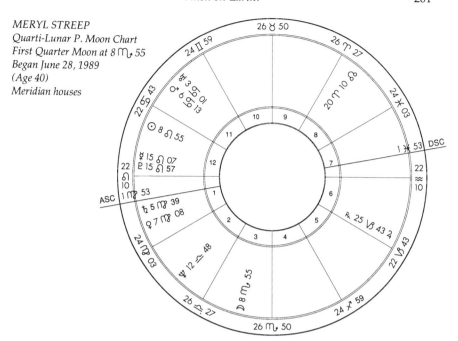

MERYL STREEP
Quarti-Lunar P. Moon Chart
First Quarter Moon at 8 ♏ 55
Began June 28, 1989
(Age 40)
Meridian houses

Meryl Streep—Quarti-Lunar Secondary Progressed Moon Chart
June 28, 1989 to October 5, 1996

fine films, including Woody Allen's *Manhattan* (1979), *Kramer vs. Kramer* (1979), and *French Lieutenant's Woman* (1980). She received numerous awards and kudos for these performances, among them an Oscar in 1980 as best supporting actress in *Kramer vs. Kramer*. During this period she also had her first of three children. The promise of Sun/Moon/Jupiter and Venus/ASC from March 1982 was certainly coming to pass, with fruitfulness and success in every area of her life.

The continuation of this theme is marked in the New Moon quarter chart starting October 8, 1982, and enduring to June 1989 (not because of P. Jupiter now but because of the implied presence of natal Jupiter on the P. Sun/Moon [1°52′ orb] and the sustained presence of P. Venus angular and conjunct P. ASC). Notice how angular P. Pluto (on the equatorial ASC) continues to lend that quality of depth, obsession, and persistence. For all her increasing wealth and professional stature, Streep has continued to place new demands on her talent, stretching herself beyond previous limits.

With P. Mars/Pluto on the Cardinal axis (a potentially violent combination), it is interesting too how she moved into more and more roles that involved either emotional, physical, or political violence. The first was *Sophie's Choice,* which was released December 10, 1982, just two months after this chart begins, and for which she won her first Oscar as best actress in the spring of 1983. Other roles echoing Mars/Pluto are those she played in *Silkwood* (1983), *Plenty* (1985), *Heartburn* (1986), *Ironweed* (1987), and *Cry in the Dark* (1988).

Meryl Streep's next chart begins June 28, 1989, shortly after her 40th birthday, and runs to October 5, 1996 (see previous page). It is not as easy or effortless a chart as the previous two, mainly due to the presence of Saturn angular and close to a P. ASC which is moving towards Saturn for the next 5-6 years. In fact, with Venus/Saturn both near the ASC, it hints of new responsibilities (Saturn) or perhaps an element of sadness (also Saturn) in either her art (Venus) or her love life and family life (Venus/ASC), or both. Yet in the past, Streep has always seemed to handle Saturn's energy well. In any case, there is certainly a rare nobility, depth, and breadth to her character, which one comes to expect from a person with such a chart and destiny whatever the cyclical patterns may bring.

Time Clues: A Stormy Celebrity Relationship
(Madonna and Sean Penn)

Celebrities have the mixed blessing of often living out their private lives in public. Some of them try to avoid that situation altogether, and sometimes they succeed. When stage and screen actor Sean Penn and rock star and budding movie actress Madonna announced they would marry in August 1985, it was done as secretively as possible. The press did not hear of it until a day or two before. Even so, they gathered their forces quickly to the appointed place by the sea in Malibu, California on August 16, 1985, and the noise from the helicopters hovering overhead, waiting for some tasty aerial shots, was positively deafening.

The invitations said 6:00 p.m. (Pacific Daylight Time). Sean and Madonna first appeared at 6:30 p.m. and were reported to exchange

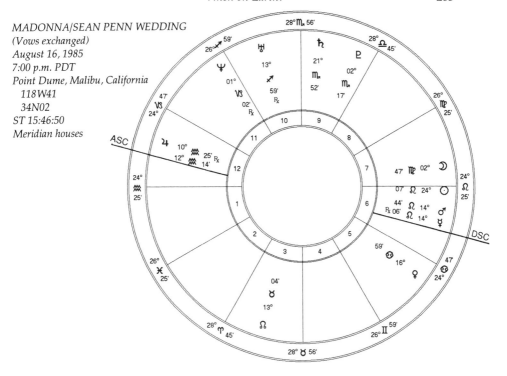

Madonna/Sean Penn Wedding

their vows at 7:00 p.m.[111] (This time is probably correct, within 0 to 30 minutes of accuracy.) The date chosen for the wedding was Madonna's 27th birthday, and the following day was Sean Penn's 25th birthday. It is not totally unheard of for a couple to share each other's birthday, either exactly or within 24 hours of it. But one might start to feel uneasy when considering the thought of two people marrying when each has three planets, including N. Sun, in the area of Sun-ruled Leo (♌). That is a lot of Leo under one roof! Being ruled by the Sun, planets in Leo like to bask in the limelight, have the center of attention, do it with dramatic flair, and have recognition from others, because it gives them the strength to

---

111. *People*, September 2, 1985, pp. 23-24.

The determination of the moment of birth or "first breath" of a marriage can be argued, of course, but my preference is for the ceremonial pronouncement of the couple as "husband and wife." There is a sacredness to the entire ceremony, however long, but this pronouncement almost always occurs at the end, and in a sense proclaims the existence of this new entity called a marriage.

In this discussion, we will review mainly the larger planetary patterns, which are unaffected by a 30-minute variation. Even so, the Jupiter/Sun/Mars/Mercury combination remains angular anytime between 6:45 p.m. and 7:30 p.m. PDT that evening.

radiate back out again. Obviously these are all excellent indicators for those performing in public. Being also a Fixed Fire sign, Leo has much energy to burn (Fire) and wants to do it in its own way (Fixed mode). Sun-ruled Leo also has a great need to believe in the theatrical intensity and fervor of the romantic love that is being experienced. In short, there is much that is very colorful as well as potentially willful about Leo.

The wedding chart (see p. 203) shows Jupiter (♃) angular, conjunct the Ascendant, which is a nice symbol for good fortune. It is opposite three planets in Leo, T. Mercury (☿), Mars (♂), and Sun (☉), all of which in turn are square T. Saturn (♄) and Moon's Node (☊). (Because these planets are angular, their energies are prominent at the actual event as well as for the duration of the marriage.) This starts to look a little more perturbing, as we now have five planets and two Personal Points in Fixed signs. Fixity in excess, which this is, related by hard contact, or waiting to manifest, corresponds to all the things discussed in Chapter 2: stubbornness, obsessiveness, and lack of ability to see alternate modes of thought or action. The Cardinal axis holds Mars/Neptune/Moon's Node, which is fitting enough for two people whose work (Mars) involves movie-making and music (both Neptune). Both are well known by the public (Aries/Moon's Node), especially Madonna, who was becoming phenomenally successful not only as a rock star, but also as an actress, notably with her role as a carefree East Village bohemian in the movie *Desperately Seeking Susan*, released in April 1985.[112] But we have already seen how Mars/Neptune can be dangerous if there is any excessive use of drugs or alcohol, which there was—not with Madonna, who drinks almost no alcohol, but with Sean Penn, who was definitely into "hard living." When the two first met, Madonna was aware of Sean's self-destructive tendencies, and even commented "He's wild ... He'll probably die young."[113]

Nevertheless, she married him—on August 16, 1985, which gives us many astrological clues even if we don't know the natal charts of the individuals involved. The bunching of the planets at

---

112. By 1988, Madonna was ninth on a list of the world's 40 highest paid entertainers, with earnings of $46 million for the two-year period 1986-87. She was also one of only five women on the list, and at the top of their numbers. (*The New Mexican*, September 19, 1988, p. A-7.)

113. *Current Biography Yearbook*, 1986, p. 331.

the Descendant, for example, shows that a great deal is expected of this partnership, that there are intense feelings (Moon, ☽) that get expressed verbally (Mercury, ☿) and sexually (Mars, ♂) and can get very heated up (also Mars) with pride or issues of personal identity (Sun, ☉), all of this greatly magnified and exaggerated by being opposite Jupiter (♃) at the Ascendant. The T. Sun and Moon are close to each other, it being only 16 hours after the exact New Moon, the energy so new and fresh that it is not certain yet of its direction and the Moon too new to even be seen in the heavens. Symbolically, the man (Sun) and wife (Moon) are too much in each other's shadow, unable to shine either alone or together.

Watching only the transits and secondary progressions to this wedding chart, we could approximate the likely outcome of this much ballyhooed event. If the correct time of the pivotal wedding moment is anywhere from 6:59 p.m. to 7:02 p.m. PDT, we have a wedding chart with an ASC (relationship axis) receiving all the same T. Saturn/Uranus/Pluto transits during 1988 that were plaguing the N. ASC of Client X (see p. 176), whose marriage grew from bad to worse during 1988, endured a split in October 1988, and ended in the first formal divorce proceedings in January 1989. This does not necessarily guarantee that this couple married August 16, 1985 will divorce; but the story we have already outlined astrologically makes that outcome a strong likelihood. (In fact, final divorce papers were filed by Madonna on January 5, 1989.)

Fortunately, we have accurate birth data for Sean Penn and Madonna, so we can fill in the blank spots by having a look at their natal charts and later on at their composite chart. [114]

Madonna and Sean Penn do have the rather unusual feature of having their N. Suns conjunct, in this case within 2° of each other. However, they were born two years apart, and in a moment we will see how that affected their timing. The shape of Madonna's natal chart is such that there is much concentration of planetary energy in the 12th, 1st, and 2nd houses, showing an intense focus to her life,

---

114. A composite chart is a blending of any two natal charts, calculated by obtaining the midpoints in celestial longitude between each person's planets and Personal Points. It gives us a picture of how the two individuals interact as a unit, as if the couple were now perceivable as a single entity.

For further details, we would examine the wedding chart for its interconnections to the two natal charts and to the composite. In this case, we do know that the two birthdays are very close and, with the wedding on the one birthday, the Sun in each chart will be at nearly the same degree. This establishes the pertinence of August 16, 1985 to both of them.

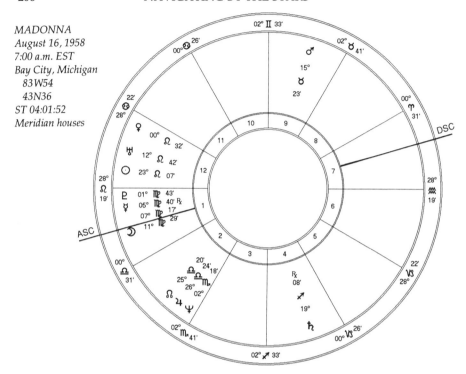

Natal Horoscope for Madonna

especially with Pluto angular (as with Meryl Streep), and Mercury/ Moon angular at the Ascendant. The N. ASC in Virgo (symbol of the Virgin), as well as N. Pluto, Mercury, Moon, and P. Sun in Virgo, is interesting considering all her preoccupation with virgins. In fact, her second album, *Like a Virgin* (Sire, 1984), and its accompanying music videos are credited with transforming her into a pop idol. At her rock concerts, she wore mod bridal outfits and punk haircuts and sang that "virginity is mine to claim...I'm pure as long as I belong to myself."[115] With N. Neptune right on the 3-9 communications axis, she magnifies (Neptune) whatever she says and does through music and/or films and theater (both Neptune). N. Mars on the Cardinal axis tends to connect her with the world through either her work (Mars) or through some aggressive and potentially violent action. Having three planets in showy Leo (including N. Sun), located in the reclusive 12th house, indicates that Madonna might have some contradictory feelings about allowing the public into her private life (Moon/ASC).

---

115. *Current Biography Yearbook*, 1986, p. 331.

At the time of her wedding to Sean Penn, Madonna (full name: Madonna Louise Ciccone, which she never uses publicly) was entering the last year of her 29-1/2 year secondary progressed Moon cycle. This is classically a time of releasing energy, not of starting something new and major. Not only that, but, to compound her difficulty, the upcoming P. New Moon chart has P. Sun/Moon = P. Saturn, within 1°. This was to start August 7, 1986. If you recall how this affected Meryl Streep in her quarter from 1967 to 1975, it tended to deny the presence of successful romantic relationships in her life and brought much steady, hard work with relatively little remuneration. Saturn is also a conservative and serious energy.

In the June 29, 1986, issue of *The New York Times*, Madonna reported on her recent change of image, from junk jewelry and underwear worn as outerwear to a new streamlined look, complete with close-cropped hair, demure dresses with flowered prints, and an old-fashioned glamour reminiscent of the 1950s. She said, "I see my new image as very innocent and feminine and unadorned. It makes me feel good."[114] Madonna was never afraid to change her image. She even startled her fans totally by playing a Christian missionary in the 1986 movie *Shanghai Surprise*, which she made with Sean Penn. (The movie, produced by ex-Beatle George Harrison, was considered a flop.) She also released her highly successful *True Blue* album in 1986, which she said expressed her husband's "very pure vision of love."[117]

Unfortunately, with the cycles of time working against them, this "very pure vision of love" was to deteriorate rather rapidly. By 1987 the Penns were already filing for divorce, although the divorce filing was later nullified. They moved together into 1988, with increasingly public displays of anger and discontent. Sean, for his part, showed his fire through a volatile temperament and was arrested and jailed at least once during this period for violent behavior, usually towards some intruding photographer assumed to be forcibly invading his privacy.

Meanwhile, Madonna, whose marital difficulties were hinted at personally with the wedding chart Saturn/Uranus midpoint (sudden separations and difficulties) right on the Moon (the woman, the wife), began to suffer in her marriage. In addition, not

116. *Ibid.*
117. *Ibid.*

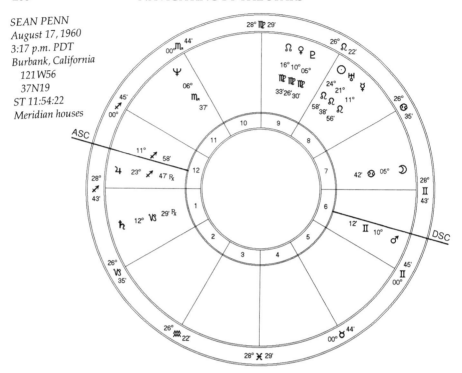

SEAN PENN
August 17, 1960
3:17 p.m. PDT
Burbank, California
121W56
37N19
ST 11:54:22
Meridian houses

Natal Horoscope for Sean Penn

only was her quarti-lunar P. New Moon chart (starting August 7, 1986) pointing in this direction, but also the factor of her first Saturn return during much of 1987, which while on the same axis, activated P. Sun/Moon/Saturn and N. Saturn. This is a heavy dose of saturnine energy and tends to cause a constriction in one's sense of well-being on every level. Of course, one could say the marriage was ripe to be cut short, or one could say it would have been fantastic at another time in their lives. Either way, destiny plays out its hand, and one's destiny tends to be indicated by the astrological chart and the timing to it.

Sean Penn's natal chart shows planets more spread out than Madonna's, evoking a wider field of interests than hers and also the possibility of less focus. Several astrological factors are notable: first, he has N. Sun (☉) closely conjunct N. Uranus (♅) (the body and personal identity [Sun] are highly excitable or eccentric [Uranus]) and, secondly, N. Moon (☽) opposite N. Saturn (♄) (the emotions and/or woman [Moon] are experienced as causing extra responsibility, heaviness, and perhaps even constriction [Saturn]). In other words, with this combination, unless fully integrated into his personality, he could feel as if his wife (Moon/Saturn) is cramping his style as a freewheeling, adventure-seeking man (Sun/Uranus). Meanwhile, she would be very important to him (N. Moon in the 7th house), perhaps too important. And, just to further his potential confusion, his N. Ascendant (what he is projecting) is located in his 12th house (a secluded place, often hidden from ourselves). Thus it would not always be clear to him what he is putting out and why he is attracting what he does. That may be one reason why destiny placed Mars on his N. Descendant, a position that tends to attract polarized situations in which the individual is tested again and again in the skills of clarity in relationship and conflict resolution. (This is discussed in Chapter 3, where comparison is made to Robert Kennedy, who also has N. Mars conjunct Descendant.)

With time, Sean Penn would hopefully grow to understand better some of these paradoxes in his nature. He could and did play some of them out in his movie characters, to some extent in *Racing with the Moon* (1984) and in a big way in *Falcon and the Snowman* (1985), in which he gives a "standout . . . performance as a desperate, amoral, drugged-out kid."[118] But unfortunately his life was to echo the movies too much, and by the end of 1988, the papers reported that Madonna had called in the police over New Year's weekend, complaining of being beaten by her husband.

Divorce papers were filed once again, on January 5, 1989. This time it was to be final, and this time it was Sean Penn who was due to experience *his* first Saturn return shortly, from February 20 through June 21, 1989. Father Time would be checking in to see how he was measuring up in the general scheme of life. (Madonna had probably glimpsed the outcome of this marriage during *her* first Saturn return two years earlier. The delay factor might have been his Saturn return, which brought the truth home now to him in early 1989.)

This relationship is also well described in the composite chart (defined in footnote 114, p. 205), which is shown on the next page. The advantage of its perspective is in being able to see the couple's interaction before they ever decide on a permanent commitment. It lets them know what to expect in terms of their ongoing inter-dynamics, in case that had not yet presented itself. It is quite

---

118. Leonard Maltin's *TV Movies and Video Guide*, 1988 edition, p. 301.

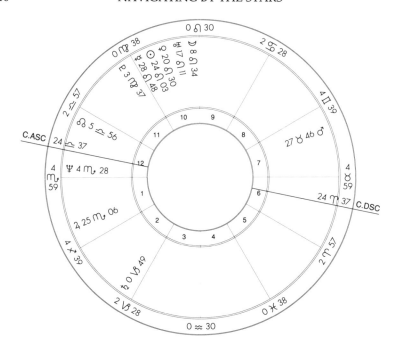

Madonna/Sean Penn Composite Chart

fascinating how this composite chart can imitate the wedding chart. Oftentimes it does, sometimes to good effect—or the opposite, as is true here.

Once again a large number of planets and Personal Points are in fixed signs: composite Moon/Uranus/Venus/Sun/Mercury (☽ / ♅ / ♀ / ☉ / ☿ , all in Fixed Fire Leo in the prominent 10th house) are square Jupiter (♃ , in the first house) and Mars (♂ , in the 7th house of partnerships and open conflicts). Mars brings in the sexual and potentially violent element, and Jupiter amplifies that as well as everything it is squaring, specifically: 1) the emotional content of the relationship and its public nature, focusing especially on the woman as a public figure (Moon at the top of the chart in the 10th house); 2) the individual opinions and desires of the man and wife (Uranus); 3) the love they share (Venus); 4) the identity they feel as a married couple (Sun); and 5) what they have to say about everything (Mercury). In addition, the excessive Fixity (even Neptune and MC are in Fixed signs) makes the likelihood of stubbornness and conflict a real issue, as well as feelings and opinions that run hot and strong. The willingness and ability to compromise is almost nowhere to be found, making it especially hard to break through the famous Leo pride.

What adds to the intrigue is Neptune (♆) angular, conjunct the equatorial ASC, providing an important clue as to why such a pair might stick it out. Neptune holds out the possibility of an idealized love (as in Madonna's *True Blue* album, 1986). It bestows glamour and mist, and ultimately can delude a couple about what they are doing together and why. When it is prominent, as it is here, they have to ask each other what they might be hiding from themselves about the real nature of the relationship. The fact is, with so much planetary action in the 10th house of public image and social position, this couple is bound to have a very public marriage. As it happened, they were constantly surrounded by crowds and the inevitable paparazzi photographers. But in this case also, the man (Mars) cannot accept or handle that fact, and becomes violent in his efforts to shield both of them from the glare of publicity—which is actually part of their *joint* destiny as public figures in a public marriage. Sean Penn was, in short, fighting their common destiny and so contributed to destroying it.

The marriage in August 1985 took place on a steep bluff overlooking the ocean near Malibu, California. The name of the place was Point Dume, pronounced Doom. The mythologist Joseph Campbell would have had something interesting to say about that.

Time Clues: A Troubled Time for a Corporation
(NASA and the Challenger Shuttle Explosion)

Many people have trouble conceiving of the idea that a meaningful astrological chart can be drawn up for anything but the birth of a human being. But as we have just seen with Sean and Madonna's wedding chart, which is within 0 to 30 minutes of accuracy, there are other pivotal starter moments in life. When anything of major importance in life begins, collectively or individually, we can cast a chart which will tell us how it will go. "The die is cast," so to speak, for the enterprise, the endeavor, the individual, whatever and whoever it is. It is not always easy to read a chart of a large collective, as there are so many trends which could develop on so many different layers of the symbols. This is why astrologers can spend years researching and observing such charts to see how they are being affected in space and time, and to develop a sense of how a collective such as a corporation reacts to certain trends and goes through its highs and lows. But just as a marriage is an "entity," so is a corporation, and it has its strengths and vulnerabilities to issues of time, locality, and relationship just as individual people do. And there are some symbols which seem to read loud and clear.

Here, then, is a brief look into the chart of the National Aeronautics and Space Administration (NASA), and the events leading up to and including the tragic Challenger shuttle disaster of January 28, 1986, from an astrological perspective.

First of all, the birth moment of this government-owned and created agency occurred when President Eisenhower signed the National Aeronautics and Space Act of 1958. Unfortunately, Eisenhower did not keep records of exactly when he signed each bill into law; he signed them in batches. But we do know from at least three different sources that he signed this bill into law July 29, 1958, and probably close to the noon hour. *The Eisenhower Appointment Records* from the Dwight D. Eisenhower Library in Abilene, Kansas show that he entered his office at 7:55 a.m. that day and left at 4:47 p.m. EDT, putting the NASA corporate Sun definitely between 5° Leo 52' and 6° Leo 13'. I have made the chart a noon chart, which is often done with corporations that have fuzzy times of incorporation or creation. But in this case we have other evidence hinting that Eisenhower probably signed the act shortly after 11:35 a.m. when he met for 11 minutes with Doctors Killian and Glennan, both due to be appointed as key administrators of the newly created NASA.

In the section of the National Aeronautics and Space Act of 1958 entitled "Declaration of Policy and Purpose," we have the following statement (Section 102a): "The Congress hereby declares that it is the policy of the United States that activities in space should be devoted to peaceful purposes for the benefit of all mankind." There is a lot of incoherent legalese which follows this statement, somehow or other seeming to make excuses in advance just in case the United States government needed to use the space program for military purposes. However, the *expressly stated purpose* of this organization is a peaceful one. This is important to remember. Just as the marriage vows have an expressly stated purpose, so do the declarations of a corporation upon its inception. In ways that are rather mysterious, but probably somewhat karmic, if a company deviates significantly from its goals, and in ways that are somehow detrimental to the welfare of others, that company tends to experience a serious retribution in some form. (Of course, with many companies, especially the heavy polluters, this retribution seems to take a long time in coming.)

Because of the condensed nature of this section, we will not cover the triumphs of NASA, which have been considerable, but only this one event which has haunted NASA and the general public ever since it occurred on January 28, 1986. That day many were watching at the site and on television as they witnessed the horrific mid-air explosion of the Challenger shuttle, its hydrogen tank disintegrating and the entire vehicle turning into a fireball at 72 seconds and 46,000 feet into flight. All seven astronauts aboard were killed, including schoolteacher/astronaut Christa McAuliffe.

For large corporations, astrologers use both long-range and short-range cyclical charts to get a sense of how that area of industry will tend to fare over a larger or smaller period. For the aeronautics and space industry (as well as the computer industry, among others), we would look at the 14-year Jupiter/Uranus cycle to see what each portends. The chart of the previous T. Jupiter/Uranus conjunction would tell us much about how things would go for that industry in a general way over the subsequent 14-year period (13.8 years, to be precise), and we watch the transits to that chart.

The most recent Jupiter/Uranus cycle began with the conjunction on September 25, 1983. It was far less fortunate for the space industry than the previous one in July 1969. (In fact, that one on July 20, 1969, at 3:59 a.m. EDT was followed within 19 hours by astronaut Neil Armstrong's first step on the surface of the Moon, part of the first-ever manned landing on the Moon. It was a fortunate 14-year period right from the beginning, with no major or minor accidents in a potentially hazardous industry.) The next period, from September 1983 to February 1997, is much less fortunate in general for the aerospace industry. We have seen this unfolding with the numerous lost and destroyed billion-dollar "payloads" internationally, and in particular on January 28, 1986, when T. Saturn was conjunct the Jupiter/Uranus conjunction chart of September 1983. This would tend to have a constrictive (Saturn) effect on the industry (expressed here as Jupiter/Uranus). Moving up closer to within a few months of the Challenger shuttle disaster,

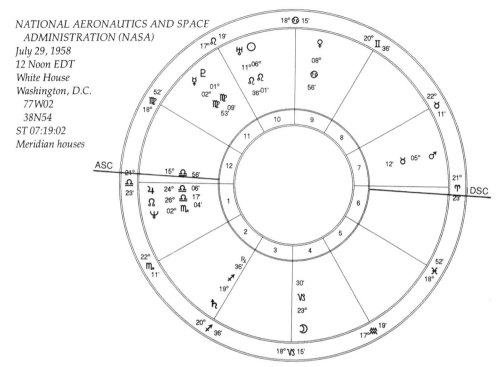

National Aeronautics and Space Administration (NASA)

we will look briefly at some key shorter-term cyclical charts. Each of them links up strongly with the NASA N. Sun, which brings us to the corporate chart of NASA (see above).

No matter where the angles are exactly, depending on the exact hour and minute of inception, we have a close Sun/Mars/Saturn (☉ / ♂ / ♄) combination by hard contact, with Uranus (♅) and Neptune (♆) hovering nearby within 4° to 5-1/2° of the N. Sun. This is a company whose identity (Sun) is linked with that of raw power (Mars) and with the necessity for utmost precision in its use (Saturn), with electronic and future-oriented equipment, especially computers (Uranus), and with a vision to move beyond any previous boundaries civilization has known in terms of space travel (Neptune). So the vision is large and the plans idealistic (Neptune), but the planet closest to the Sun by hard contact (Mars) hints of dangers in using this very explosive energy (Mars/Uranus) for mainly military purposes (also Mars). If this happens, there is the possibility of deaths suffered by the company (Sun/Mars/Saturn), especially if high-precision work (Mars/Saturn) is not vigilantly maintained. Meanwhile also, in this noon NASA chart, which works well on many levels, Jupiter hovers near the ASC (that which is projected to the world), reflecting not only the ongoing optimism (Jupiter) of NASA's official spokesmen, even in the face of catastrophic problems and setbacks, but its extraordinarily good press (Jupiter/ASC = good luck with the public), again despite all odds at times, especially after the Challenger disaster. Everyone, including the investigative journalists, wants to believe that NASA serves only the highest good of the people in its efforts to conquer the wilds of outer space and bring back new information about our solar system, and that this is NASA's major activity.

What seems particularly poignant about the NASA chart is Saturn within 1° of the 3-9 communications axis. This is the axis concerned with the internal communications within a corporation and its manner of expressing information within those bounds. This is not necessarily intended for the public, as is the Jupiter/ASC axis, but it filters through nonetheless. In the case of a disaster such as the Challenger shuttle, this was to be a crucial factor. Saturn as a symbol of a communicator can be tightlipped, cautious, and conservative, representing the establishment to the point where official memorandums and regimented procedures, such as meeting deadlines, become more important than observing and reacting to real potential crisis information with upsetting implications. Such was the case when, for seven to eight years, NASA management people systematically ignored the warnings of their own engineers that the infamous "O-rings" would not be likely to endure the explosive energy of the takeoff, especially in temperatures below freezing—which Cape Canaveral had on the morning of January 28, 1986. (The O-rings had eroded on previous flights and were treated as an "accepted flight risk.") What they *had* made sure of was a massive publicity campaign with much fanfare, so that everyone, especially all the school children, was cued up to watch teacher-in-space Christa McAuliffe. She had been specially selected in a national competition in which she "won out" over 10,000 other applicants.

Meanwhile the important short-term cyclical charts were starting to signal big warnings, even if NASA managers ignored their own engineers' latest warnings in August 1985 (as was documented in the low-key but somewhat stern Rogers Commis-

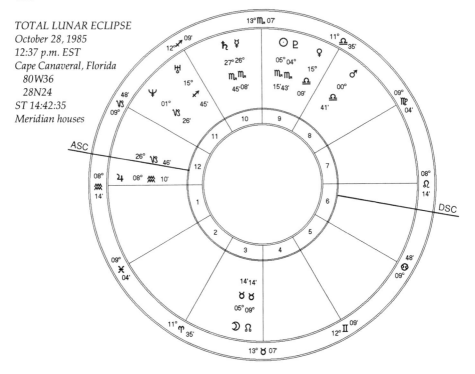

TOTAL LUNAR ECLIPSE
October 28, 1985
12:37 p.m. EST
Cape Canaveral, Florida
80W36
28N24
ST 14:42:35
Meridian houses

Total Lunar Eclipse—October 28, 1985

sion Report released June 9, 1986.[119]) A lunar eclipse on October 28, 1985, charted for Cape Canaveral, Florida, shows Jupiter (♃), planet of optimism, currently angular, although more telling is Sun/Moon/Pluto (☉/ ☽ / ♇) in paran 31 minutes earlier, and Mars/Neptune (♂ / ♆) in paran 2 hours and 40 minutes earlier. Mars/Neptune is also on the Cardinal axis, a combination which Witte-Lefeldt defines as "general infection, destruction, dissolution." (*Rules for Planetary Pictures,* 5th edition, 1959, p. 192.) The Sun/Mars/Pluto is significant being at 4°-5° Scorpio/Taurus, within 1°-2° exactly square the NASA N. Sun/ Mars/Saturn combination, making it in effect now Sun/Mars/ Saturn/Pluto, a very foreboding and potentially violent astrological combination for NASA, and specifically for NASA at Cape Canaveral, Florida. Pluto is moving slowly, as the outermost planet, and so stays in this

---

119. On the ABC Evening News June 9, 1986, television anchorman Peter Jennings announced that the Rogers Commission Report "does not say who was responsible [for the Challenger shuttle disaster]." However, later studies of the report made it clear that, due to budgetary restrictions, NASA had decided to trim 70 percent of its safety and quality-control staff in recent years.

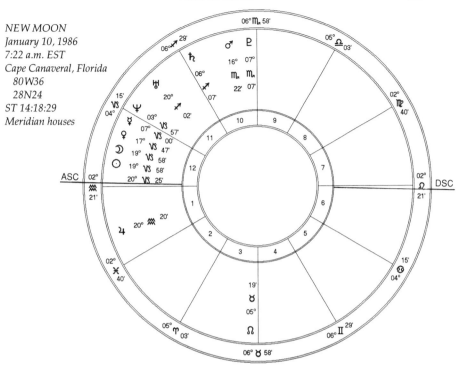

NEW MOON
January 10, 1986
7:22 a.m. EST
Cape Canaveral, Florida
  80W36
  28N24
ST 14:18:29
Meridian houses

New Moon—January 10, 1986

degree area for a significant amount of time. It shows up again on the pivotal Winter Solstice chart for December 21, 1985, forming a conjunction (within 2°) with Mars, only now Pluto at 6° Scorpio 39′ is even tighter to its hard contact with the NASA N. Sun/ Mars/Saturn.

By the New Moon chart on January 10, 1986, calculated for Cape Canaveral, Pluto is also hovering within 8′ orb to exactly conjunct the MC, with Sun/Moon rising. T. Saturn is by now within 18′ of an exact conjunction to the cyclical 14-year chart of Jupiter/Uranus (beginning September 23, 1983). T. Pluto is also within 16′ of its Stationary Retrograde degree, due February 8, 1986, lending additional force to its already potent energy. All of these factors, especially with Pluto relentlessly angular at Cape Canaveral, suggest that NASA was due to undergo an ordeal of enormous proportions at that location, very likely within the lunar period starting January 10, 1986.

After six delays in allowing the launch of the Challenger shuttle, NASA selected as its launch date Tuesday, January 28, 1986. The takeoff was precisely at 11:38 a.m. EST (Eastern Standard Time). The astrological chart for Challenger's takeoff, and therefore also its ultimate destiny, is shown on the facing page. Although there are numerous factors which could be analyzed, especially on a 90° dial, the major factors, and therefore the loudest and clearest signals, are given as follows:

1) T. Pluto = T. ASC (56' orb)

2) T. ASC = T. Mercury/Sun/Venus/Pluto/Uranus/Moon's Node (0° to 4° orb) = NASA N. Sun/Mars/Saturn/Neptune/Uranus/3-9 (Sun/Mars/Saturn, 0° to 1° orb)

3) T. Moon = T. Saturn (3° orb)

4) T. Mars = T. 2-8 axis (1-1/2° orb)

The warning signals from the previous cyclical charts had all centered around the degree area of 5° to 7° of the Fixed signs (i.e. Taurus, Leo, Scorpio, and Aquarius), but especially in Scorpio, ruled by Pluto, the planet of death, rebirth, and all life's more drastic and deep-level transformations. So, when one looks at the moment NASA finally "chose" for its demise, with no fewer than 14 mostly negative astrological factors connecting the NASA corporate chart with the moment of the Challenger launch, one is overcome with awe and horror—awe, at the precision of the planets and angles to mark the exact moment of the destruction, and horror, that despite all the precursor warning signals, nothing was done to change the destiny of this moment, which killed seven brave and valiant astronauts in their prime of life.

Muffled reports later revealed that a large portion of the "payload" on the Challenger was of a military nature. Some reports even hinted that the payload itself was extremely dangerous and beyond any previous level of military/space efforts. (Since the early 1970s, general lack of financial support for strictly scientific investigations of space had, in fact, been pushing NASA more and more into military work. The Reagan administration [1981-1989] made no secret of its desire to have NASA "dedicate the bulk of its future shuttle payloads and research programs to the military, particularly missions for the Strategic Defense Initiative."[120]) Whatever the truth of the matter, NASA paid dearly and would be

---

120. *Time*, Vol. 127, No. 23, June 9, 1986, p. 16.

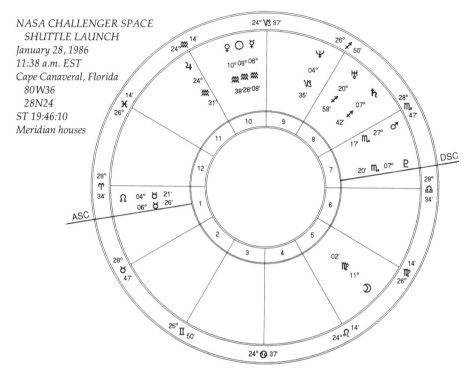

NASA CHALLENGER SPACE
  SHUTTLE LAUNCH
January 28, 1986
11:38 a.m. EST
Cape Canaveral, Florida
  80W36
  28N24
ST 19:46:10
Meridian houses

NASA Challenger Space Shuttle Launch

unlikely to recover from this blow at least until February 1997, marking the end of the current Jupiter/Uranus 14-year cycle generally unfavorable to the aeronautics and space industry. This is in spite of NASA's ongoing habit of putting on a smiling, optimistic face to the world.

A quick look at the planetary combinations for Challenger's liftoff show that, of all the planets, Pluto's influence is the most prominent and that it hooks into almost everything: the massive news coverage of the event (Pluto/Mercury), the sense of everyone identifying with what should have been a glorious moment (Sun), the outpouring of love and sympathy for these seven astronauts and their families (Venus), the amazing suddenness of it all (Uranus), and the shattered dreams (Mars/Saturn/Neptune/Pluto). The mood of the people (Moon) was dark and somber (Saturn), as violence (Mars) brought sudden death (Mars/2-8 axis), witnessed by the millions who watched on television.

When it came time to assess the faults and assign blame, the Presidential Commission on the Space Shuttle Challenger Accident was typically overprotective of the government-owned and sponsored agency—with the exception of one independent-minded commission member. This was the astute and maverick physicist Richard Feynman, who found consistent errors in the NASA scientists' methods and claims, including their analysis that projected the chance of such an accident happening as 1 in 100,000.[121] They had used these calculated projections to assure Congress and the nation that the shuttle was safe. After four months on the commission, Feynman refused to sign the report unless his scathing criticism would be a part of it. Chairman Rogers thought Feynman's remarks would be too damaging to NASA, so a compromise was reached. Feynman softened his comments somewhat, and they were published later as Appendix F: "Personal Observations on the Reliability of the Shuttle Program":

> NASA owes it to the citizens from whom it asks support to be frank, honest, and informative; [and] so that these citizens can make the wisest decisions for the use of their limited resources for a successful technology, reality must take precedence over public relations, for nature cannot be fooled.[122]

Fine-tuning for Auspicious Dates: The Electional Chart

It has probably already dawned on you by now that if certain times present such pitfalls, individually and collectively, then why not select a time one knows to be astrologically auspicious? That is exactly what the electional chart is all about. The astrologer helps the client to select the best possible date and time, given the parameters of one's schedule, which may also involve numerous other people. The personal or collective natal chart as well as the ongoing planetary patterns (called mundane transits) are checked for upcoming timing, and the event is scheduled accordingly.

---

121. Richard Feynman, whose birth chart shows a close hard contact of N. Mercury/Jupiter/Mars, has a fast-moving (Mars) and expansive (Jupiter) mind and intellect (Mercury) that pushes beyond what the ordinary perception would seem to deduce, especially with scientific factors.

122. Appendix to the *Report of the Presidential Commission on the Space Shuttle Challenger Accident*, released June 9, 1986.

For a much less censored version of Feynman's thoughts as well as experiences while on the Presidential Commission, I recommend *"What Do You Care What Other People Think?"* (1988). This is Feynman's personal account of the above, and also includes pictures and diagrams pertaining to the NASA Challenger shuttle disaster.

We have already seen how the beginning moment of anything is imprinted with planetary energy. This is not to say that the planets are causing the situation, but they are reflective of what is going on, as described in Chapter 1. Therefore, if you do not want your situation, whatever it may be, to start off with a particular imprint and destiny, you simply avoid it and wait for something better.

Here is where it gets tricky. Sometimes there is no optimum time for the person or the circumstances anywhere in the near future. Many people do not want to wait, so they go ahead anyway and have an experience that is less than perfect and sometimes disastrous. But even the best electional chart is not perfect, because life is not perfect. However, it does facilitate moving through the experience with greater ease and enjoyment.

For individuals, this applies to such things as selecting dates for weddings, important trips and meetings, and the signing of important contracts. For corporations, it applies to choosing the time of incorporation, and, if a business is not incorporated, then the time when it first opens its doors to the public is significant.

Obviously you do not want to monitor everything, such as when you leave the house to go to the grocery store. That would be an example of misuse, or excessive use, of an extremely valuable astrological technique. So, whenever possible, it is exciting and sometimes even life-saving to decide with astrology the best possible time to do something of consequence.[123]

---

123. There are other related astrological charts, called the event chart and the horary chart. These are still further methods to examine the advisability of a course of action, either before or after the fact. If, for instance, a date is unalterable, one works in advance to minimize its weaknesses and maximize its strengths as much as possible. The Challenger shuttle launch (January 28, 1986) is an event chart one would obviously *not* have chosen, but it can be studied after the fact so that the mistake is not repeated.

For people with an intermediate to advanced knowledge of astrology, I recommend Bruce Scofield's *The Timing of Events: Electional Astrology*, 1986. Suggested books on horary astrology are given in Appendix H, p. 280.

V

Postscript:
Our Plutonian Heritage

All matters pursued beyond reason and
harmony encounter their opposites.
— Paracelsus

So much that has to do with issues of accumulated power on both an individual and collective level has gotten so increasingly out of hand in the 20th century, that one looks longingly for ways in which all of these trends might be resolved. The astrological symbol for power and control, its uses and misuses, is the planet Pluto. We should accordingly pay close attention to its passage in the heavens and to the signals it gives along the way.

As a reminder, Pluto was discovered on February 18, 1930, and even the chart of its exact time of discovery gives us many clues as to how it might manifest itself in human terms (see chart on next page). Pluto (♇) itself is just rising, but is considered in astrology to be hidden away in the 12th house, i.e. the full force of its effect might be hard to detect, especially since it is in close hard contact to Neptune (♆) in the 2nd house of values and financial resources. Mars (♂) is angular, on the Descendant, indicating the potential violent energy to be unleashed, especially on our enemies (7th house). But Mercury (☿) is nearby, so one could either spend a lot of time negotiating or get distracted just talking about the violence without being fully aware that it is there, especially with Mercury/Mars in close soft aspect (120° here) to Jupiter (♃). This inclines one to exaggerate, and to think one will be lucky with the aggressive and intellectually derived forces (Mars/Mercury), such as plutonium and atomic energy. But as we have seen before with soft aspects, it is easy to think we have everything under control, and it is easy to just keep going without looking to see what havoc one might be wreaking on so many levels (Mars/DSC).

Saturn/Uranus in a tight square (8′ orb) and in paran (1 hour 6

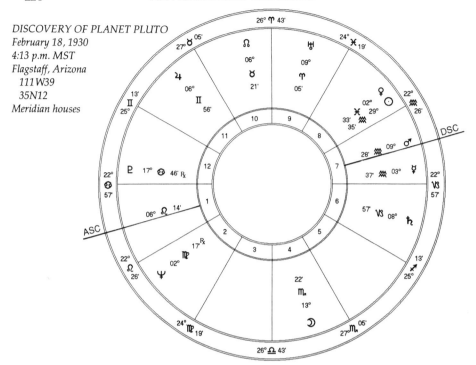

Discovery of Planet Pluto

minutes earlier) tells us that the release of Plutonian energies will pit the conservative versus the liberal forces in our civilization. In reaction to Plutonian issues, Saturn's placement in the 6th house indicates that conservatives will respond by defending jobs and military spending, perhaps downplaying health matters. Liberals will focus on the effects of Plutonian issues on the environment (3-9 axis), working through educational and legal channels (both 9th house), and at times through media events (3-9 axis).

The Sun (☉) at 29° of Uranus-ruled Aquarius shows the potential for desiring technological advancement (Uranus) at all costs and without regard to the consequences. (The 29th degree is an exaggerated position wherever it is located. Here, being in Aquarius, it applies to Uranus-ruled activities.) In addition Venus (♀) conjunct the Sun in the 8th house tends to assume a great deal of confidence in matters of financial resources, and with Venus closely opposite Neptune and in hard contact to Pluto (i.e. Venus/Neptune/Pluto), we have a sense that money matters and creature comforts (Venus) on a large scale (Pluto) have a way of moving out of our hands and into a realm that seems like it should be an advantage, but in fact is potentially insidious in its lack of clarity (all Neptune). Does any of this begin to sound familiar?

Pluto in Scorpio, 1984-1995: Industrial Power Abuses

Pluto is considered to have astrological rulership over the zodiacal area called Scorpio, and so when Pluto enters Scorpio, especially for the first time since it was discovered (i.e. brought into the conscious awareness of human beings), we have the real possibility that all the numerous levels of Pluto's symbology will come tumbling out one by one. Given that Pluto's energies tend to move very slowly and clandestinely over long periods of time, and then reveal themselves with huge dramatic force, we would expect to see something like this happening in full force during Pluto's passage through Scorpio.

Pluto first moved into the sign of Scorpio November 6, 1983, through May 18, 1984 (for the first time in 248.4 years), but it was not to make its full-fledged entry—i.e. without retrograding back into Libra—until August 28, 1984, and lasting a relatively short cycle in one sign, up to mid-November 1995. One of the first notable events within months of late August 1984 was the Union Carbide disaster in Bhopal, India on December 3, 1984. Over 2000 people were killed in a chemical leak of the pesticide manufacturing plant. It was an immense disaster and one for which Union Carbide was clearly responsible. The plant was not safely run or maintained and had not been for many years; it was oversized and too near a population center. How to compensate the victims and their families was a matter which is still probably entangled in the courts.

Strangely enough, 54 years earlier, in 1930 (the year of Pluto's discovery), there was another much less publicized incident involving Union Carbide.[124] The situation was eerily similar. It occurred in a town in West Virginia called Gauley Bridge, starting in April 1930. The country was in the midst of a deep economic depression, so when Union Carbide announced it was looking for miners to help build a tunnel, they were swamped with men looking for work. The tunnel was to be approximately four miles

---

124. Diana Rosenberg and Arlene Nimark, "Union Carbide and 'The Mills of God,'" *NCGR Journal*, Winter 1985-86, Vol. 4, No. 2, pp. 11-16.

long, and it was to divert a water supply to a power plant. There was also a large amount of highly lethal silica dust underneath. Union Carbide was made aware of this danger and informed that silica-bearing rock must be worked wet. Nevertheless, Union Carbide foremen refused to allow the miners to wet down the rock, as it was faster to drill it dry. The men quickly started to sicken and die, though more men came to replace them, and none of them was informed of the deadly situation lying ahead of them. Out of some 5000 employed, 2500 of them died at Gauley Bridge. Even when Congressional hearings were finally held in 1936, Union Carbide officials acted as if they sincerely did not know that silica dust could be lethal. Meanwhile, they had bribed judges, jurors, and legislators in West Virginia to prevent workers or workers' families from making any claims against them. At the Congressional hearings, Union Carbide got off with a relatively light fine and reprimand.

Union Carbide is certainly not alone in its amazing lack of humanity, let alone corporate responsibility. In fact it is not as if the corporations are on one side and the government on the other. What we have is an increasing amount of evidence that at times government officials and administrators who are supposed to protect the consumers seem to be either blatantly accepting bribes, or are strangely inactive in their efforts to halt circumstances that could be detrimental to ordinary citizens. (We saw how that happened with tragic results in the case of NASA and the Challenger shuttle disaster.)

Recently the issue of safe pesticides has come to public attention, especially one called Daminozide, or Alar, which is used chiefly on apples. (A byproduct of Daminozide is used in rocket fuel.) Dr. Moore, an Assistant Administrator of the Environmental Protection Agency, was interviewed in February 1989 by *Sixty Minutes'* Mike Wallace. When Wallace asked Dr. Moore why he could not take the dangerous pesticide off the market, Moore said that it had been legalized some 25 years ago and, until the laws changed, there was nothing he could do to pull it off the market. This, even though conclusive proof has come to light that many young children who eat apples (or products from apples) sprayed with the troublesome pesticide are dying of cancer.

On many occasions the corporation will seem to be acting responsibly when in fact it is not. When there are large and powerful public relations machines working on behalf of the company, it is easy to have this develop. For example, McDonald's (hamburgers) made front page news in 1987 when they announced they would be using a new kind of box for their hamburgers that did not contain chlorofluorocarbons (known to deplete the ozone layer, which is an increasingly urgent environmental issue that was first made public in the early 1960s). However, tucked away in South America, away from the glare of publicity, are the many rain forests that McDonald's is stripping away in vast quantities in order to provide grazing land for their cattle. Stripping too many rain forests is now shown to be causing even further damage in the delicate ecological balance that, among other things, also helps to maintain the ozone layer (which in turn protects us from the Sun's harmful ultraviolet rays).

Financial and Sexual Abuses

So we are beginning to see the persistence of this theme hinted at in the Pluto discovery chart, that powerful forces would be at work behind the scenes and cause potentially violent results unless something was done to uncover the *source* of the power—or uncover the secret, since Plutonian power works most insidiously when it is anonymous and unidentified. This is an important clue, and in the end a very positive one, I believe, because since Pluto's final entry into Scorpio in August 1984, a whole series of things have been made public which in another era would have gone undetected. And the messages are potent as to what has been going on in the abuse of power both on an individual level and on a corporate or collective level. They have to do with the uses of money, and the power of money to corrupt (implicating both government and industry in its use of privilege to buy favors from each other on a grand scale), and also the uses of sexuality and violence (and the burgeoning incidences, or at least reports of incidences, such as child abuse and wife battering). It is as if some extraordinarily wild and ruthless energy has been let loose.

One of the stories I ran across in 1987 seemed to epitomize the amazing crosscurrents of this abuse of power both sexually and financially. It deals with John Fedders, a former head of the Securities and Exchange Commission, an organization created to enforce securities laws and investigate any irregularities in the financial markets, i.e. the policemen for Wall Street bankers, investors, and brokers. Fedders was a chief executive at the SEC for some years and presumably did a reasonable job at it. What was remarkable was the revelation that he was accused of a high level of physical abuse and violence against his wife and children. This came to light when his wife took him to court and wrote a book about it. So here was a man entrusted with enforcing the largest financial securities market in the world. He wielded exceptional power and influence in his professional life, and it was entrusted to him. Yet domestically the power turned inward and perverted itself into violent physical behavior against his wife and children.

Terrorism, Censorship, and AIDS: February 16, 1989 (Pluto Station)

This level of violence on a larger scale has another Plutonian manifestation: terrorism. It works mostly underground, usually anonymously, and will do anything to achieve its ends, which are considered fanatically important. On February 16, 1989, the day that Pluto turned Stationary Retrograde (within 11' of the Cardinal axis), there were at least two remarkable occurrences, both related to Pluto and its passage through Scorpio. First, apropos terrorism, was the announcement by Iran's Ayatollah Khomeini that he was sending death squads after Salmon Rushdie, the author of *The Satanic Verses*, an allegorical novel which satirizes the prophet Mohammed and implies that Islam is not the only true religion. (Rushdie was born a Moslem in Bombay, India, but no longer practiced Islam. He was living in England with his American-born wife.) This caused an incredible international furor, and in America security forces were increasingly wary that some fanatical Iranian students living in the United States might firebomb bookstores selling the Rushdie book. Rushdie, meanwhile, was in hiding with police protection in England, as Iran had offered a $2.6 million bounty to any group or individual who carried out the death sentence on Rushdie and his publishers.

In terms of timing, the odd thing was that Rushdie's book had been published in September 1988, and one would think such a vehement reaction on the part of Khomeini and Iran would have occurred upon publication of the book. But either they were unaware of its existence or did not care enough about the book until it became important for political reasons to jump on the Moslem fundamentalist bandwagon. In any case, the very day they selected for this unprecedented and tempestuous international censure of a literary man was February 16, 1989, the day when T. Pluto's station on the Cardinal axis would mirror a maximal level of potency for Plutonian forces in society.

The second event of note on February 16, 1989, was the announcement in Los Angeles of the verdict in the case of Marc Christian against the estate of Rock Hudson. Christian had lived with Hudson during the last two years of the actor's life, and although they continued to have high-risk sex together, Christian did not learn of Hudson's diagnosis as an AIDS victim until eight months later. Hudson died on October 2, 1985, and Christian filed suit against him for $11 million in damages. The judge and jury awarded him $14.5 million from Hudson's estate, and lawyers regard this as a landmark case in terms of demanding full disclosure to a sexual partner if you have AIDS.

Timewise, again, Hudson had died 3-1/2 years earlier, and this case had been in the courts for months. The echo from June 1985 was to be important, because in the time span following Pluto's entry into Scorpio August 28, 1984, Hudson's was the first case of a public announcement of a well-known celebrity contracting AIDS. I find his case notable, because during his entire career as a movie actor, Rock Hudson had gone to great lengths to keep his homosexuality a carefully guarded secret. An early marriage to Phyllis Gates was arranged by the movie studio strictly for publicity purposes, apparently unbeknownst even to the bride. His movie image was that of a suave and handsome leading man/ladies' man, but in his private life he was a very active homosexual. The fact that his secret was not only finally made known, but unleashed alongside his image as rapidly deteriorating and emaciated, and facing an understandably furious male lover—this was a rather cruel end for Hudson, though a typically Plutonian one.

Plutonian Crimes Coming to Light 1984-1995

What is important to remember here is that transiting Pluto's influence in Scorpio is bringing a large number of hidden Plutonian elements to the surface, thus completely blowing apart the previous image of the person or corporation. Along these lines we have covert operations such as the Iran-Contra affair coming to light; we have more spies caught than ever before; and a record number of Mafia notables are being taken to court and prosecuted, along with insider-traders on Wall Street such as Ivan Boesky (probably the biggest scandal ever to hit Wall Street, implicating a host of other high rollers as Boesky plea-bargained in exchange for revealing names of other individuals and firms involved in insider trading). Even the United Nations' Nazi War Crimes files were unveiled in 1987 for the first time since World War II ended, although in typical Plutonian fashion 400 of the files were missing, raising questions about who had access to the files and why they had reason to protect some reputations. One such reputation was that of Austrian President and former United Nations Secretary General (1972-1981) Kurt Waldheim. It came to light in 1986-87 that Waldheim was most likely guilty of Nazi war crimes himself, as shown in photographs and documents bearing his name, although he has hotly denied that he had any knowledge of wrongdoing on the part of the Nazi army, in which he was an officer. In any case, Waldheim has never been prosecuted, but he has lost face in America and his presence is generally not welcomed in the United States.

Global Policy on Nuclear Energy and Nuclear Weapons

Issues about nuclear energy, chemical and nuclear leaks, and the problems of solid and nuclear waste are all very Plutonian, and have come into prominence for the first time ever as urgent national and global issues since Pluto entered Scorpio in August 1984. These issues have been around for some time, to be sure, but the absolute necessity of dealing with them wisely is in the forefront right now. Pluto's maximal prominence both on the equator in 1987 and on the Cardinal axis in 1989 and 1990 assures that no one will escape thinking about or at least knowing about the consequences of policy decisions on these matters at this time. In fact, the potential dangers and problems of the nuclear industry are so enormous that many private citizens are starting to get educated fast, realizing that in addition to the level of industrial pollution we have already allowed to be perpetrated on our environment, this new threat to global environmental safety is too big to be left strictly in the hands of government and industry alone. This is also because government and industry have been showing themselves too often to be irresponsible in making decisions that more often profit their own interests to the detriment of the environment and the consumers.

Similarly, much needed financial resources have been misused too often in the interest of military spending, creating military buildups where none would have existed without the heavy pressure of the defense industries, which have much to gain. President (and former General) Dwight D. Eisenhower warned of this development back in the 1950s, and so does author Norman Cousins in his book *The Pathology of Power*, 1987, p. 29:

> There is danger in allowing the military to have an unreasonably large part in decision-making in matters concerning the life of the nation, all the way from domestic economic policy to foreign policy.

Plutonian Power and the Bush Administration
January 20, 1989-January 20, 1993

We know that President George Bush will be dealing with many of these Plutonian issues prominently during his four-year term that began January 20, 1989, given that Pluto is exactly angular (on the Descendant) in his inauguration chart (see next page).[125] In fact, with Pluto/Sun/Mars (♇ / ☉ / ♂) all angular it promises that President Bush will encounter greater forces for change than he might think, given his inaugural speech pressing for "unity, diversity, generosity... and compromise."

In the fall of 1990 Bush first spoke of "a new world order" based on the "rule of law." (Note the inauguration chart's active 9th house, which includes matters of law.) And by October 25, 1990, Congress did pass a bill which was signed into law November 5th— "[It] calls for the President to report to the Congress by Oct. 1, 1991 the results of his efforts in regard to the establishment of an International Criminal Court." (The Foreign Operations Appropriations Bill became Public Law #101-513.) This was an idea that the United Nations had been considering for several years, and for the first time since the Nuremberg Trials of Nazi war criminals in 1945-46.) It was

---

125. The inauguration chart is determined from the moment the Oath of Office is concluded, in this case at 12:03:26 p.m. Eastern Standard Time, January 20, 1989, U.S. Capitol Building, Washington, D.C. This chart gives the destiny of the President and his administration for the next four years.

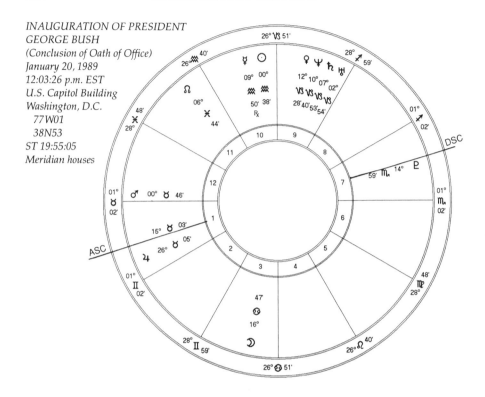

INAUGURATION OF PRESIDENT
GEORGE BUSH
(Conclusion of Oath of Office)
January 20, 1989
12:03:26 p.m. EST
U.S. Capitol Building
Washington, D.C.
    77W01
    38N53
ST 19:55:05
Meridian houses

Inauguration of President George Bush

also a hopeful sign that a global court system might finally supercede military war as a method of solving world problems.

However, the 9th house of an event chart shows more about talk and *proposed* philosophy, whereas the angular planets show what is more likely to happen—what words get put into action. We soon saw the real thrust of the Bush Administration, echoing the aggressive Pluto/Sun/Mars angular in the inauguration chart, and Moon/Mars paran, or angular simultaneously 45 minutes earlier— indicating an easily agitated public that can be galvanized into war. In spite of his talk of "a new world order" based on the "rule of law," as of early fall and winter 1990 Bush made the forceful decision to deploy American military troops to the Mideast. This was in response (Sun/Mars) to Iraqi Saddam Hussein's coercive takeover of Kuwait on August 2, 1990 (Pluto/DSC).

Bush had previously been following a ten-year-long Republican

Party policy to appease the oil-rich Iraq, no matter how much Saddam and his military-backed government wreaked havoc on others inside and outside Iraq. (For example, there is evidence that Saddam killed at least 20,000 of his own Kurdish peoples with poison gas in 1988. In response to this, in September 1988, the U.S. Senate voted for Democratic Senator Clairborne Pell's "Prevention of Genocide Act," which would have imposed strict sanctions against Iraq. The sanctions lost momentum and died in the House due to pressure from the Reagan administration.)

According to American journalists, just eight days before the August 2nd invasion, Bush's State Department instructed April Glaspie, the U.S. Ambassador to Iraq, to tell Saddam, "We have no opinion on... your border dispute with Kuwait."[126] Bush was confirming that the United States had no commitment to Kuwait.

On March 20, 1991, speaking before the U.S. Senate Foreign Relations Committee, Ambassador Glaspie broke an eight-month-long public silence on the subject. She told how the Iraqis deliberately skewed the report of her July 25th meeting with Saddam Hussein. If so, one wonders why Ambassador Glaspie waited so long to tell "the truth." It sounds more like Republican Party damage control.

The 9th house of the Bush inauguration chart defines—among other things—the dissemination of ideas by any means, and political propaganda and censorship. With four planets (Uranus, Saturn, Neptune, and Venus, i.e. ♅ / ♄ / ♆ / ♀) heating up activity in this arena, we have reason to believe that Iraq would not be the only country guilty of distorting the news. In addition to the odd eight-month hiatus in Ambassador Glaspie's testimony, we have many other potentials for biased American reporting, especially war reporting. For example, General Electric, America's fourth largest defense contractor, also owns NBC (National Broadcasting Corp.) since a merger December 11, 1985.

The inauguration chart tells us that, with Mercury Retrograde (☿ R) in the 10th house, Bush would be likely to reverse his position on appeasing Iraq—as well as a number of other issues. And he would be likely to be lucky in doing so, with Jupiter 11° away from rising, strong in a Stationary Direct position that morning, and in

---

126. *The New Mexican*, March 12, 1991, p. A-11. (Quoted from Katie Sherrod, syndicated columnist for the *Fort Worth Star-Telegram*.)

hard contact to Venus and Neptune, which together add elements of self-delusion and transitoriness, i.e. passing luck.

On January 16, 1991, some 500,000 Allied forces, led primarily by President Bush and American troops, initiated a war against Iraq in order to "liberate" Kuwait. After six weeks, with Iraqi casualties of more than 100,000 (American casualties were around 100), Allied forces declared victory and a cease-fire.

This inauguration chart also suggests that, whether or not there is another course of action available, such as economic sanctions, during his first term in office Bush would choose a military solution over a non-military one. (Earlier in his term Bush also initiated the American military invasion of Panama.) And he would give preference to military weapons spending (again, Sun/Mars angular). As of March 1991, U.S. defense equipment firms are running out of American contracts and seek congressional support to sell their wares abroad. The Bush administration stands prepared to support a package of $18 billion in weapons sales to five Middle Eastern countries alone. This means that the pace of U.S. arms exports could more than double in the early 1990s.

Meanwhile, the U.S. will proceed to disarm Iraq, to whom we have already sold significant military technology, including the capacity for nuclear and chemical weapons. We will also proceed to help clean up the largest acts of environmental terrorism ever set in motion—many miles of Saudi coastline contaminated by deliberate oil spills and some 1000 Kuwaiti oil wells either damaged or set ablaze by Saddam Hussein in the six-week war initiated by the United States. The current Bush administration has no constructive domestic policy on oil conservation or alternative energy sources, which insures an ongoing cycle of money for weapons for oil for weapons, at least through January 20, 1993.

A combination of angular Sun/Mars/Pluto also suggests that each leader might pit his manhood against the other. Bush asked for unity among Americans and rationalized the use of dangerous weapons for a cause that he said was "morally right and just." (He also warned Saddam not to use his chemical weapons.) Saddam Hussein in turn rallied his country in a Holy War when he assured Iraqis: "God is on our side." In both cases a compromise could not be reached because too much perceived manhood (translated as patriotism and military might) was at stake. Each leader was appealing to that need in himself and in the collective, as well as an unwillingness to back down. In the process, "the enemy" became dehumanized to the point where mass killing could be justified.

In such a pivotal chart as a U.S. Presidential Inauguration chart, Pluto can intensify the meaning of any other planets it contacts. In this case it is contacting the two most masculine planets, Sun and Mars (because they are all angular simultaneously), suggesting a concentration on masculine behavior as well as on wartime violence and terrorism—in this instance, environmental terrorism surpassing anything the world has yet seen.

If we remember that Pluto is also about the drastic overhaul and transformation of whatever it is contacting, then at this time we would also expect to see controversy around the issue of what is masculine and warrior-like about the American male, and what is appropriate and inappropriate behavior.

While President Bush (1924-   ) was amassing American troops in Saudi Arabia for the fight in the Mideast, on the home front the American poet and storyteller Robert Bly (1926-   ) was making another kind of headline. His book *Iron John: A Book About Men* climbed to the top of *The New York Times Book Review* "Best Seller list"—a major cultural barometer for Americans—where it remained for more than five months as of April 1991. Bly has continually explored the connections between American political policy and the American psyche, and here he applies that line of thinking to the American male and his warrior instincts.

> Contemporary war, with its mechanical and heartless destruction, has made the heat of aggression seem disgraceful.... [There has been a] decline from warrior to soldier to murderer, but it is important to notice the result. The disciplined warrior, made irrelevant by mechanized war, disdained and abandoned by the high-tech culture, is fading in American men. The fading of the warrior contributes to the collapse of civilized society. A man who cannot defend his own [interior] space cannot defend women and children. The poisoned warriors called drug lords prey primarily for recruits on kingless, warriorless boys.
>
> —Robert Bly, *Iron John: A Book About Men*, 1990, p. 156.

Policemen who brutalize the people they are entrusted to protect are also "poisoned warriors." Within days of welcoming home its first troops from the Mideast, Americans learned of widespread police brutality across the United States, triggered by a videotape March 3rd of Los Angeles police officers clubbing, kicking, and stomping an unarmed black man. This incident accelerated the intent of the Department of Justice to review some 15,000 complaints received in the previous six years of police brutality in America.

Robert Bly zeroes in on some important truths here. And even if we are not eager to hear them, we have to admit that events all around us are verifying the ideas he presents so well. He has correctly identified the Plutonian reality.

> If a culture does not deal with the warrior energy—take it
> in consciously, discipline it, honor it—it will turn up
> outside in the form of street gangs, wife beating, drug
> violence, brutality to children, and aimless murder.
> —*Ibid.*, p. 179.

I look forward to seeing the constructive uses of Plutonian power, because no planetary energy manifests itself in a solely negative way for all time. But it seems that with Pluto, we do not reap the benefits of its tremendous revitalizing force until it has ripped through like a scourge. It keeps hammering home its message, asking each individual to be more responsible for his or her own personal power, so that a blind and unconscious collective does not swallow it up.

Pluto asks us to be continually more aware of who has the power, who we give it to, and what we are willing to pay whom in order to get what we want. For those groups and individuals who have misused their power and privilege, the Plutonian energy— especially while in Scorpio 1984-1995—will tend to dissipate those powers and privileges, especially the more their secrets are made known. This retribution process seems painfully slow, but we have already seen many instances since 1984 where it is gradually occurring. And once the secrets of power abusers are made known, their source of strength is weakened—and then healing on all levels of society, including our environment, can begin to take place.

Appendices

Appendix A
Astrological Timetables in General: Planning for the Year, Quarter, Month, Day

1. The Yearly Rhythm: The Four Quarters

Even if you have no idea of the particulars of your natal chart or anyone else's, there are astrological guidelines that can be used to help smooth your decision-making over the long haul. They will not necessarily have the fine-tuning of *your* personal timetable, but they will work well in a pinch.

Astrologers focus on the Solstices and Equinoxes as the key guide to the changing of the light, and thus the key turning points in the year. As we look at the 360° dial on the next page, we observe the key fourth and eighth harmonics of the 360° circle. The Solstices and Equinoxes mark the four points of the compass of the year, though on the astrological chart the points are just opposite from where you might expect. At least this is where they are relevant from the vantage point of the Northern Hemisphere. (The dates given here can also vary up to 48 hours due to the slight variations in the yearly movement of the Earth around the Sun.)

When we look at the year on a linear graph, it looks like the graph below the 360° dial. Around the Solstices, the movement of the light appears to be standing still, which is exactly where the word "Solstice" comes from—the Latin *sol* (Sun) plus *sistere* (to cause to stand still). This describes a basic rhythm of the year, where essentially all of the increasing light begins at the Winter Solstice for the Northern Hemisphere. In the *I Ching, or Book of Changes,* the Winter Solstice is called "The Return" or "Turning Point" (Hexagram 24).

> After a time of decay comes the turning point. The powerful light that has been banished returns. There is movement, but it is not brought about by force ... The old is discarded and the new is introduced. Both measures accord with time; therefore no harm results ... Movement

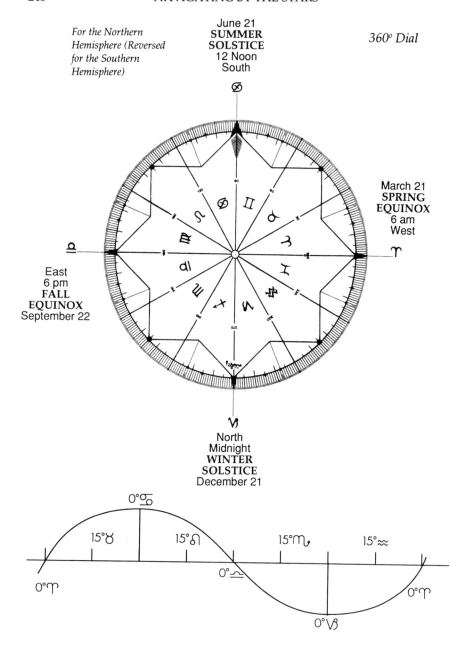

For the Northern
Hemisphere (Reversed
for the Southern
Hemisphere)

June 21
**SUMMER
SOLSTICE**
12 Noon
South

360° Dial

March 21
**SPRING
EQUINOX**
6 am
West

East
6 pm
**FALL
EQUINOX**
September 22

North
Midnight
**WINTER
SOLSTICE**
December 21

15♉ to 15♌ : **May 7-Aug 9: slow change, high stability**
15♌ to 15♏ : **Aug 9-Oct. 31: fast change, decreasing light**
15♏ to 15≈ : **Oct. 31 -Feb. 7: slow change, low stabilty**
15≈ to 15♉ : **Feb. 7-May 7: fast change, increasing light**

is just at its beginning; therefore it must be strengthened by rest, so that it will not be dissipated by being used prematurely. This principle, i.e. of allowing energy that is renewing itself to be reinforced by rest, applies to all similar situations. The return of health after illness, the return of understanding after an estrangement: everything must be treated tenderly and with care at the beginning, so that the return may lead to a flowering.

> —*I Ching, or Book of Changes*, Richard Wilhelm translation rendered into English by Cary F. Baynes, ©1950 (Bollingen Foundation), 3rd edition, 1968, pp. 97-98.

2. The Yearly Rhythm: The Retrograde and Eclipse Schedules

Within the yearly scheme marked by the regular intervals of the Solstices and Equinoxes lie the retrograde and eclipse schedules, which need to be factored in as additional fine-tuning information and *can* contradict somewhat the yearly rhythms as measured by the Solstices and Equinoxes. On the next page is a visual representation of the retrograde planetary periods for the year 1988. The months during which retrograde motion occurs vary from year to year, but in the mid to late 1980s the outer planets were retrograde from early spring through summer.

A planet is retrograde when its relative motion, from the viewpoint of the Earth and its orbital speed, appears to go backwards for a time. Be especially aware of the chunks of time when a large number of planets are retrograde. This tends to inhibit the sweeping forward movement of plans, either individual or collective or corporate. At this time you may experience a sense of matters churning in place—at worst, static, at best, an overhaul and review to make them stronger.

Notice also that during the mid-1980s, including 1988, the retrograde block is punctuated on either side by solar and lunar eclipses, when the Sun and Moon, respectively, are partially or totally obscured from our view somewhere on Earth. Solar eclipses occur about every six months, accompanied by lunar eclipses two weeks before or after—and occasionally both before *and* after. During an eclipse it is known that the Earth's atmosphere becomes more highly charged with electrons (or negatively charged

1988 Retrogrades & Eclipses

	JAN.	FEB.	MAR.	APR.	MAY	JUNE	JUL.	AUG.	SEPT.	OCT.	NOV.	DEC.
☿		Feb. 2 / Feb. 23			May 31	June 24			Sept. 28	Oct. 20		
♀					May 22		July 4					
♂								Aug. 26		Oct. 27		
♃									Sept. 24			Jan. 20
♄				Apr. 10				Aug. 30				
♅				Apr. 4					Sept. 5			
♆		Feb. 14		Apr. 11			July 19		Sept. 18			
♇		Feb. 14					July 19					
☉E & ☽E			Mar. 3 ☽E / Mar. 18 ☉E					Aug. 27 ☽E	Sept. 10 ☉E			

particles), which may account for why eclipses tend to bring sudden and drastic changes in the weather, usually in the time period closely surrounding the eclipses, but especially during the two week period between eclipses. I have noticed that events such as meetings or appointments scheduled within hours of an exact solar or lunar eclipse are unsettling in some way. People seem to be thrown off balance temporarily, either by other personalities or by major details or items of importance that have been forgotten or mislaid.

An eclipse may be affecting you very personally, especially if it is conjunct or opposite one of your six Personal Points (Aries point, Ascendant, Moon's Node, Sun, Moon, or Midheaven). However, in general, an eclipse marks a more intensified period, implying a greater excitability on the part of the people for up to six weeks before and six weeks after, but especially during the two-week period between eclipses and during the actual eclipse, when the Earth's electromagnetic field is drastically altered for about 24 hours. Astrologers study the precise degree area where the eclipse is occurring, and for greater fine-tuning, they observe where in a given chart the eclipse is occurring. Even if it is not making a hard contact to a natal Personal Point or planet, an eclipse will still in some way affect the natal house in which it occurs.

Larger movements in the stock market, either up or down, have been observed during the eclipse time frame. If you wanted to schedule an event maximally for intense emotional reactions with staying power, such as the opening of a play or movie, you might want to zero in on a time within the eclipse envelope, so to speak, but not too close to the exact eclipse, bearing in mind the various other factors such as the retrogrades.

Let us discuss the implications of each retrograde planet. First, one takes the inherent qualities and description of that planet astrologically and turns it inwards upon itself. (Astrologers also note the exact degrees where planets go Stationary Retrograde [SR] and Stationary Direct [SD], and there is oftentimes a correlation to events when the planet by transit returns to pass again over the degree where it went SR.)

Mercury Retrograde (☿ R): Occurs three times per year for approximately three weeks each time. Communication (mail, phone, in person) and travel plans at all levels can experience a far greater than usual number of delays, disorder, mistakes, and confusion. One's vehicle can be more prone to problems at this time. Not recommended for travel or for doing large or important mailings. Worst possible time (also Mars Retrograde) to sign any important contract. Good time to review matters pending, tend to old business, clean closets in all respects, focus the mind more introspectively. While not generally the best time for a company to incorporate or open for business, the exceptions are those businesses that profit from Mercury-Retrograde events, such as car repairs and/or mechanical repairs of communications equipment.

Venus Retrograde (♀ R): Occurs once every two years for approximately six weeks. Matters related to love, finances, and/or the arts may need further attention before forward movement can take place. Review and introspection on all of these is a good idea. While marriage is not ideal during this time frame, it depends on the position of transiting Venus in the natal chart.

Mars Retrograde (♂ R): Occurs once every two years for approximately nine weeks. Avoid surgery at this time, even outpatient surgery, as even a small, seemingly very containable situation can easily get botched if done now. Extremely dangerous to purchase a car or vehicle of any sort during this period, as the inherent physical energy of Mars then backfires, and that car or vehicle then has an ongoing tendency to be accident-prone. Have any car or vehicle repairs done before Mars Retrograde period, especially before Mars and Mercury are retrograde simultaneously. Avoid scheduling a marriage ceremony at this time, as the sexual love energy also symbolized by Mars is more internalized and less accessible. Also avoid starting a job during Mars Retrograde, as this is essentially a review period for work as well as for physical and sexual energy. The ironic part about a Mars-Retrograde period, especially if your personal orientation tends to be rather Mars-like (via angular Mars, Sun/Mars in hard contact, or Personal Points located in the sign of Aries) is that the urge is very strong to take the initiative and to be aggressive, partly because we unconsciously sense that there is a temporary pulling back or a curtailing of this aggressive energy.

Jupiter Retrograde (♃ R): Occurs annually for approximately four months. Jupiter's natural expansiveness and sense of optimism might be slightly impeded during this time. The idealism and philosophical proclivities are more introspective. Jupiter Retrograde can impede negotiations regarding financial matters (loans from banks, gifts or loans from wealthy people) and foreign travel. It can also slow down upward momentum in the stock market, unless ♃ R is also in an Earth sign. (In the mid-late 1980s, Jupiter's retrograde period has begun after most of the other outer planets have gone direct, so it has not been associated with as much relative slowdown of plans.) Not ideal to start a job at this time.

Saturn Retrograde (♄ R): Occurs annually for approximately 4-1/2 months.

Uranus Retrograde (♅ R): Occurs annually for approximately 5 months.

Neptune Retrograde (♆ R): Occurs annually for approximately 5-1/4 months.

Pluto Retrograde (♇ R): Occurs annually for approximately 5-1/4 months.

The four outermost planets tend to be retrograde in overlapping simultaneous blocks, and they relate to larger organizations (world and national governing bodies and corporations) which are having to do some housecleaning or review before they can make bold steps forward. The rest of us are affected in that our individual plans may be temporarily slowed down by this chain reaction.

3. The Monthly Rhythm: The Lunar Phases

The lunar cycle of 29-1/2 days is a crucial one in aligning human beings with the monthly ebb and flow of life. It is closely associated with the emotional flow and human excitability, women's menstrual cycles, and the oceans' tides. In the waxing phase of the Moon, from the New Moon to the Full Moon, we usually experience fresh new energy with which to move our projects—not only physically, but emotionally and mentally. The waning phase, from Full Moon (or two days after) to the exact New Moon, tends to symbolize the implementation and also the implications of the plans and actions we set in motion during the waxing phase.

When scheduling an important event, such as a wedding, the founding of a company, or the kickoff of any major project, it is more highly recommended to do so during the waxing Moon (and for a wedding, one avoids getting too close to the Full Moon by at least two to three days minimum, and one avoids the Last or Fourth Quarter Moon).[1] The waxing Moon reflects energy which is in the growth, flowering, and blooming stages, which is why it is ideal symbolically for the start of a major venture. During the last two days or so of the waning phase we can often experience less energy available, especially if the physical energy is low to begin with, in which case it is almost immediately perceptible when the New Moon has taken place.

Here are some exceptions to this usual ebb and flow of the lunar month:

1) When the Moon is above the horizon during the business day, which happens for five days *before* the New Moon and five days *after* the New Moon. The Earth's magnetic field is known to be generally stronger each day from about two hours after moonrise until about two hours after moonset. Because of the stronger magnetic field, we have increased energy levels, but they are probably less stable and more outwardly induced during the last two days of the waning Moon.

2) When there is a New Moon solar eclipse, which causes the energy level to be more excitable due to alterations in the Earth's electromagnetic field (discussed on pp. 241 and 243). Thus the usual sense of decreasing energy during the last two days of the waning Moon is less likely just before an eclipse.

3) When the New or Full Moon is also in perigee (closest approach to the Earth), called a "SuperMoon." During a SuperMoon, there is a history of evidence to confirm correlations with upheavals in weather and seismic activity, as well as in mass psychology, including social and economic disruptions. When SuperMoons form close hard contacts to Personal Points in the natal chart, a major emotional effect can be felt in the weeks following the SuperMoon. (The Moon's perigee and apogee [its furthest position

---

1. There are certain exceptions to avoiding the Full Moon wedding, such as when both parties have many key planetary factors, especially their own Sun and Moon tying into that Full Moon.

from the Earth] are commonly listed in yearly astrological calendars.)

4) When there is a simultaneous convergence of hard contacts between planets, measured heliocentrically—which can temporarily upset or even amplify the natural monthly rhythm. (See text pp. 18; 28-29). This occurs much less often, several times a year on average. Known to coincide with short-wave radio disturbances and magnetic storms in the Earth's ionosophere, it is not surprising that these configurations also coincide with disturbances in the human energy field. The dates when such phenomena occur are listed annually in *Valliere's Natural Cycles Almanac*. During 1991, major stellar combinations of this type (again, measured heliocentrically) occurred March 18-22 and April 18-25.[2]

4. The Daily Rhythm:
Angular Planets and Moon Void of Course

As we have learned from much evidence, especially from the Gauquelin research, angular planets, particularly when rising or culminating, are very strong in their influence. In daily rhythms, we also examine the planets that set, come to the lower meridian, and east and west of the Midheaven. Depending on the nature of the planets that come to the angles, we have periods of time throughout the day that are easier and go more smoothly than others. Such times are shown in the shaded areas of the kinetic mundascope graphs in *Valliere's Natural Cycles Almanac*, and they vary in their frequency and time length every month.[3] The lines here are perfectly calibrated for New York City's longitude and latitude, but at the back of the Almanac are simple instructions for how to make time corrections for your locality (cities in the continental USA only, anywhere between 25° and 49° north latitude). Generally speaking, when Mars, Saturn, Uranus, Neptune, and/or Pluto get involved, it is no longer such smooth sailing as it is with Sun, Venus, Jupiter, and

---

2. There is also a noticeably heightened effect when, *geocentrically,* a cluster of planets converges in one sign, or are in hard aspect. Though neither of these combinations has been known to coincide with changes in the Earth's electromagnetic field (as do clusters of heliocentric hard contacts), nevertheless they are important in concentrating planetary energy in a certain arena of life for the individual or the collective. Clusters of five or more planets within 20° of arc are listed in Michelsen's *Tables of Planetary Phenomena*. It covers a time period from 1700 to 2050.

3. See illustration on page 249 from *Valliere's Natural Cycles Almanac,* 1989, published by Astrolabe, Inc. (See Appendix G, p. 276, for information on how to order *Valliere's.)*

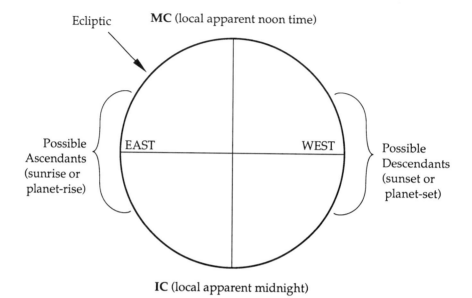

*The Angles of the Chart: Measuring
the Diurnal Movements of the Planets*

MC: *Midheaven, where the upper meridian intersects the ecliptic. MC =
        abbreviation of the Latin* medium coeli, *middle of the sky. A planet culminates
        at the MC.*

IC: *Abbreviation of the Latin* immum coeli, *bottom of the sky. The point where the
        lower meridian intersects the ecliptic. A planet anti-culminates at the IC.*

ASC: *Ascendant, where the easterm horizon meets the ecliptic, and where the Sun
        can be seen rising early in the day. The angle of the ASC in relation to the MC is
        not always 90°, but depends on latitude and time of year. The Sun, being on the
        ecliptic, is always at 0° celestial latitude (measured north or south of the ecliptic)
        and thus always rises within a few minutes of reaching the ASC from below the
        horizon. Other planets, especially Pluto, but also at times Moon and Mercury,
        go to high latitudes and thus may rise or set up to an hour before or after
        reaching the exact degree (expressed in zodiacal longitude) of the ASC or DSC,
        respectively. Regardless of whether it is actually 90° from the MC, the ASC is
        shown as such in most computerized astrological charts.*

DSC: *Desendant, where the western horizon meets the ecliptic and where the Sun can
        be seen to set.*

EAST: *The exact East Point, or Equatorial Ascendant, is where the eastern horizon
        intersects the prime vertical and the celestial equator. When a planet is Easting
        or Westing, it is very close to 90° east or west of the MC. When the MC is within
        a few degrees of the Cardinal axis (i.e. 0° ♈, ♋,   , or ♑) the East Point
        coincides with the ASC.*

ECLIPTIC: *The Sun's apparent path around the Earth.*

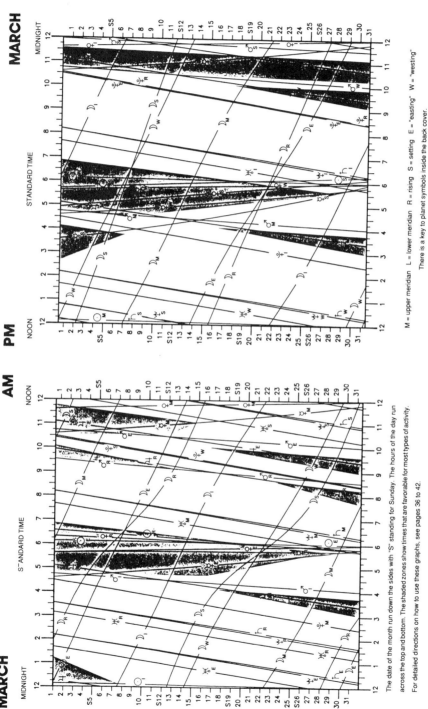

MARCH

MIDNIGHT · STANDARD TIME · NOON

PM

AM

NOON · STANDARD TIME · MIDNIGHT

MARCH

M = upper meridian   L = lower meridian   R = rising   S = setting   E = "easting"   W = "westing"

There is a key to planet symbols inside the back cover.

The date of the month run down the sides with "S" standing for Sunday. The hours of the day run across the top and bottom. The shaded zones show times that are favorable for most types of activity.

For detailed directions on how to use these graphs, see pages 36 to 42.

more marginally, Mercury. We've already seen how this is true with the planetary lines on the Astro·Carto·Graphy maps.

However, just as with the yearly and monthly rhythms, there are other factors that could periodically contradict what should normally be a smooth situation. The main factor that can account for daily mixups or confusion is Moon Void of Course. Astrologers speak of the Moon as Void of Course (VOC) when, while in a certain zodiac sign, it is no longer in an angular relationship (in aspect) with other planets that can be measured in the classical Ptolemaic terms (i.e. 0°, 60°, 90°, 120°, 180°). Any astrological calendar or ephemeris will normally list the VOC Moon periods month by month, usually in Greenwich Mean Time (GMT) or Eastern Standard Time (EST). When the Moon enters the next zodiacal sign (called an "ingress") the Moon VOC period is over.

For the layperson, these standard Moon VOC periods will generally suffice for useful daily information, when needed. However, if you want to look more deeply, especially in planning or studying an event, there are some exceptions to using only the classical Ptolemaic aspects. For example, some astrologers consider the true VOC period to begin *after* the completion of the so-called "minor" aspects, especially by 8th and 16th harmonics—such as the 45° (semi-square) or 135° (sesquiquadrate)—or the parallels (which are measured by the planet's declination, or angular distance, from the celestial equator). These aspects are all listed in a Daily Aspectarian (see p. 252).

The Moon stays in each sign for about 2-1/2 days, so there can be Moon VOC as often as every other day, for as short as a few minutes to as long as nearly two days. The effect can be similar to experiencing Mercury Retrograde, in that the daily efficient functioning of ordinary affairs is not particularly grounded. In astrological terms, the Moon VOC is not linked up with the other planets, so it is in a kind of limbo, ideal for internalized, introspective, and inspirational work, but not so ideal for getting things done with practical and precise results.[4] Other people are apt to be temporarily unreachable or unreliable. And you could be too.

---

4. In the case of James Dean's fatal automobile accident around dusk on September 30, 1955 (discussed in Chapter 4), we notice that not only is Mercury going Stationary Retrograde that very day at 6:14 p.m. Pacific Standard Time, but also the Moon is Void of Course the same day from 7:26 a.m. to 9:56 p.m. PST, further corroborating the number of overwhelming negative astrological factors.

When there are longish periods of Moon VOC, longer than an hour or two, especially when combined with Mercury Retrograde, obviously you do not want to plan something that needs precision or at least advantageous results. This is because the Moon is symbolic of our ability to flow towards our desired goals in life, and when the Moon is VOC it contradicts the best laid plans, astrologically-speaking. It represents a situation where the people involved usually drift and get sidetracked from their intended goals. (This does not apply to the natal chart with Moon VOC.)

For example, you would not want Moon VOC for the scheduling of an important event, such as a wedding, an incorporation, or any major starting point celebrated as an event in life. Nor would you want a Moon VOC within a few hours *after* the event, unless you desire little to no developments from the event. The exceptions are minor hard aspects, as mentioned above, although they too can be risky, and the final aspect the Moon makes before leaving a sign should be favorable. (This gives a hint of the complexity of electional and horary astrology.)

5. The Ephemeris: What It Is and How to Use It

In ancient times astrologers determined the planets' positions by direct observation and with the use of various handmade instruments. Modern astrologers are fortunate to have a publication called an ephemeris to tell where the planets are located.[5] The word comes from the Greek *ephemeros,* existing no longer than a day, and as you can see from the sample page, each planet is listed in its new position every 24 hours throughout the month, beginning at midnight Greenwich Mean Time (GMT). Ephemerides exist for one or more celestial bodies, but the example on the next page is typical of the ones used by modern astrologers, especially in the United States. It includes the Sun, Moon, Moon's Node (measured two different ways), and planets Mercury through Pluto. Heliocentric ephemerides are also available, though most are geocentric, and sometimes heliocentric positions are given right alongside geocentric positions for each day. They are two separate sets of coordinates, however, and heliocentric and geocentric positions

---

5. Ephemerides are available from various specialized publishers in the United States and abroad. I recommend those published by Astro Communications, Inc. (See Appendix G, p. 275, for information on ordering an ephemeris.)

NOVEMBER 1977

LONGITUDE

Day	Sid. Time	☉	☽	☽ 12 Hour	Mean ☊	True ☊	☿	♀	♂	♃	♄	♅	♆	♇
	h m s	° ' "	° ' "	° ' "	° '	° '	° '	° '	° '	° '	° '	° '	° '	° '
1	2 40 40	8♏ 27 12	3♋ 36 56	9♋ 32 46	13♎ 47	15♎ 0R	16♏ 36	18♎ 33	2♌ 9	6♋ 3R	29♌ 4	11♏ 53	14♐ 32	15♎ 2
2	2 44 37	9 27 14	15 29 27	21 27 30	13 44	14 57	18 10	19 48	2 33	6 1	29 9	11 57	14 34	15 4
3	2 48 33	10 27 18	27 27 27	3♌ 29 51	13 41	14 55	19 43	21 3	2 56	5 59	29 13	12 1	14 36	15 6
4	2 52 30	11 27 24	9♌ 35 16	15 44 18	13 38	14 55D	21 16	22 18	3 19	5 57	29 17	12 4	14 38	15 8
5	2 56 26	12 27 32	21 57 32	28 15 31	13 34	14 55	22 48	23 33	3 42	5 55	29 20	12 8	14 40	15 10
6	3 0 23	13 27 43	4♍ 38 46	11♍ 7 48	13 31	14 56	24 20	24 48	4 4	5 53	29 24	12 12	14 42	15 13
7	3 4 19	14 27 55	17 43 2	24 24 46	13 28	14 58	25 52	26 3	4 25	5 50	29 28	12 16	14 44	15 15
8	3 8 16	15 28 10	1♎ 13 16	8♎ 8 35	13 25	15 0R	27 24	27 18	4 47	5 47	29 32	12 19	14 46	15 17
9	3 12 13	16 28 26	15 10 42	22 19 20	13 22	15 0	28 54	28 33	5 8	5 44	29 35	12 23	14 48	15 19
10	3 16 9	17 28 45	29 34 6	6♏ 54 23	13 18	14 59	0♐ 25	29 48	5 28	5 41	29 39	12 27	14 50	15 21
11	3 20 6	18 29 5	14♏ 19 23	21 48 10	13 15	14 57	1 55	1♏ 3	5 48	5 38	29 42	12 31	14 52	15 23
12	3 24 2	19 29 27	29 19 38	6♐ 52 35	13 12	14 53	3 25	2 18	6 8	5 34	29 45	12 34	14 54	15 25
13	3 27 59	20 29 51	14♐ 25 47	21 58 2	13 9	14 48	4 54	3 33	6 27	5 30	29 48	12 38	14 56	15 27
14	3 31 55	21 30 16	29 28 7	6♑ 55 1	13 6	14 42	6 24	4 48	6 45	5 26	29 51	12 42	14 58	15 29
15	3 35 52	22 30 42	14♑ 17 47	21 35 40	13 3	14 37	7 52	6 4	7 4	5 22	29 54	12 45	15 0	15 31
16	3 39 48	23 31 10	28 48 6	5♒ 54 44	12 59	14 33	9 20	7 19	7 21	5 18	29 57	12 49	15 3	15 33
17	3 43 45	24 31 40	12♒ 55 19	19 49 50	12 56	14 31D	10 48	8 34	7 38	5 13	0♍ 0	12 53	15 5	15 35
18	3 47 42	25 32 10	26 38 22	3♓ 21 8	12 53	14 30	12 15	9 49	7 55	5 9	0 2	12 57	15 7	15 37
19	3 51 38	26 32 42	9♓ 58 24	16 30 32	12 50	14 31	13 42	11 4	8 11	5 4	0 5	13 0	15 9	15 39
20	3 55 35	27 33 15	22 57 55	29 20 58	12 47	14 33	15 8	12 20	8 27	4 59	0 7	13 4	15 11	15 41
21	3 59 31	28 33 49	5♈ 40 7	11♈ 55 45	12 44	14 34R	16 33	13 35	8 42	4 54	0 10	13 8	15 13	15 43
22	4 3 28	29 34 25	18 8 16	24 18 2	12 40	14 34	17 57	14 50	8 56	4 48	0 12	13 11	15 16	15 45
23	4 7 24	0♐ 35 1	0♉ 25 23	6♉ 30 36	12 37	14 33	19 21	16 5	9 10	4 43	0 14	13 15	15 18	15 46
24	4 11 21	1 35 39	12 33 59	18 35 45	12 34	14 29	20 44	17 21	9 24	4 37	0 16	13 19	15 20	15 48
25	4 15 17	2 36 18	24 36 7	0♊ 35 17	12 31	14 22	22 5	18 36	9 37	4 31	0 18	13 22	15 22	15 50
26	4 19 14	3 36 59	6♊ 33 27	12 30 45	12 28	14 14	23 25	19 51	9 49	4 25	0 19	13 26	15 24	15 52
27	4 23 11	4 37 41	18 27 24	24 23 33	12 24	14 4	24 44	21 7	10 0	4 19	0 21	13 29	15 27	15 54
28	4 27 7	5 38 24	0♋ 19 25	6♋ 15 13	12 21	13 53	26 1	22 22	10 11	4 13	0 23	13 33	15 29	15 55
29	4 31 4	6 39 9	12 11 11	18 7 38	12 18	13 43	27 17	23 37	10 22	4 7	0 24	13 36	15 31	15 57
30	4 35 0	7♐ 39 56	24♋ 4 52	0♌ 3 14	12♎ 15	13♎ 34	28♐ 30	24♏ 53	10♌ 31	4♋ 0	0♍ 25	13♏ 40	15♐ 33	15♎ 59

DECLINATION and LATITUDE

Day	☉ Decl	☽ Decl	☽ Lat	☽ 12 Hr. Decl	☿ Decl	☿ Lat	♀ Decl	♀ Lat	♂ Decl	♂ Lat	♃ Decl	♃ Lat	♄ Decl	♄ Lat
1	14S19	18N16	5S 8	17N54	17S25	0S38	5S50	1N33	21N 6	1N27	22N57	0S21	12N55	1N12
2	14 39	17 21	5 14	16 36	17 58	0 45	6 19	1 33	21 2	1 29	22 58	0 21	12 54	1 12
3	14 58	15 39	5 7	14 33	18 29	0 51	6 47	1 32	20 58	1 31	22 58	0 21	12 53	1 12
4	15 16	13 16	4 46	11 49	19 0	0 58	7 16	1 32	20 55	1 32	22 58	0 21	12 51	1 12
5	15 35	10 14	4 11	8 30	19 30	1 4	7 44	1 31	20 51	1 34	22 58	0 21	12 50	1 13
6	15 53	6 39	3 23	4 42	19 60	1 10	8 12	1 30	20 48	1 36	22 58	0 21	12 49	1 13
7	16 11	2 39	2 24	0 32	20 28	1 16	8 40	1 30	20 45	1 38	22 58	0 20	12 48	1 13
8	16 29	1S38	1 15	3S48	20 55	1 22	9 8	1 29	20 42	1 40	22 59	0 20	12 47	1 13
9	16 46	5 58	0N 1	8 4	21 21	1 28	9 35	1 28	20 38	1 42	22 59	0 20	12 46	1 13
10	17 3	10 6	1 19	11 59	21 46	1 33	10 3	1 27	20 35	1 44	22 59	0 20	12 45	1 14
11	17 20	13 42	2 33	15 12	22 10	1 39	10 30	1 26	20 32	1 46	22 59	0 20	12 44	1 14
12	17 36	16 27	3 38	17 26	22 33	1 44	10 57	1 25	20 29	1 48	22 59	0 20	12 43	1 14
13	17 53	18 5	4 28	18 26	22 54	1 49	11 23	1 24	20 27	1 50	22 60	0 20	12 42	1 14
14	18 8	18 27	4 60	18 8	23 15	1 54	11 50	1 23	20 24	1 52	22 60	0 20	12 41	1 14
15	18 24	17 32	5 11	16 38	23 34	1 59	12 16	1 21	20 21	1 55	23 0	0 20	12 40	1 15
16	18 39	15 29	5 1	14 7	23 53	2 3	12 42	1 20	20 19	1 57	23 0	0 20	12 40	1 15
17	18 54	12 34	4 34	10 51	24 10	2 7	13 7	1 19	20 17	1 59	23 1	0 20	12 39	1 15
18	19 9	9 1	3 51	7 6	24 26	2 11	13 32	1 17	20 14	2 1	23 1	0 20	12 38	1 15
19	19 23	5 6	2 57	3 5	24 40	2 14	13 57	1 16	20 12	2 3	23 1	0 19	12 37	1 16
20	19 37	1 2	1 54	0N59	24 53	2 17	14 22	1 14	20 10	2 5	23 2	0 19	12 37	1 16
21	19 51	2N59	0 48	4 56	25 5	2 20	14 46	1 13	20 8	2 8	23 2	0 19	12 36	1 15
22	20 4	6 49	0S19	8 37	25 16	2 23	15 9	1 11	20 7	2 10	23 2	0 19	12 36	1 16
23	20 17	10 18	1 25	11 52	25 25	2 25	15 33	1 9	20 5	2 12	23 2	0 19	12 35	1 16
24	20 29	13 18	2 25	14 35	25 33	2 26	15 56	1 8	20 4	2 15	23 3	0 19	12 35	1 17
25	20 41	15 43	3 19	16 39	25 40	2 28	16 18	1 6	20 3	2 17	23 3	0 19	12 34	1 17
26	20 53	17 25	4 3	17 59	25 45	2 28	16 41	1 4	20 2	2 19	23 3	0 19	12 34	1 17
27	21 4	18 22	4 36	18 32	25 48	2 28	17 2	1 2	20 1	2 22	23 4	0 19	12 33	1 17
28	21 15	18 29	4 57	18 15	25 51	2 28	17 23	1 0	20 0	2 24	23 4	0 19	12 33	1 18
29	21 25	17 49	5 5	17 11	25 52	2 27	17 44	0 58	19 60	2 27	23 4	0 18	12 33	1 18
30	21S35	16N22	5S 0	15N22	25S51	2S25	18S 5	0N56	19N59	2N29	23N 5	0S18	12N32	1N18

Day	♅ Decl	♅ Lat	♆ Decl	♆ Lat	♇ Decl	♇ Lat
1	15S 2	0N23	21S 8	1N26	9N22	16N34
5	15 7	0 23	21 9	1 26	9 20	16 35
9	15 11	0 23	21 10	1 26	9 18	16 36
13	15 16	0 23	21 11	1 25	9 16	16 38
17	15 20	0 23	21 12	1 25	9 14	16 39
21	15 25	0 23	21 13	1 25	9 13	16 40
25	15 29	0 23	21 14	1 25	9 11	16 42
29	15S33	0N23	21S15	1N25	9N10	16N44

☽ PHENOMENA

d	h	m	
4	3	59	☾
11	7	10	●
17	21	53	☽
25	17	32	○

d	h	° '
7	15	0
13	19	18S28
20	6	0
27	16	18N32

1	23	5S14
9	0	0
15	1	5N11
21	17	0
29	3	5S 5

VOID OF COURSE ☽

Last Aspect		☽ Ingress		
2	9am41	3	♌	5am 4
5	2pm 7	5	♍	3pm17
7	4pm26	7	♎	9pm52
10	0am25	10	♏	0am43
12	0am41	12	♐	1am 4
14	0am37	14	♑	0am51
15	2pm32	16	♒	2am 1
17	9pm53	18	♓	5am59
20	9am21	20	♈	1pm14
21	11pm36	22	♉	11pm10
24	10am37	25	♊	10am49
27	2pm15	27	♋	11pm21
30	1am48	30	♌	11am54

d	h	
12	12	PERIGEE
27	20	APOGEE

DAILY ASPECTARIAN

Day	Aspect	Time
1 T	☽☌♃	4am53
	☉△☽	10 42
	☽∥☿	3pm21
	☽△♅	4 49
	☽∠♄	9 16
	☽×♆	10 8
	☽□♇	11 8
2 W	☽△☿	6am11
	☽□♀	9 41
3 Th	☽×♄	3am31
	☽⚼♆	4 17
	☽∥♅	6 29
	☉∥☽	6 48
	☉∥♅	9 16
	☽☌♂	11 14
	☽×♃	4pm53
	☿⚼♃	7 18
4 F	☽∥♄	3am32
	☉□☽	3 59
	☽□♅	4 53
	☽△♆	9 53
	☽⚹♇	10 52
	☉☌♅	3pm42
	☽∠♃	10 1
5 S	☽□☿	1am51
	☽⚹♀	3 23
	☽∥♇	6 22
	☽☌♄	2pm 7
	☽∥♀	3 8
	☽∠♇	3 40
	☽×♂	10 53
6 Su	☽⚹♃	2am17
	☽∠♀	10 33
	☽⚹♅	2pm 1
	☉⚹☽	5 37
	☽□♆	6 34
	☽×♇	7 31
7 M	☽∠♂	3am10
	☉×♆	6 35
	☿∥♂	1pm27
	☿×♀	3 29
	☽×♀	4 24
	☽⚹☿	4 26
	☽∠♅	5 7
	☉×♇	7 21
	☽×♄	9 1
	☉∠☽	10 35
8 T	☽⚹♂	6am21
	☽□♃	7 55
	♀∥♇	8 52
	☿∥♆	1pm26
	☽×♅	7 14
	☽∠☿	9 35
	☽∠♄	10 59
	☽⚹♆	11 21
9 W	☽☌♇	0am14
	☉×☽	2 21
	☿□♄	11 11
	☿ ♐	5pm21
	☽∥♇	7 8
	♀⚹♄	8 52
	☿∠♇	10 55
	☽∥♀	11 40
10 Th	☽⚹♄	0am 7
	☽☌♀	0 25
	☽∠♆	0 26
	♀∠♆	0 42
	☽×☿	1 33
	♀ ♏	3 52
	☽□♂	9 53
	☽△♃	9 58
	♂×♃	1pm15
	☽∥♄	5 7
	☽☌♅	9 4
11 F	☽×♆	0am53
	☽×♇	1 43
	☉☌☽	7 10
	☽⚼♃	10 5
	☽∥♅	12pm19
12 S	☽□♄	0am41
	☽∠♇	1 45
	☽×♀	5 10
	☽☌☿	7 13
	☽×♃	9 53
	☽△♂	11 3
	☉∥☽	6pm21
	☽×♅	9 8
13 Su	☉⚼♃	0am11
	☽☌♆	0 49
	☽⚹♇	1 38
	☿∥♃	6 11
	☽∠♀	7 9
	☿×♃	9 15
	☉×☽	10 21
	☽⚼♂	11 25
	☽∠♅	9pm 9
14 M	☽△♄	0am37
	☿△♂	7 28
	☉∥☽	9 2
	☽⚹♀	9 23
	☽☍♃	9 34
	♀△♃	11 31
	☽×♂	11 59
	☉∠☽	12pm10
	☽×☿	12 23
	☽⚹♅	9 29
15 T	☽⚼♄	1am 0
	☽×♆	1 10
	☽□♇	2 0
	☉⚹☽	2pm32
	☽∠☿	3 43
	♀∥♄	10 14
16 W	♀□♂	1am 4
	☽∥♅	1 32
	☽×♄	1 56
	☽∠♆	2 5
	☽×♃	10 54
	☽☍♂	2pm45
	☽□♀	3 47
	☽⚹☿	7 55
	☽∥♀	8 21
	☽∥♄	11 22
	☽□♅	11 56
17 Th	♄ ♍	2am51
	☽⚹♆	3 44
	☽△♇	4 37
	☽⚼♃	12pm37
	☉□☽	9 53
	☽∥♇	10 39
18 F	☽☍♄	6am 4
	☽⚼♇	7 7
	☿×♅	12pm 0
	☽△♃	3 9
	☽×♂	8 41
19 S	☽△♀	2am13
	☽△♅	5 34
	☽□☿	7 39
	☽□♆	9 31
	☽×♇	10 26
20 Su	☽⚼♂	0am55
	☿☌♆	1 3
	☽⚼♀	9 5
	☉△☽	9 21
	☿⚹♇	9 34
	☽⚼♅	9 37
	☽×♄	1pm30
	♀☌♅	2 53
	☽□♃	10 32
21 M	☽△♂	5am55
	☽×♅	2pm23
	☉⚼☽	4 29
	☽×♀	4 53
	☽⚼♄	6 17
	☽△♆	6 25
	☽☍♇	7 21
	☽△☿	11 36
22 T	☉∥♂	5am 7
	♀×♆	8 23
	☉ ♐	10 8
	☉□♄	3pm18
	☽∥♇	4 7
	♀∥♅	5 42
	♀×♇	5 50
	☽△♄	11 37
	☽⚼♆	11 45
23 W	☉×☽	0am21
	☉∠♇	4 40
	☽⚹♃	8 23
	☽⚼☿	8 43
	☽□♂	5pm36
	☽∥♄	5 47
24 Th	☽☍♅	1am29
	☽×♆	5 31
	☽×♇	6 27
	☽☍♀	10 37
	☽∠♃	1pm56
	☽×☿	6 20
	☽∥♅	9 26
25 F	☽∥♀	9am 9
	☽□♄	11 26
	☽⚼♇	12pm31
	♀⚼♃	4 22
	☉☍☽	5 32
	☽×♃	7 45
26 S	☽⚹♂	6am40
	☽×♅	1pm55
	☉×♃	5 24
	☽☍♆	5 54
	☽△♇	6 48
27 Su	☿⚼♂	5am49
	☽×♀	6 0
	☽∠♂	1pm27
	☽☍☿	2 15
	☽⚼♅	8 23
	☉∥♆	10 55
28 M	☽⚹♄	0am 7
	☽☌♃	7 49
	☉×☽	11 46
	☽⚼♀	3pm56
	☽×♂	8 16
29 T	☽∥♀	1am18
	☽△♅	2 53
	☽∠♄	6 31
	☽×♆	6 45
	☽□♇	7 37
	☉⚼☽	8pm53
30 W	☽△♀	1am48
	☿∠♅	3 30
	☽∥♅	9 35
	☽×☿	9 52
	☽×♄	12pm46
	☽⚼♆	1 3
	☽×♃	7 43

Page from The American Ephemeris: 1931-1980 & Book of Tables, *compiled and programmed by Neil F. Michelsen, published by Astro Communications Services, Inc. (formerly ACS Publications and Astro Computing Services, Inc.), 1976.*

should not be mixed at random.

The layperson might want to go through an ephemeris to observe when planets go retrograde and direct, when the lunar phases and eclipses occur, when Moon Void of Course occurs, and, later on, when the planets enter new zodiacal signs (called ingresses), especially the Sun, geocentrically, at the Solstices and Equinoxes. Astrologers also observe declination of planets (measured north and south of the celestial equator), and their celestial latitude (measured north and south of the ecliptic). "Sid. time" is short for sidereal (pronounced si-deér-ial) time, from the Latin *sidus, sideris,* constellation or star. The time given is reckoned from the vantage point of the fixed stars for a specific locality, which is then translated by the astrologer through calculations (nowadays usually on a computer) to get a usable clock time for a specific longitude and latitude.

The "Daily Aspectarian" is also for more advanced use. It shows the aspects, or angular planetary relationships, which occur daily. The time given in GMT is when the new planetary contact begins. The astrologer uses these for further nuances that provide more detail to the larger picture shown by angular planets and the Moon Void of Course.

Appendix B
A Listing of All the Birth Data Used in This Book (In Alphabetical Order by Name), with Data Sources

Standards of longitude and latitude have been obtained from the following atlases:

1) *The American Atlas: US Latitudes and Longitudes, Time Changes and Time Zones,* compiled and programmed by Thomas G. Shanks, 5th revised edition, 1990.

2) *The International Atlas: World Latitudes, Longitudes and Time Changes,* compiled and programmed by Thomas G. Shanks, 1985.

The following abbreviations for data sources will be found in the listing of birth data:

ABC *The American Book of Charts,* by Lois M. Rodden, 1980. (Reprinted under the title Astro–Data II.)

ADIII *Astro–Data III,* by Lois M. Rodden, 1986.

CBC *The Circle Book of Charts,* compiled by Stephen Erlewine, revised edition, 1982.

GBAC *The Gauquelin Book of American Charts,* by Michel and Francoise Gauquelin, 1982.

PW *Profiles of Women: A Collection of Astrological Biographies,* by Lois M. Rodden, 1979.

1) **Bundy, Theodore:** Nov. 24, 1946, 10:35 p.m. EST (Zone +5), Burlington, Vermont, 73W12, 44N29. (Died Jan. 24, 1989.) Data source: T. Patrick Davis, astrologer, quotes birth certificate. (Quoted in ADIII).

2) **Burton, Richard:** Nov. 10, 1925, 7:58 p.m. Zone +00, Pontrhydyfendigaid, South Wales, 3W51, 52N17. (Died Aug. 5, 1984.) Data source: Ronald Davison, astrologer, in his book *Synastry: Understanding Human Relations Through Astrology,* in

which he writes "from an American source, rectified. . . ." (Quoted in ABC.) There are still various proposed birth times for Richard Burton, none of them absolutely confirmed.

3) **Campbell, Joseph:** March 26, 1904, 7:25 p.m. EST (Zone +5), New York, N.Y., 73W57, 40N45. (Died Oct. 30, 1987.) Data source: From his mother to Erin Cameron, astrologer, 1981. (Quoted in ADIII.)

4) **Dean, James:** Feb. 8, 1931, 9:09 p.m. CST (Zone +6), Marion, Indiana, 85W40, 40N32. (Died Sept. 30, 1955.) Data source: Church of Light Research and Data Dept., Los Angeles, CA, quotes birth certificate. (Quoted in ABC. New data of 2 a.m. birth time presented in Rodden's ABC, *Supplement to First Edition*, Jan. 1, 1988, from biography source *James Dean: A Short Life Story*, by V. Hearndon. However, this title is *not* listed in *Books in Print* or in the Library of Congress data base, which covers some 15 million titles. As a privately published book it may lack in qualified research data. In addition, a time close to, if not in fact 9:09 p.m. more accurately fits Dean's character and timing.)

5) **Diana, Princess:** July 1, 1961, 7:45 p.m. BST (Zone –1), Sandringham, England, 52N50, 0E30. Data source: Charles Harvey, astrologer, quotes Diana's mother. (Quoted in ADIII.)

6) **Feynman, Richard:** May 11, 1918, time not available, Far Rockaway, New York, 73W45, 40N36. (Died Feb. 15, 1988.) Data source: Date of birth in *Current Biography Yearbook* 1986, p. 128. Place of birth given in Feynman's autobiographical account, *"Surely You're Joking, Mr. Feynman!": Adventures of a Curious Character*, 1985.

7) **Ford, Gerald:** July 14, 1913, 00:43 a.m. CST (Zone +6), Omaha, Nebraska, 96W01, 41N17. Data source: Jeff Mayo, astrologer, in [American Federation of Astrologers] *AFA Bulletin*, March 1976, from data recorded in Ford's baby book. (Quoted in ADIII.)

8) **Gacey, John Wayne:** March 17, 1942, 12:20 a.m. CST (Zone +6), Chicago, Illinois, 87W39, 41N52. Data source: Edith Custer, astrologer, quoted in *Mercury Hour*, April 1979, "hospital birth record." Standard time confirmed by the hospital. (Quoted in ABC.)

9) **Gandhi, Indira:** Nov. 19, 1917, 11:39 p.m. (Zone –5.5), Allahabad, India, 81E50, 25N27. (Died Oct. 31, 1984.) Data source:

Zipporah Dobyns, astrologer, obtained birth data in India, 1977. (Quoted in PW.)

10) **Gandhi, Mahatma:** Oct. 2, 1869, 7:12 a.m. LMT, Porbandar, India, 69E37, 21N38. (Died Jan. 30, 1948.) Data source: Cyril Fagan, astrologer, quoted in *AFA Bulletin,* March 1948, "Shake 1791, Bhadrapad Vadya 12th, three ghatis and 12 Palas after sunrise [i.e. 7:11:48 a.m. LMT], from Yeshawant K. Pradhan in *Voice of India,* Feb. 1924...." Other birth times from other sources differ, though most are around sunrise. (Quoted in ABC, p. 304.)

11) **Garbo, Greta:** Sept. 18, 1905, 7:30 p.m. MET (Zone –1), Stockholm Sweden, 18E03, 59N20. (Died April 15, 1990.) Data source: Ivan Wilhelm, astrologer, quotes birth certificate in hand. (Quoted in PW, *Supplement,* 4th printing Feb. 1986.)

Grace, Princess: see Kelly, Grace

12) **Griffin, Merv**: July 6, 1925, 4:45 a.m. PST (Zone +8), San Mateo, California, 37N34, 122W19. Data source: *Contemporary Sidereal Horoscopes,* compiled by Clark, Gilchrist, Mackey and Dorminy, 1976. (Quoted in ABC.)

13) **Hauptman, Bruno:** Nov. 26, 1899, 1:00 p.m. MET (Zone –1), Kamenz, Germany, 14E06, 51N16. Data source: T. Patrick Davis, astrologer, quotes a radiogram "from [Hauptman's] mother to Paul Clancy [astrologer]." (Quoted in ABC.)

14) **Hoffman, Dustin:** August 8, 1937, 5:07 p.m. PST (Zone +8), Los Angeles, California, 118W15, 34N04. Data source: Lockhart, astrologer, quotes birth certificate. (Quoted in ABC.)

15) **Jones, Jim:** May 13, 1931, 10:00 p.m. CST (Zone +6), Lynn, Indiana, 84W56, 40N03. Data source: Zipporah Dobyns, astrologer, quotes Beverly Good "from newspaper sources in Indiana." (Quoted in ABC.)

16) **Jung, Carl Gustav:** July 26, 1875, 7:26 p.m. GMT (Zone +00), Kesswil, Switzerland, 9E19, 47N36. Data source: Various, all qualified to around local sunset. Exact time unknown. (Quoted in ABC.)

17) **Kelly, Grace:** Nov. 12, 1929, 5:31 a.m. EST (Zone +5), Philadelphia, Pennsylvania, 75W10, 39N57. (Died September 14, 1982.) Data source: Confirmed on birth certificate from Bob Garner via Edwin Steinbrecher, astrologer. (Quoted in PW, *Supplement*, 4th printing, Feb. 1986.)

18) **Kennedy, David Anthony:** June 13, 1955. No time or location currently available. (Died April 25, 1984.) Data source: The author obtained from newspapers during last week of April 1984. Not verifiable in *Facts on File, Who's Who* volumes, or other biographical sources to date.

19) **Kennedy, John F.:** May 29, 1917, 3:00 p.m. EST (Zone +5), Brookline, Massachusetts, 71W07, 42N20. (Died Nov. 22, 1963.) Data source: Garth Allen, astrologer, in *American Astrology*, May 1960, from JFK's mother. (Quoted in ADIII.)

20) **Kennedy, Robert:** Nov. 20, 1925, 3:11 p.m. EST (Zone +5), Brookline, Massachusetts, 71W07, 42N20. (Died June 5, 1968.) Data source: T. Patrick Davis, astrologer, in *Mercury Hour*, July 1981, data from RFK's office. (Quoted in ADIII.)

21) **Lennon, John:** Oct. 9, 1940, 6:30 p.m. BDT (Zone −1), Liverpool, England, 2W58, 53N25. (Died Dec. 8, 1980.) Data source: His stepmother, Pauline Stone. (Quoted in ABC, *Supplement to First Edition*, Jan. 1, 1988.)

22) **Ludwig Rudolph of Hanover, Prince:** Nov. 28, 1955. No time or location currently available. (Died Nov. 29, 1988.) Data source: *People* magazine, Jan. 9, 1989, p. 51.

23) **MacLaine, Shirley:** April 24, 1934, 3:57 p.m. EST (Zone +5), Richmond, Virginia, 77W27, 37N33. Data source: Church of Light, Los Angeles, California, quotes birth certificate. (Quoted in PW.)

24) **Madonna** [birth name: Madonna Louise Ciccone]: Aug. 16, 1958, 7:00 a.m. EST (Zone +5), Bay City, Michigan, 83W54, 43N36. Data source: Lois Rodden, astrologer, birth certificate in hand.

25) **Manson, Charles:** Nov. 12, 1934, 4:40 p.m. EST (Zone +5), Cincinnati, Ohio, 84W31, 39N06. Data source: Family written records. (Quoted in *Contemporary Sidereal Horoscopes*, by Clark, Gilchrist, Mackey, and Dorming, 1976.)

26) **Mountbatten, Lord Louis:** June 25, 1900, 6:00 a.m. GMT (Zone +00), Windsor, England, 0W38, 51N29. (Died Aug. 27, 1979.) Data source: Dana Holliday, astrologer, quotes *Mountbatten's 80 Years in Pictures* (Viking Press), 1979. (Quoted in ADIII.)

27) **Nader, Ralph:** Feb. 27, 1934, 4:52 a.m. EST (Zone +5), Winsted, Connecticut, 73W04, 41N55. Data source: J.L. Ahern, astrologer, quotes Ralph Nader. (Quoted in ADIII.)

28) **National Aeronautics and Space Administration (NASA):** July 29, 1958, 12 noon EDT (Zone +4), White House, Washington, D.C., 77W02, 38N54. Data source: For the signing of The National Aeronautics and Space Act of 1958 by President Eisenhower, as determined by 1) *The Public Papers of the President,* Vol. 1958; 2) *The Eisenhower Appointment Records,* from the Dwight D. Eisenhower Library, Abilene, Kansas; and 3) *The Laws of the 85th Congress, 2nd Session,* under The National Aeronautics and Space Act of 1958. *The ... Appointment Records* do not indicate exactly when he signed the bill into law, but they do show Eisenhower's office hours on July 29, 1958, to be from 7:55 a.m. to 4:47 p.m., and a visit from Doctors Killian and Glennan (future administrators of NASA) from 11:24-11:35 a.m. same day. The author assigned the 12 noon time, although it is very likely within 0 to 30 minutes of exactness, and a 12 noon chart is appropriate for a company whose exact time of official inception or incorporation is unknown. *The Public Papers of the President,* Vol. 1958 quote Eisenhower on July 29, 1958: "I have today signed The National Aeronautics and Space Act of 1958."

29) **Nicholas II, Czar, and Emperor of Russia:** May 31, 1868 (New Style Gregorian Calendar), 00:30 a.m. LMT, St. Petersburg (now Leningrad), USSR, 30E15, 59N55. Data source: Lois Rodden, astrologer, who quotes *Nicholas II, The Last of the Tzars,* by Princess C. Radziwell, 1931, p. 16.

30) **Nixon, Richard:** Jan. 9, 1913, 9:35 p.m. PST (Zone +8), Yorba Linda, California, 117W49, 33N53. Data source: *Real Nixon,* by B. Kornitzer, "as recorded by Nurse H. Shockney." (Quoted in CBC, p. 268, #784.)

31) **Onassis, Christina:** Dec. 11, 1950, 3:00 p.m. EST (Zone +5), New York City, N.Y., 73W59, 40N46. (Died Nov. 19, 1988.) Data source: Ruth Dewey, astrologer, quotes hospital records in *Mercury Hour,* Jan. 1977. (Quoted in PW.)

32) **Ono, Yoko:** Feb. 18, 1933, 8:30 p.m. (Zone –9), Tokyo, Japan, 139E45, 35N40. Data source: From Yoko Ono to Roger Elliot, astrologer. (Quoted in PW, *Supplement,* 4th printing Feb. 1986.)

33) **Pahlavi, Mohammed Reza, Shah of Iran:** Oct. 26, 1919, 8:15 a.m. (Zone –3.5), Teheran, Iran, 51E26, 35N45. Data source: Church of Light Research Dept., Los Angeles, quotes Marion Meyer Drew, astrologer. Date of birth given in autobiography *Mission for My Country,* 1960, p. 51. The exact time of birth is still not absolutely confirmed. (Quoted in ABC, p. 349.)

34) **Penn, Sean:** Aug. 17, 1960, 3:17 p.m. PDT (Zone +7), Burbank, California, 121W56, 37N19. Data source: Lois Rodden, astrologer, birth certificate in hand.

35) **Quinlan, Karen Ann**: March 29, 1954, 11:43 p.m. EST (Zone +5), Scranton, Pennsylvania, 75W40, 41N25. (Went into coma April 15, 1975. Died June 11, 1985.) Data source: Doris Kaye, astrologer, in *Mercury Hour,* July 1978. Birth time speculative/rectified. (Quoted in ABC, p. 357.)

36) **Redford, Robert:** Aug. 18, 1936, 8:02 p.m. PST (Zone +8), Santa Monica, California 118W29, 34N01. Data source: Lockhart, astrologer, quotes birth certificate. (Quoted in ABC.)

37) **Schwarzenegger, Arnold**: July 30, 1947, 4:10 a.m. METD (Zone –2), Graz, Austria, 15E26, 47N05. Data source: Doris Chase Doane, astrologer, who quotes "from [Schwarzenegger] to a colleague," 1979. (Quoted in ABC.)

Simpson, Wallis: see Windsor, Duchess of

38) **Speck, Richard:** Dec. 6, 1941, 1:00 a.m. CST (Zone +6), Monmouth, Illinois, 90W39, 40N55. Data source: 1:00 a.m. CST confirmed in ABC *Supplement* to 1st edition, Jan. 1, 1988. Location confirmed by Lois Rodden Jan. 1989, replacing Kirkwood, Illinois, as listed in *Supplement* above.

39) **Spitz, Mark:** Feb. 10, 1950, 5:45 p.m. PST (Zone +8), Modesto, California, 121W00, 37N39. Data source: Lockwood, astrologer, quotes birth certificate. (Quoted in ABC.)

40) **Springsteen, Bruce:** Sept. 23, 1949, 10:50 p.m. EDT (Zone +4), Freehold, New Jersey, 74W17, 40N16. Data source: *Current Biography* 1978. (Quoted in GBAC, which contains only "officially confirmed" birth data.)

41) **Streep, Meryl:** June 22, 1949, 8:05 a.m. EDT (Zone +4), Summit, New Jersey, 74W22, 40N43. Data source: Edwin Steinbrecher, astrologer, quotes birth certificate in hand. (Quoted in *Data News* [Lois M. Rodden], No. 14, Dec. 1988, p. 3.)

42) **Taylor, Elizabeth:** Feb. 27, 1932, 2:00 a.m. (Zone +00), London, England, 0W06, 51N31. Data source: Liz Taylor, her birth date and hour signed by her on a photo to Bob Prince, astrologer. (Quoted in PW, Supplement to 3rd printing, April 1984. Confirmed in *Data News* [Lois M. Rodden], No. 10, April 1988.)

43) **Trotsky, Leon:** Nov. 7, 1879 (New Style Gregorian Calendar), 10:09 p.m. LMT (Zone –2), Yanavka (now Ivanovka) in the Ukraine, USSR, near Odessa; Ivanovka, Ukraine, USSR, 30E28, 46N58. Data source: Date and time from *Sabian Symbols in Astrology*, by Marc Edmund Jones, 1966, p. 363. (Quoted in CBC.) As there are ten Ivanovkas listed in *The International Atlas*, Trotsky's birthplace Ivanovka is confirmed as near Odessa in *The New Encyclopedia Britannica*, Vol. II of the Micropaedia, Chicago, 1987, p. 944. *The Columbia Lippincott Gazeteer of the World* confirms this Ivanovka (Yanovka to 1945) as 35 miles NNW of Odessa. The coordinates for Odessa are given as 30E44, 46N28.

44) **Windsor, Duchess of (Wallis Simpson):** June 19, 1896, 10:30 p.m. EST (Zone +5), Blue Ridge Summit, Pennsylvania, 77W28, 39N43. Data source: Ruth Hale Oliver, astrologer, who quotes a letter of the attending physician, given in *American Astrology*, Jan. 1937, "as he recalled the unusual circumstances of her birth" with a time of 10:30 p.m. EST. (Quoted in PW. In *Data News* No. 15, Jan. 1989, there is a discussion of conflicting data given in the Charles Higham biography *The Secret Life of the Duchess of Windsor*. This data, based on frequently erroneous census data, which changes the year of birth in this case, has been disregarded as of late March 1989 by Lois Rodden, author of *Data News*.)

45) **Windsor, Duke of:** June 23, 1894, 9:55 p.m. GMT (Zone +00), Richmond, England, 0W18, 51N27. Data source: Cyril Fagan, astrologer, in *American Astrology*, Nov. 1976, quoting an "official news release." (Quoted in ABC.)

Appendix C
Meridian House Tables

How to Use the Meridian House Tables

Many computer programs now provide the option of Meridian houses. However, if you want to check your Meridian houses by using these tables, there are two ways to use them.

1) If you know the sidereal time of the astrological chart but not the Midheaven.

2) If you know the Midheaven of the astrological chart.

1) If you know only the sidereal time, proceed as follows to calculate the Midheaven:

   a) As an example, your sidereal time is 20 hours: 2 minutes: 25 seconds.
   b) Turn to page 1 of the Meridian House Tables.
   c) Check the top of the hours column under minutes until you come to 20 hours.
   d) Check the left-hand column until you come to 2 minutes.
   e) Coordinate the two pieces of information and you come to 28 \\Vg 23.
   f) To add the 25 seconds, interpolate 25/60 = .41666 x the distance between 28 \\Vg 23 and 28 \\Vg 38 (20 hours: 3 minutes), i.e. 15 minutes. Thus .41666 x 15 = 6 minutes. Add 6 minutes to 28 \\Vg 23.
   g) The Midheaven is 28 \\Vg 29 for a sidereal time of 20 hours: 2 minutes: 25 seconds.

2) Once you have determined the Midheaven of the astrological chart, proceed as follows:

   a) Using the same example, if the Midheaven is 28 \\Vg 29, look directly to the right along the same horizontal line.
   b) The next set of numbers directly to the right of the MC tells you the Meridian house cusp of the 11th house—in this case, 28 ≈ 26. Add 6 minutes to each house cusp figure, exactly the same amount added to determine the Midheaven.

c) The 12th house cusp is then 0 ♈ 39, 1st house 2 ♉ 48, 2nd house 2 ♊ 40, and 3rd house 0 ♋ 34.

d) The 1st Meridian house cusp is also called the Equatorial Ascendant or the East Point. To derive the usual Ascendant (the intersection of horizon and ecliptic) you will need a different house table.

e) Notice when you move to the end of the far-right column you continue to the far left-hand column, staying on the same horizontal line of numbers, reversing the astrological sign if you move to the left.

f) That is, if you are using ♑ and ♒ at the far right-hand column, you now switch to ♈, ♉, ♊, and ♋ to the left.

MIN.	12 hrs. / 0 hours	14 hrs. / 2 hrs.	16 hrs. / 4 hrs.	18 hrs. / 6 hrs.	20 hrs. / 8 hrs.	22 hrs. / 10 hrs.
0	♈00°00♎	♉2°11♏	♊2°05♐	♋00°00♑	♋27°55♑	♌27°49♒
1	16	27	20	14	28°09	28°05
2	33	42	34	28	23	20
3	49	58	48	41	38	36
4	1°05	3°13	3°03	55	52	52
5	22	29	17	1°09	29°06	29°07
6	38	44	31	23	21	23
7	54	4°00	45	36	35	39
8	2°11	16	4°00	50	49	54
9	27	31	14	2°04	♌0°04♒	♍0°10♓
10	43	47	28	18	18	26
11	3°00	5°02	42	31	33	41
12	16	18	57	45	47	57
13	32	33	5°11	59	1°02	1°13
14	49	48	25	3°13	16	29
15	4°05	6°04	39	26	31	44
16	22	19	54	40	45	2°00
17	38	35	6°08	54	59	16
18	54	50	22	4°08	2°14	32
19	5°10	7°06	36	22	28	48
20	27	21	50	35	43	3°03
21	43	36	7°04	49	58	19
22	59	52	19	5°03	3°12	35
23	6°16	8°07	33	17	27	51
24	32	23	47	30	41	4°07
25	48	38	8°01	44	56	23
26	7°05	53	15	58	4°10	4°39
27	21	9°09	29	6°12	25	54
28	37	24	43	26	39	5°10
29	♈54♎	♉39♏	♊57♐	♋39♑	♌54♒	♍26♓

MIN.	12 hrs. / 0 hours	14 hrs. / 2 hrs.	16 hrs. / 4 hrs.	18 hrs. / 6 hrs.	20 hrs. / 8 hrs.	22 hrs. / 10 hrs.
30	♈8°10♎	♉9°58♏	♊9°12♐	♋6°53♑	♌5°09♒	♍5°42♓
31	26	10°10	26	7°07	23	58
32	43	25	40	21	38	6°14
33	59	40	54	35	53	30
34	9°15	56	10°08	48	6°07	46
35	31	11°11	22	8°02	22	7°02
36	48	26	36	16	37	18
37	10°04	41	50	30	51	34
38	20	56	11°04	44	7°06	50
39	36	12°12	18	58	21	8°06
40	53	27	32	9°11	35	22
41	11°09	42	46	25	50	38
42	25	57	12°00	39	8°05	54
43	41	13°12	14	53	20	9°10
44	58	27	28	10°07	34	26
45	12°14	42	42	21	49	42
46	30	58	56	34	9°04	58
47	46	14°13	13°10	48	19	10°14
48	13°03	28	24	11°02	34	30
49	19	43	38	16	48	46
50	35	58	52	30	10°03	11°02
51	51	15°13	14°06	44	18	18
52	14°07	28	20	58	33	34
53	24	43	34	12°11	48	50
54	40	58	48	25	11°03	12°06
55	56	16°13	15°02	39	17	22
56	15°12	28	16	53	32	39
57	28	43	30	13°07	47	55
58	45	58	43	21	12°02	13°11
59	♈16°01♎	♉17°13♏	♊ 57♐	♋ 35♑	♌ 17♒	♍ 27♓

MIN.	13 hrs. / 1 hour	15 hrs. / 3 hrs.	17 hrs. / 5 hrs.	19 hrs. / 7 hrs.	21 hrs. / 9 hrs.	23 hrs. / 11 hrs.
0	♈ 16°17 ♎	♉ 17°28 ♏	♊ 16°11 ♐	♋ 13°49 ♑	♌ 12°32 ♒	♍ 13°43 ♓
1	33	43	25	14°03	47	59
2	49	58	39	16	13°02	14°15
3	17°05	18°13	53	30	17	32
4	21	28	17°07	44	32	48
5	37	42	21	58	47	15°04
6	54	57	35	15°12	14°02	20
7	18°10	19°12	49	26	17	36
8	26	27	18°02	40	32	53
9	42	42	16	54	47	16°09
10	58	57	30	16°08	15°02	25
11	19°14	20°12	44	22	17	41
12	30	28	58	36	32	57
13	46	41	19°12	50	47	17°14
14	20°02	56	26	17°04	16°02	30
15	18	21°11	39	18	18	46
16	34	26	53	32	33	18°02
17	50	40	20°07	46	48	18
18	21°06	55	21	18°00	17°03	35
19	22	22°10	35	14	18	51
20	38	25	49	28	33	19°07
21	54	39	21°02	42	48	24
22	22°10	54	16	56	18°04	40
23	26	23°09	30	19°10	19	56
24	42	23	44	24	34	20°12
25	58	38	58	38	49	29
26	23°14	53	22°12	52	19°04	45
27	30	24°07	25	20°06	20	21°01
28	46	22	39	20	35	17
29	♈ 24°02 ♎	♉ 37 ♏	♊ 53 ♐	♋ 34 ♑	♌ 50 ♒	♍ 34 ♓

MIN.	13 hrs. 1 hour	15 hrs. 3 hrs.	17 hrs. 5 hrs.	19 hrs. 7 hrs.	21 hrs. 9 hrs.	23 hrs. 11 hrs.
30	♈24°18♎	♉24°51♏	♊23°07♐	♋20°48♒	♌20°06♒	♍21°50♓
31	34	25°06	21	21°03	21	22°06
32	50	21	34	17	36	23
33	25°06	35	48	31	51	39
34	21	50	24°02	45	21°07	55
35	37	26°04	16	59	22	23°12
36	53	19	30	22°13	37	28
37	26°09	33	43	27	53	44
38	25	48	57	41	22°08	24°01
39	41	27°02	25°11	56	24	17
40	57	17	25	23°10	39	33
41	27°12	32	38	24	54	49
42	28	46	52	38	23°10	25°06
43	44	28°00	26°06	54	25	22
44	28°00	15	20	24°06	41	38
45	16	29	34	21	56	55
46	31	44	47	35	24°11	26°11
47	47	58	27°01	49	27	27
48	29°03	29°13	15	25°03	43	44
49	19	27	29	17	58	27°00
50	34	42	42	32	25°13	17
51	50	56	56	46	29	33
52	♉00°06♏	♊00°10♐	28°10	26°00	44	49
53	21	25	24	14	26°00	28°06
54	37	39	37	29	16	22
55	53	54	51	43	31	38
56	1°08	1°08	29°05	57	47	55
57	24	22	19	27°12	27°02	29°11
58	40	37	32	26	18	27
59	55	51	46	40	33	44
60	♉2°11♏	♊2°05♐	♋00°00♑	♋27°55♑	♌27°49♒	♎00°00♈

Appendix D
Sample of Unmarked 360° Dial

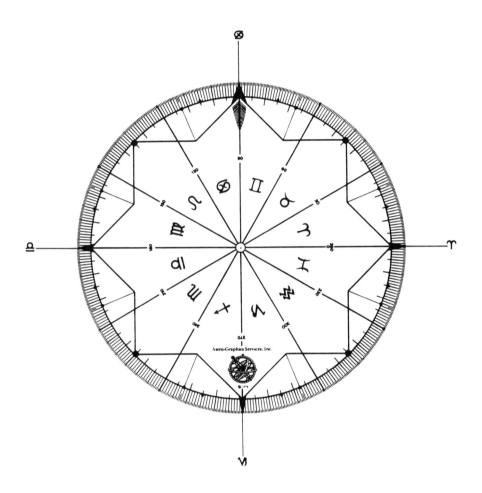

Appendix E
Sample of Unmarked 90° Dial

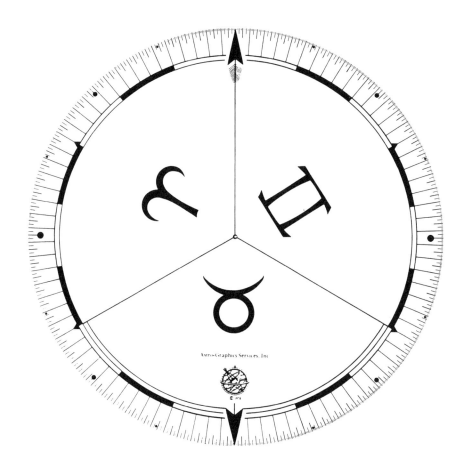

Appendix F
Sample of A∗C∗G Latitude Crossings

John F Kennedy
May 29, 1917 3:00 PM EST

NORTH LATITUDES		CENTRAL LATITUDES		SOUTH LATITUDES	
		55N48	SU/IC * NE/DSC		
69N19	UR/MH * NE/ASC	55N45	Moscow	6N27	Lagos
69N14	SA/IC * PL/ASC	55N41	Copenhagen	1N55	MO/MH * VE/DSC
68N59	SU/IC * PL/DSC	54N38	MO/DSC * UR/ASC		
68N54	SA/ASC * PL/ASC	53N24	MO/MH * JU/DSC	1S55	MO/IC * VE/ASC
68N52	ME/ASC * UR/ASC	52N55	SA/IC * ME/ASC		
68N49	NE/IC * SA/ASC	52N32	NE/IC * SU/ASC	16S27	UR/MH * JU/ASC
68N32	ME/ASC * NE/DSC	52N30	Berlin		
68N20	SU/DSC * PL/DSC	52N19	VE/IC * UR/ASC	20S20	JU/IC * UR/ASC
68N12	NE/IC * PL/ASC	51N30	London	22S54	Rio De Janeiro
68N06	VE/IC * SU/ASC	50N27	VE/MH * MO/ASC	23S11	UR/IC * SU/DSC
68N00	UR/ASC * NE/DSC			24S19	MO/IC * SU/ASC
67N56	MO/DSC * SU/ASC	49N14	Vancouver	25S16	ME/DSC * JU/DSC
67N47	ME/ASC * SA/DSC	48N59	SA/IC * JU/ASC	25S50	UR/MH * ME/ASC
67N40	JU/IC * SU/DSC	48N50	Paris	26S00	ME/IC * UR/ASC
67N36	PL/IC * NE/DSC	47N36	Seattle	26S12	Johannesburg
67N29	ME/IC * SU/DSC	45N56	ME/DSC * MA/DSC	28S48	MA/MH * NE/ASC
67N09	JU/ASC * NE/DSC	45N32	Montreal		
67N07	MA/IC * SU/DSC	44N59	Minneapolis	30S05	UR/MH * MA/ASC
67N07	PL/IC * UR/ASC	43N46	NE/IC * ME/ASC	32S12	NE/MH * MA/ASC
66N52	MO/DSC * VE/ASC	43N39	Toronto	33S40	SU/MH * UR/DSC
66N50	MA/ASC * NE/DSC	43N38	JU/IC * SA/DSC	33S55	Sydney
66N48	PL/IC * SA/DSC	43N13	SA/IC * MA/ASC	34S36	Buenos Aires
66N46	JU/ASC * UR/ASC	42N22	Boston	34S53	MA/IC * UR/ASC
66N42	JU/ASC * SA/DSC	42N20	Detroit	34S58	ME/MH * NE/ASC
66N38	SU/ASC * NE/DSC	41N54	Rome	36S47	MA/MH * SA/ASC
66N37	SA/DSC * UR/ASC	41N53	Chicago	36S52	Auckland
66N35	SU/IC * VE/DSC	41N22	ME/IC * SA/DSC	37S43	UR/IC * VE/DSC
66N35	UR/MH * SA/ASC	40N43	New York	37S50	Melbourne
66N31	PL/IC * JU/ASC	40N41	NE/IC * JU/ASC	38S01	JU/MH * NE/ASC
66N25	MA/ASC * SA/DSC	40N41	MO/IC * PL/ASC		
66N22	SU/ASC * SA/DSC			40S41	MO/MH * PL/DSC
66N21	VE/ASC * NE/DSC	39N44	Denver	40S41	NE/MH * JU/DSC
66N17	MA/ASC * UR/ASC	38N53	Washington	41S22	ME/MH * SA/ASC
66N16	SU/ASC * UR/ASC	38N37	St. Louis	43S13	SA/MH * MA/DSC
66N14	SU/ASC * MA/ASC	38N01	JU/IC * NE/DSC	43S38	JU/MH * SA/ASC
66N11	VE/ASC * SA/DSC	37N47	San Francisco	43S46	NE/MH * ME/DSC
66N04	VE/ASC * MA/ASC	37N43	UR/MH * VE/ASC	45S56	ME/ASC * MA/ASC
65N56	PL/IC * SU/ASC	36N47	MA/IC * SA/DSC	48S59	SA/MH * JU/DSC
65N56	VE/ASC * MA/ASC	36N10	Las Vegas		
65N50	PL/IC * VE/ASC	35N40	Tokyo	50S27	VE/IC * MO/DSC
65N40	SU/ASC * VE/ASC	34N58	ME/IC * NE/DSC	52S19	VE/MH * UR/DSC
65N37	PL/IC * MA/ASC	34N53	MA/MH * UR/DSC	52S32	NE/MH * SU/DSC
65N26	VE/ASC * JU/ASC	34N04	Los Angeles	52S55	SA/MH * ME/DSC
65N09	SU/ASC * JU/ASC	33N45	Atlanta	53S24	MO/IC * JU/ASC
65N09	JU/IC * PL/DSC	33N40	SU/IC * UR/ASC	54S38	MO/ASC * UR/DSC
64N51	MO/IC * NE/ASC	33N27	Phoenix	55S48	SU/MH * NE/ASC
64N50	JU/IC * VE/DSC	32N47	Dallas	56S29	SA/MH * SU/DSC
64N31	ME/IC * PL/DSC	32N12	NE/IC * MA/ASC	56S46	NE/MH * VE/DSC
64N31	ME/IC * VE/ASC	30N05	UR/IC * MA/DSC	57S12	SU/MH * SA/ASC
64N30	VE/DSC * PL/DSC	30N03	Cairo	58S43	MO/IC * MA/ASC
63N52	MA/IC * VE/DSC			59S25	SA/MH * VE/DSC
63N15	MA/IC * PL/DSC	29N58	New Orleans	59S58	SU/DSC * ME/DSC
63N07	SA/DSC * NE/DSC	29N46	Houston		
62N54	ME/ASC * VE/ASC	28N48	MA/IC * NE/DSC		
62N43	MO/DSC * SA/DSC	28N39	Delhi		
62N38	MO/DSC * NE/DSC	26N00	ME/MII * UR/DSC		
61N54	VE/IC * SA/DSC	25N50	UR/IC * ME/DSC		
61N38	VE/IC * NE/DSC	25N47	Miami		
61N13	Anchorage	25N16	ME/ASC * JU/ASC		
60N42	MO/MH * ME/DSC	24N19	MO/MH * SU/DSC		
60N32	UR/MH * PL/ASC	23N11	UR/MH * SU/ASC		
60N28	MO/IC * SA/ASC	22N34	Calcutta		
		22N16	Hong Kong		
59N58	SU/ASC * ME/ASC	21N19	Honolulu		
59N25	SA/IC * VE/ASC	20N26	Mexico City		
59N20	Stockholm	20N20	JU/MH * UR/DSC		
58N43	MO/MH * MA/DSC				
57N12	SU/IC * SA/DSC	16N27	UR/IC * JU/DSC		
56N46	NE/IC * VE/ASC	14N35	Manila		
56N29	SA/IC * SU/ASC	10N30	Caracas		

273

Appendix G
Selected List of Astrological
Reference Tools (Including Software) and
Their Sources

Atlases (Software or Book Format)

1) *The American Atlas: US Longitudes and Latitudes, Time Changes and Time Zones,* compiled and programed by Thomas G. Shanks, 5th revised edition, 1990.

2) *The International Atlas: World Latitudes, Longitudes and Time Changes,* compiled and programmed by Thomas G. Shanks, 1985.

Both available from specialized bookstores, or their publisher: Astro Communications Services, Inc. (formerly ACS Publications and Astro Computing Services, Inc.), P.O. Box 16430, San Diego, CA 92116; phone 1–800–888–9983. Also available from Astrolabe, Inc.: phone 1–800–THE NOVA; in Massachusetts, 1–508–896–5081.

Ephemerides

1) *The American Ephemeris for the 20th Century, 1900 to 2000,* compiled and programmed by Neil F. Michelsen, revised edition, 1983. (Order either noon or midnight version.)

2) *The American Ephemeris for the 21st Century, 2001–2100,* compiled and programmed by Neil F. Michelsen, 1982. (Order either noon or midnight version.)

3) *The American Midpoint Ephemeris, 1991–1996,* compiled from programs by Neil F. Michelsen, due in 1991.

4) 45° Graphic Ephemeris, available in software format. (Astrolabc's *Timegruphs,* ©1989: You decide the dates and planets you want to include. Add–on module for either *Nova, Chartwheels,* or *Advanced Report Programs.* Also, Matrix Software's *Quick·Graphs,* ©1991.)

1-3) Available from specialized bookstores, or from their publisher, Astro Communications Services, Inc., as listed above.

275

4) Available in software format from Astrolabe, Inc. (phone 1-800-THE NOVA), or from Matrix Software (phone 1-800-PLANETS.) Available in computer printout from Astro Communications Services, Inc. (formerly ACS Publications and Astro Computing Services, Inc.), P.O. Box 16430, San Diego, CA 92116; phone 1–800–888–9983.

Other Timing Tools

1) 90° Dials, available from Astrolabe, Inc. in software or non–software format.

2) *Solar Arc Tables: Sonnenbogentabelle,* compiled by Arthur Kickbusch. Available from specialized bookstores or from publisher Ludwig Rudolph (Witte–Verlag), Hamburg, Germany. (Directions in English and German.)

3) *Source Book of Mundane Maps,* published annually by Astro•Carto•Graphy, c/o Astro–Numeric Service, Box 425, San Pablo, CA 94806. Phone: 1–800–MAPPING. Available in Europe in the German language from: Claude Weiss, Astrodata AG, Lindenbachstr. 56, CH – 8042, Zurich, Switzerland. Phone: 01–363–60 60.

4) *Tables of Planetary Phenomena,* compiled by Neil F. Michelsen, ©1990.

5) *Valliere's Natural Cycles Almanac,* published annually by Astrolabe, Inc., Box 28, Orleans, MA 02653. Phone: 1-800-THE NOVA; in Massachusetts 1–508–896–5081 or FAX: 1–508–896–5289.

Astrological Software

A wide range of astrological software programs are available from:

1) Astrolabe, Inc., Box 28, Orleans, MA 02653. Phone: 1–800–THE NOVA (1–800–843–6682), for Master Card and VISA orders.

2) Astrolabe's European outlet for software only: Astrolabe (Europe Ltd.), Villa Tortue, 28, Chemin des Daillettes, CH–1012, Lausanne, Switzerland. Phone: 021–29–58–31.

3) Matrix Software, 315 Marion Ave., Big Rapids, MI 49307. Phone: 1–800–PLANETS (free catalog request and order line.)

Astrological Libraries*

Heart Center Library
315 Marion Ave.
Big Rapids, Michigan 49307
Phone: 1-616-796-3940

IAO Library
Toronto, Canada
Inquiries to: Robin Armstrong

Urania Trust
5 Victoria Rd.
Frome, Somerset BA 11 1RR
United Kingdom

*There are also permanent collections belonging to some of the larger astrological organizations, such as the AFA and the NCGR. (See listings in Appendix I, p. 283.)

Please Note: The works of astrologers from previous centuries are becoming increasingly available in reprint editions.

Regulus Publishing Co., Ltd. (London, England) specializes in publishing facsimile editions of William Lilly, Guido Bonatus, and Jerom Cardan.

Justus & Associates (Issaquah, Washington, USA), publisher of *The Horary Practitioner*, has published the complete works of William Lilly (1602-1681) in modern type.

Appendix H
Selected Bibliography

Introductory Texts
    Hand, Robert, *Horoscope Symbols*, ©1981.
    Oken, Alan, *Alan Oken's Complete Astrology*, revised edition, 1988.

Astronomy
    Filbey, John & Peter, *Astronomy for Astrologers*, ©1985.

General Survey
    Campion, Nicholas, *The Practical Astrologer*, ©1987.

General Reference Books
    Brau, Jean-Louis, Helen Weaver and Allan Edmands, *Larousse Encyclopedia of Astrology*, ©1977.
    DeVore, Nicholas, *Encyclopedia of Astrology*, ©1947, reprinted 1977.
    Dean, Geoffrey, compiler, *Recent Advances in Natal Astrology: A Critical Review 1900-1976*, ©1977.

Historical Survey (to 1700)
    Tester, Jim, *A History of Western Astrology*, ©1987.

Research
    Gauquelin, Michel, *Birthtimes: A Scientific Investigation of the Secrets of Astrology*, ©1983.
    Gauquelin, Michel, *The Cosmic Clocks: From Astrology to a Modern Science*, ©1967.
    Gauquelin, Michel, *Cosmic Influences on Human Behavior*, ©1973.

Forecasting and Cycles
    Greene, Liz, *The Outer Planets & Their Cycles: The Astrology of the Collective*, ©1983.
    *Hand, Robert, *Planets in Transit: Life Cycles for Living*, ©1976.
    Rudhyar, Dane, *The Lunation Cycle: A Key to the Understanding of Personality*, ©1967, 1971.
    Ruperti, Alexander, *Cycles of Becoming: The Planetary Pattern of Growth*, ©1978.

*For regular use.

Astro-Mapping
Lewis, Jim and Ariel Guttman, *The Astro·Carto·Graphy Book of Maps,* ©1989.

Reference Guides for Planetary Pictures
Ebertin, Reinhold, *The Combination of Stellar Influences,* ©1940, 1972.

Witte-Lefeldt [Alfred Witte & Hermann Lefeldt], *Rules for Planetary-Pictures: The Astrology of Tomorrow,* ©1928, 5th edition, 1959.

Uranian Astrology
Jacobson, Roger A., *The Language of Uranian Astrology,* ©1975.

Simms, Maria Kay, *Dial Detective: Investigations with the 90° Dial (An Illustrated Introduction to Uranian Astrology),* ©1989.

See also Witte-Lefeldt, *Rules for Planetary Pictures* (listed above).

Hindu Astrology
Braha, James T., *Ancient Hindu Astrology for the Modern Western Astrologer,* ©1986.

Frawley, David, *The Astrology of the Seers: A Guide to Vedic (Hindu) Astrology,* ©1990.

Electional Astrology
Scofield, Bruce, *The Timing of Events: Electional Astrology,* ©1985.

Horary Astrology
Barclay, Olivia, *Horary Astrology Rediscovered,* ©1990.

Louis, Anthony, *Horary Astrology: The History and Practice of Astro-Divination,* ©1991.

Watters, Barbara H., *Horary Astrology and the Judgment of Events,* ©1973.

Mundane Astrology (politics, history, world affairs)
Baignent, Michael, Nicholas Campion and Charles Harvey, *Mundane Astrology: An Introduction to the Astrology of Nations and Groups,* ©1984.

Campion, Nicholas, *The Book of World Horoscopes: An Annotated Sourcebook of Mundane Charts,* ©1988.

McEvers, Joan, editor, *Financial Astrology for the 1990s,* ©1989.

Chart Collections (natal charts): currently available in software format only

The Blackwell Data Collection, compiled by Arthur Blackwell. Program by Robert Hand. Astrolabe, Inc., ©1989.

*Compact Data Collection. Volumes 1-17+. Compiled by Mark Penfield, Stephen Erlewine, Michael Erlewine, *et al.* Matrix Software, ©1988-

The Mackey-Saunders Data Collection, compiled by Janice Mackey and Jessica Saunders. Program by Robert Hand. Astrolabe, Inc., ©1990.

*One of these volumes contains Stephen Erlewine's *Circle Book of Charts.* See below.

Chart Collections (natal charts): available in book format

*The American Book of Charts, by Lois M. Rodden, ©1980. (Reprinted under the title *Astro-Data II.*)

*Astro-Data III, by Lois M. Rodden, ©1986.

*Astro-Data IV, by Lois M. Rodden, ©1990.

The Circle Book of Charts, by Stephen Erlewine, ©1972, revised edition 1982.

The Gauquelin Book of American Charts, by Michel and Francoise Gauquelin, ©1982.

*Profiles of Women: A Collection of Astrological Biographies, by Lois M. Rodden, ©1979.

*Rodden's works are currently updated with annual supplements on Jan. 1st of each year. New birth data information is also available on a bimonthly basis through Rodden's *Data News.* If you are interested in either of these, contact the author directly at 11736 3rd St., Yucaipa, CA 92399.

Chart Collections (corporate charts): available in book format

Standard and Poor's 500, by Carol S. Mull, ©1984.

Chart Collections (charts of countries, states, cities): available in book format

The Book of World Horoscopes: An Annotated Sourcebook of Mundane Charts, by Nicholas Campion, ©1988.

Horoscopes of the U.S., States & Cities, by Carolyn R. Dodson, ©1975, 1980.

Please note: The horoscope of the United States has been a subject of much discussion and debate over the years. My personal preference is for a time between 4:47 p.m. and 4:50 p.m. LMT (Local Mean Time), July 4, 1776, Philadelphia, Pennsylvania. Campion gives a time of either 4:50 or 5:10 p.m. LMT on July 4th, and the weight of historical evidence puts these times closest to the probable time of the actual signing of the Declaration of Independence. (The vote was taken on July 2nd, 1776.) A time in the 4:47 p.m. to 4:50 p.m. range on July 4th gives a 7°–8° Sagittarius Ascendant, as opposed to the perennially popular 7°–8° Gemini Ascendant. Dodson presents the latter in her book listed above. That time is based on a time of 2:13 a.m. LMT and has scant historical evidence to support its validity. Campion recommends a time of 5:10 p.m. LMT.

Appendix I
Selected List of Astrological
Organizations and Periodicals

Organizations:

1) **AFA (American Federation of Astrologers, Inc.)**, P.O. Box 22040, Tempe, AZ 85285–2040.

*2) **AFAN (Association for Astrology Networking)**, 8306 Wilshire Blvd., #537, Beverly Hills, CA 90211.

3) **Aquarius Workshops**, P.O. Box 556, Encino, CA 91426.

*4) **Astrological Association Of Great Britain**, P.O. Box 39, North P.D.O., Nottingham NG5 5PD, U.K.

*5) **Astrological Lodge Of London**, 6 Queen Sq., Bloomsbury, London WC1 3AR, U.K.

6) **Church Of Light**, P.O. Box 76862, Los Angeles, CA 90076.

7) **DAV (Deutsche Astrologen–Verband)**, Dr. Peter Niehenke, Merzhauser Strasse 145–B, 7800 Freiburg, West Germany.

8) **FAA (Federation of Australian Astrologers)**, c/o Keven Barrett, 41 Argyle Street, Bigola Plateau 2107 NSW, Australia.

9) **FABEF (Federation Astrologique Belge d'Expression Francaise)**, 1/B34 Clos du Parnasse, B 1040, Bruxelles, Belgium.

10) **FCA (Fraternity for Canadian Astrologers)**, Membership Secretary Nancy Atwood, 13155 24th Ave., Surrey B.C. V4A 2G2, Canada.

11) **FSC (Foundation for the Study of Cycles)**, Dr. Jeffrey Horovitz, Executive Director, 3333 Michelson Dr., #210, Irvine, CA 92715–1607.

*12) **ISAR (International Society for Astrological Research)**, P.O. Box 38613, Los Angeles, CA 90038–0613.

*13) **NCGR (National Council for Geocosmic Research)**, NCGR Headquarters, Secretary, 105 Snyder Ave., Ramsey, NJ 07446.

14) **Stichting Astro–kring,** Tees Reitsma, 362 Leyweg, 2545 EE, The Hague, Netherlands.

15) **Urania Trust,** 5 Victoria Rd., Frome, Somerset BA11 1RR, U.K.

16) **World ARC Center (Astrological Registration and Communication),** P.O. Box 5153, Walter Blaser, CH–8800 Thalwil, Switzerland.

*especially recommended

Periodicals:

1) *American Astrology.* Monthly. Available at newsstands.

2) *Above & Below.* Quarterly. P.O. Box 5645, 40 Bay St., Toronto, Ontario, Canada M5W 1N8.

3) *Aspects.* Quarterly. Aquarius Workshops, P.O. Box 556, Encino, California 91426.

4) *Astrological Monthly Review.* Monthly. Dengar Publications, P.O. Box 426, Leichardt NSW 2040, Australia.

5) *Astro*Talk.* Bimonthly. Matrix Software, 315 Marion Ave., Big Rapids, Michigan 49307.

6) *Considerations.* Quarterly. P.O. Box 491, Mt. Kisco, New York 10549.

7) *Correlation.* Semiannually. 2 Waltham Close, Abbey Park, West Bridgeford, Nottingham NG2 6LE, U.K.

8) *Data News.* Bimonthly. Lois Rodden, 11736 3rd St., Yucaipa, California 92399.

9) *Dell Horoscope.* Monthly. Available at newsstands.

10) *The Horary Practitioner.* Quarterly. Just Us & Associates, 1420 N.W. Gilman #2154, Issaquah, Washington 98027–5327.

11) *Mercury Hour.* Quarterly. Edie Custer, C7 3509 Waterlick Rd., Lynchburg, Virginia 24502.

12) *Meridian.* Bimonthly, in German. Ebertin–Verlag, Kronenstrasse 2, Postfach 167, 7800 Freibug im Breisgau, West Germany.

13) *The Monthly Aspectarian.* Monthly. P.O. Box 1342, Morton Grove, Illinois 60053.

14) *The Mountain Astrologer.* Bimonthly. P.O. Box 11292, Berkeley, California 94701.

15) *The Mutable Dilemma.* Quarterly. CCRS, 838 Fifth Ave., Los Angeles, California 90005. (Zipporah Dobyns and family.)

16) *NCGR Journal.* Biannually (quarterly through 1990). National Council for Geocosmic Research (NCGR), P.O. Box 34487, San Diego, California 92163.

17) *Planet Watch.* Monthly. Planet Watch Publications, P.O. Box 515, Old Chelsea Station, New York, New York 10113. (Eleanor Bach)

18) *Welcome To Planet Earth.* Monthly. Great Bear Press, P.O. Box 5164, Eugene, Oregon 97405.

Index

A

Adams, Evangeline, 20
Adams, John C., 48
AFAN (Association for
  Astrology Networking),
  22, 283
Air element, 62
Angles of the chart,
  description of, 248
Anti-astrology manifesto
  (1975), 17
Apted, Michael, 148
Aquinas, St. Thomas, 66
Aries point
  see Cardinal axis
Ascendant, description of,
  33-4, 54, 248
Aspectarian
  see Daily aspectarian
Astro·Carto·Graphy
  see Astro-mapping
Astro Communications
  Services, Inc., 24, 164, 175,
  275, 276
Astrolabe, Inc., 73, 165, 175,
  275, 276
Astrolocality maps
  see Astro-mapping
Astrology
  autonomy and, 65-7
  Christian theology and, 12
  Church view on, 2
  comparison to reading
    music, 63-5
  electional, 202-5, 217-21,
    231-6, 251, 280
  geocentric, 12, 28, 31, 247

Astrology (cont'd.)
  harmonics in, 28, 32, 178-80
  heliocentric, 12, 28
  Hindu, 2, 23, 28, 55, 64
  legal issues, 20-2
  psychiatry and, 13
  psychology and, 12-6, 52
  psychotherapy and, 13-6
  reference tools, 275-7
  scientific validation of, 18-9
  software available, 26, 164,
    174, 175, 275, 276
  study in the universities, 2
  sun-sign, 1
  Uranian system, 12, 23,
    28-37, 53-5, 165
Astro-mapping
  computerized system, 24,
    26-8
  description, 26-8
  latitude crossings, 27, 65, 77,
    273
  planetary lines, 27, 73, 73-8
Astronauts
  location indicators, 132-3
  timing indicators, 133
  see also Challenger shuttle
    explosion, NASA
    (1-28-86)
Ayatollah Khomeini
  see Khomeini, Ayatollah

B

Baumann-Jung, Gret, 14
Bell's theorem, 3-5

STAY IN TOUCH

On the following pages you will find listed, with their current prices, some of the books now available on related subjects. Your book dealer stocks most of these, and will stock new titles in the Llewellyn series as they become available. We urge your patronage.

However, to obtain our full catalog, to keep informed of new titles as they are released and to benefit from informative articles and helpful news, you are invited to write for our bi-monthly news magazine/catalog. A sample copy is free, and it will continue coming to you at no cost as long as you are an active mail customer. Or you may keep it coming for a full year with a donation of just $2.00 in U.S.A. ($7.00 for Canada & Mexico, $20.00 overseas, first class mail). Many bookstores also have *The Llewellyn New Times* available to their customers. Ask for it.

Stay in touch! In *The Llewellyn New Times'* pages you will find news and reviews of new books, tapes and services, announcements of meetings and seminars, articles helpful to our readers, news of authors, advertising of products and services, special money-making opportunities, and much more.

The Llewellyn New Times
P.O. Box 64383-Dept. 366, St. Paul, MN 55164-0383, U.S.A.
• • •

TO ORDER BOOKS AND TAPES

If your book dealer does not have the books described on the following pages readily available, you may order them direct from the publisher by sending full price in U.S. funds, plus $1.50 for postage and handling for orders *under* $10.00; $3.00 for orders *over* $10.00. There are no postage and handling charges for orders over $50. UPS Delivery: We ship UPS whenever possible. Delivery guaranteed. Provide your street address as UPS does not deliver to P.O. Boxes. UPS to Canada requires a $50 minimum order. Allow 4–6 weeks for delivery. Orders outside the U.S.A. and Canada: Airmail—add retail price of book; add $5 for each non-book item (tapes, etc.); add $1 per item for surface mail.

FOR GROUP STUDY AND PURCHASE

Because there is a great deal of interest in group discussion and study of the subject matter of this book, we feel that we should encourage the adoption and use of this particular book by such groups by offering a special "quantity" price to group leaders or "agents."

Our Special Quantity Price for a minimum order of five copies of *Navigating by the Stars* is $44.85 cash-with-order. This price includes postage and handling within the United States. Minnesota residents must add 6% sales tax. For additional quantities, please order in multiples of five. For Canadian and foreign orders, add postage and handling charges as above. Credit card (VISA, Master Card, American Express) orders are accepted. Charge card orders only may be phoned free ($15.00 minimum order) within the U.S.A. or Canada by dialing 1-800-THE-MOON. Customer service calls dial 1-612-291-1970. Mail Orders to:

LLEWELLYN PUBLICATIONS
P.O. Box 64383-Dept. 366 / St. Paul, MN 55164-0383, U.S.A.

THE ASTRO*CARTO*GRAPHY BOOK OF MAPS
by Jim Lewis and Ariel Guttman
Everyone believes there is a special person, job and place for him or her. This book explores those special places in the lives of 136 celebrities and famous figures. The maps, based on the time of birth, graphically reveal lines of planetary influence at various geographic locations. A planet affecting a certain area is correlated with a person's success, failure or activities there. Astro*Carto*Graphy can also be used to bring about the stronger influence of a certain planet by showing its angular positions. Angular positions involve the Ascendant, the IC, the Descendant and the Midheaven. The maps show where planets would have been had you been born at different locations than at your birthplace.

Charts and maps of personalities in the entertainment field, such as Joan Crawford, Marilyn Monroe, Grace Kelly, James Dean, John Lennon and David Bowie, are included in this compilation. Activists like Martin Luther King, Jr. and Lech Walesa, spiritual pioneers like Freud, Jung and Yogananda and events in the lives of painters, musicians and sports figures as well as the successes, problems and tendencies of such politicians as FDR, Harry Truman, JFK, Richard Nixon, Ronald Reagan, George Bush, and Margaret Thatcher.
0–87542–434–1, 300 pgs., 8–1/2 x 11, charts, softcover   **$15.95**

HORARY ASTROLOGY
by Anthony Louis
This new book delves deeply into the heritage and the modern applicability of the horary art. Author Anthony Louis is a practicing psychiatrist, and he brings the compassion and erudition associated with his field to this scholarly textbook.

Written beautifully and reverently in the tradition of William Lilly, the book translates Lilly's meaning into modern terms. Other features include numerous case studies; tables; diagrams; and more than 100 pages of appendices, including an exhaustive planetary rulership list, planetary key words and a lengthy astrological/horary glossary. Dignities and debilities, aspects and orbs, derivative houses, Arabic parts, fixed stars, critical degrees and more are explored in relation to the science of horary astrology. Worksheets supplement the text.
0-87542-394-9, 600 pgs., 6 x 9, softcover   **$18.95**

FINANCIAL ASTROLOGY
Edited by Joan McEvers

This third book in Llewellyn's anthology series edited by well–known astrologer Joan McEvers explores the relatively new field of financial astrology. Nine well–known astrologers share their wisdom and good fortune with you.Learn about the various types of analysis and how astrology fine–tunes these methods. Covered cycles include the Lunar Cycle, the Mars/Vesta Cycle, the 4-1/2-year Martian Cycle, the 500-year Civilization Cycle used by Nostradamus, the Kondratieff Wave and the Elliot Wave. Included topics are:

- Michael Munkasey: A Primer on Market Forecasting
- Pat Esclavon Hardy: Charting the U.S. and the NYSE
- Jeanne Long: New Concepts for Commodities Trading Combining Astrology & Technical Analysis
- Georgia Stathis: The Real Estate Process
- Mary B. Downing: An Investor's Guide to Financial Astrology
- Judy Johns: The Gann Technique
- Carol 5. Mull: Predicting the Dow
- Bill Meridian: The Effect of Planetary Stations on U.S. Stock Prices
- Georgia Stathis: Delineating the Corporation
- Robert Cole: The Predictable Economy

0–87542–382–5,368 pgs., 5-1/4 x 8, illus., softcover　　　　　　**$14.95**

ASTROLOGICAL COUNSELING: The Path to Self-Actualization
Edited by Joan McEvers

The sixth Joan McEvers anthology explores the challenges for today's counselors and gives guidance to those interested in seeking an astrological counselor to help them win their own personal challenges. Articles by 10 well-known astrologers, including:

- David Pond: Astrological Counseling
- Maritha Pottenger: Potent, Personal Astrological Counseling
- Bill Herbst: Astrology and Psychotherapy: A Comparison for Astrologers
- Gray Keen: Plato Sat on a Rock
- Ginger Chalford, Ph.D.: Healing Wounded Spirits: An Astrological Counseling Guide to Releasing Life Issues
- Donald L. Weston, Ph.D.: Astrology and Therapy/Counseling
- Susan Dearborn Jackson: Reading the Body, Reading the Chart
- Doris A. Hebel: Business Counseling
- Donna Cunningham: The Adult Child Syndrome, Codependency, and Their Implications for Astrologers
- Eileen Nauman: Medical Astrology Counseling

0-87542-385-X, 336 pgs., 5-1/4 x 8, charts, softcover　　　　　　**$16.95**

THE ASTROLOGY OF THE MACROCOSM
Edited by Joan McEvers
Joan has done it again! This fifth volume of Llewellyn's anthology series meets the challenges and explores the possibilities of Mundane Astrology with chapters by 11 competent astrologers. Topics include:
• Jimm Erickson: A Philosophy of Mundane Astrology
• Judy Johns: The Ingress Chart
• Jim Lewis: Astro*Carto*Graphy—Bringing Mundane Astrology Down to Earth
• Richard Nolle: The SuperMoon Alignment
• Chris McRae: The Geodetic Equivalent Method of Prediction
• Nicholas Campion: The Age of Aquarius—A Modern Myth
• Nancy Soller: Weather Watching with an Ephemeris
• Marc Penfield: The Mystery of the Romanovs
• Steve Cozzi: The Astrological Quatrains of Michel Nostradamus
• Diana K. Rosenberg: Stalking the Wild Earthquake
• Caroline W. Casey: Dreams and Disasters—Patterns of Cultural and Mythological Evolution into the 21st Century
0-87542-384-1, 420 pgs., 5-1/4 x 8, charts, softcover   **$19.95**

THE HOUSES: POWER PLACES OF THE HOROSCOPE
Edited by Joan McEvers
The fourth in Llewellyn's astrology anthology series, this volume explores each house of the natal chart with clarity and understanding, drawing on the knowledge and talents of 11 respected astrologers. Various house systems are briefly described in Joan McEvers' introduction. Learn about house associations and planetary influences upon each house's activities with the following experts.
• Peter Damian: The First House and the Rising Sun
• Ken Negus: The Seventh House
• Noel Tyl: The Second House and The Eighth House
• Spencer Grendahl: The Third House
• Dona Shaw: The Ninth House
• Gloria Star: The Fourth House
• Marwayne Leipzig: The Tenth House
• Lina Accurso: Exploring Your Fifth House
• Sara Corbin Looms: The Eleventh: House of Tomorrow
• Michael Munkasey: The Sixth House
• Joan McEvers: The Twelfth House: Strength, Peace, Tranquillity
0–87542–383–3, 400 pgs., 5-1/4 x 8, illus., softcover   **$12.95**

ASTROLOGY FOR THE MILLIONS
by Grant Lewi

First published in 1940, this practical, do-it-yourself textbook has become a classic guide to computing accurate horoscopes quickly. Throughout the years, it has been improved upon since Grant Lewi's death by his astrological proteges and Llewellyn's expert editors. This, the first new edition since 1979, presents updated transits and new, user-friendly tables to the year 2050, including a new sun ephemeris of revolutionary simplicity. It's actually easier to use than a computer! Also added is new information on Pluto and rising signs, and a new foreword by Carl Llewellyn Weschcke and introduction by J. Gordon Melton.

Of course, the original material is still here in Lewi's captivating writing style—all of his insights on transits as a tool for planning the future and making the right decisions. His historical analysis of U.S. presidents has been brought up to date to include George Bush. This new edition also features a special In Memoriam to Lewi that presents his birthchart.

One of the most remarkable astrology books available, *Astrology for the Millions* allows the reader to cast a personal horoscope in 15 minutes, interpret from the readings and project the horoscope into the future to forecast coming planetary influences and develop "a grand strategy for living."

0-87542-438-4, 300 pgs., 6 x 9, tables, charts, softcover   **$12.95**

PLUTO: The Evolutionary Journey of the Soul
by Jeff Green

If you have ever asked "Why am I here?",or "What are my lessons?," then this book will help you to objectively learn the answers from an astrological point of view. Green shows you how the planet Pluto relates to the evolutionary and karmic lessons in this life and how past lives can be understood through the position of Pluto in your chart.

Beyond presenting key principles and ideas about the nature of the evolutionary journey of the Soul, this book supplies practical, concise and specific astrological methods and techniques that pinpoint the answers to the above questions. If you are a professional counselor or astrologer, this book is indispensable to your practicc. The reader who studies this material carefully and applies it to his or her own chart will discover an objective vehicle to uncover the essence of his or her own state of being. The understanding that this promotes can help you cooperate with, instead of resist, the evolutionary and karmic lessons in your life.Green describes the position of Pluto through all of the signs and houses, explains the aspects and transits of Pluto, discusses Pluto in aspect to the Moon's Nodes, and gives sample charts and readings. It is the most complete look at this "new" planet ever.

0–87542–296–9, 360 pgs., 6 x 9, softcover   **$12.95**

URANUS: Freedom From the Known
by Jeff Green
This book deals primarily with the archetypal correlations of the planet Uranus to human psychology and. behavior to anatomy/physiology and the chakra system, and to metaphysical and cosmic laws. Uranus' relationship to Saturn, from an individual and collective pointofview, is also discussed.

The text of this book comes intact in style and tone from an intensive workshop held in Toronto. You will feel as if you are a part of that workshop.

In reading Uranus you will discover how to naturally liberate yourself from all of your conditioning patterns, patterns that were determined by the "internal" and "external" environment. Every person has a natural way to actualize this liberation. This natural way is examined by use of the natal chart and from a developmental point of view.

The 48–year sociopolitical cycle of Uranus and Saturn is discussed extensively, as is the relationship between Uranus, Saturn and Neptune. With this historicalperspective,you can see what lies ahead in 1988, a very important year.

0–87542–297–7, 192 pgs., 5-1/4 x 8, softcover $7.95

HEAVEN KNOWS WHAT
by Grant Lewi
What better way to begin the study of astrology than to actually do it—while you learn. *Heaven Knows What* contains everything you need to cast and interpret complete natal charts without memorizing any symbols, without confusing calculations, and without previous experience or training. The tear-out horoscope blanks and special "aspect wheel" make it amazingly easy.

The author explains the influence of every natal Sun and Moon combination, and describes the effects of every major planetary aspect in language designed for the modern reader. His readable and witty interpretations are so relevant that even long-practicing astrologers gain new psychological insight into the characteristics of the signs and meanings of the aspects.

Grant Lewi is sometimes called the father of "do-it-yourself" astrology, and is considered by many to have been astrology's forerunner to the computer.

0-87542-444-9, 352 pgs., 6 x 9, tables, charts, softcover $12.95